MICROSOFT
FRONTPAGE 2000
NO EXPERIENCE REQUIRED

MICROSOFT®
FRONTPAGE® 2000
NO EXPERIENCE REQUIRED™

Gene Weisskopf

SYBEX®

San Francisco • Paris • Düsseldorf • Soest • London

Associate Publisher: Amy Romanoff
Contracts and Licensing Manager: Kristine O'Callaghan
Acquisitions & Developmental Editor: Cheryl Applewood
Editor: Dann McDorman
Technical Editor: Susan Glinert
Book Designers: Patrick Dintino, Catalin Dulfu, Maureen Forys
Graphic Illustrator: Tony Jonick
Electronic Publishing Specialist: Nila Nichols
Production Coordinators: Julie Sakaue, Susan Berge
Proofreader: Blythe Woolston
Indexer: Lynnzee Elze
Cover Designer: Design Site
Cover Illustrator/Photographer: Jack D. Myers

Library of Congress Card Number: 99-60022
ISBN: 0-7821-2482-8

Manufactured in the United States of America

10 9 8 7 6 5 4 3 2 1

SYBEX is a registered trademark of SYBEX Inc.

No Experience Required is a trademark of SYBEX Inc.

Screen reproductions produced with Collage Complete. Collage Complete is a trademark of Inner Media Inc.

Netscape Communications, the Netscape Communications logo, Netscape, and Netscape Navigator are trademarks of Netscape Communications Corporation.
Netscape Communications Corporation has not authorized, sponsored, endorsed, or approved this publication and is not responsible for its content. Netscape and the Netscape Communications Corporate Logos are trademarks and trade names of Netscape Communications Corporation. All other product names and/or logos are trademarks of their respective owners.

TRADEMARKS: SYBEX has attempted throughout this book to distinguish proprietary trademarks from descriptive terms by following the capitalization style used by the manufacturer.

The author and publisher have made their best efforts to prepare this book, and the content is based upon final release software whenever possible. Portions of the manuscript may be based upon pre-release versions supplied by software manufacturer(s). The author and the publisher make no representation or warranties of any kind with regard to the completeness or accuracy of the contents herein and accept no liability of any kind including but not limited to performance, merchantability, fitness for any particular purpose, or any losses or damages of any kind caused or alleged to be caused directly or indirectly from this book.

Photographs and illustrations used in this book have been downloaded from publicly accessible file archives and are used in this book for news reportage purposes only to demonstrate the variety of graphics resources available via electronic access. Text and images available over the Internet may be subject to copyright and other rights owned by third parties. Online availability of text and images does not imply that they may be reused without the permission of rights holders, although the Copyright Act does permit certain unauthorized reuse as fair use under 17 U.S.C. Section 107.

To my niece Amanda, an Oxford scholar and a great kid.

Acknowledgments

I would like to thank everyone at Sybex for all their talent, good spirits, and willingness to help out when needed. Producing a book with them is always a very gratifying experience.

There are several people at Sybex who played a major role in bringing this book to life. My thanks go to Kristine O'Callaghan, contracts and licensing manager, whose pleasant demeanor and willingness to help are always appreciated. Many thanks to editor Dann McDorman, who has that uncanny editorial talent of making sense out of four layers of revision marks. Thanks to developmental editor Cheryl Applewood for getting the whole thing going, and to technical editor Susan Glinert for ensuring that this was truly a work of nonfiction. I'd also like to thank the electronic publishing specialist Nila Nichols, production coordinators Julie Sakaue and Susan Berge, proofreader Blythe Woolston, and indexer Lynnzee Elze.

As always, my thanks go out to fellow authors Peter Dyson and Pat Coleman for helping to maintain the creative fires amidst the more usual infernos of the schedule and beta cycle.

Contents at a Glance

skills

Table of Contents

Introduction

In the early days of the PC revolution, if you wanted to underline or boldface text in a document, you probably have had to look up the control codes for those effects in your printer manual. Unless you were something of a programmer type (and there were plenty of them back then, by necessity), your word processor offered little more than an IBM Selectric Typewriter. Less than 20 years later, feature-rich word processors, such as Microsoft Word, have transformed the PC into a lot more than the glamorous typewriter it was when the PC was in its infancy.

In the 1990s, the Internet and the World Wide Web have created another dramatic spark in the computer revolution. And once again, a major contender in the PC revolution is struggling to move out of its infancy. In the earliest years, only those users who were willing to master the Hypertext Markup Language (HTML) using a text editor and a lot of code were able to publish their ideas to this remarkable new medium.

Thankfully, the early days of the Web are waning quickly, and Microsoft Front-Page 2000 is one of the primary reasons. With FrontPage in hand, you don't need a deep understanding of HTML to produce attractive and informative pages that work together to create well-designed, fully functional Web sites. With *Microsoft FrontPage 2000: No Experience Required* in your other hand, you'll be well-prepared to set out on the Information Highway.

Who Should Read This Book

The Internet is, by far, the fastest growing component in the computer industry today. As a result, the demand for Internet-savvy professionals is skyrocketing. The No Experience Required series from Sybex is designed to teach you the skills that are essential to being successful in some aspect of this revolutionary field. This book, which focuses on Microsoft FrontPage, gives you the skills you need to become a player in the Internet revolution.

Microsoft FrontPage 2000: No Experience Required introduces you to Microsoft FrontPage, while at the same time introducing you to the process of designing Web sites and pages. Whether you're building a home page for your personal Web site on the Internet or a departmental Web site on your corporate intranet, this book and FrontPage will help you get the job done quickly and easily, impressing your coworkers, your best friend, or maybe even your boss.

This book helps you in two important ways:

- If you are new to publishing on the Web, you'll gain a solid grounding in the basics of Web design while learning how to apply the powerful features of FrontPage to build an attractive, well-coordinated Web site.

- If you are already familiar with the Web and HTML, you'll see how to use FrontPage to cut your development time in half, taking advantage of its highly regarded Web-site management and page-editing tools.

You certainly don't need to be a computer expert to use this book, but you should have a general working knowledge of Windows and Windows-based word processing. Creating web pages in FrontPage is really not all that different from creating documents in your word processor. Understanding folders and file management helps you work with the web-related tools in FrontPage, where creating and managing Web sites become very straightforward tasks.

What's New in FrontPage 2000

If you've used previous versions of FrontPage, you'll undoubtedly be impressed with the new and enhanced features in FrontPage 2000, and its refreshing new look. If you'd like to see a list of new features, choose the What's New option in the Contents of the FrontPage help system.

If you're a previous FrontPage user, however, two changes to the program are worth noting. First, there is now just a single FrontPage program that incorporates the page-editing features of the FrontPage Editor and the web-management tools of the FrontPage Explorer.

Second, building webs in FrontPage no longer requires the presence of a FrontPage-aware Web server. Therefore, when you install FrontPage 2000, the Microsoft Personal Web Server is no longer automatically installed. You can, of course, install that Web server or another if you want to test your FrontPage webs outside of FrontPage.

What's Inside

The best way to start reading this book is from the beginning. Skill 1, *Web Publishing with FrontPage 2000*, is an introduction to the Internet and the World Wide Web. It explains how FrontPage is a well-rounded solution to the issues involved with creating, running, and managing a Web site.

Skill 2, *Creating a Web and Web Pages*, shows you how to create a new Web site in FrontPage, and gives you an overview of creating and editing pages in Front-Page. You can either save your pages in a FrontPage web or use them elsewhere. Skills 3, 4, and 6 through 13 all cover various page-creation issues in FrontPage.

Skill 3, *Working with Lists and Headings*, and Skill 4, *Formatting Your Pages*, both focus on the basics of editing and formatting your web pages, including the ways you can change the appearance of a page by formatting text, paragraphs, or the entire page.

Skill 5, *Managing Webs in FrontPage*, shows you how to manage files and folders in a web and the ways FrontPage helps you understand the hyperlinks in the files in your site. Most importantly, it shows you how to add pages to your web's structure that are automatically linked to other pages.

Perhaps the most important feature of any Web site—creating and using hyper-links—is covered in Skill 6, *Linking Your Pages to the Web*. You'll learn how to create hyperlinks from text or images and how to specify the target files and bookmarks. You'll also learn how to apply navigation bars to make your web easy to get around.

The HTML table is discussed in Skill 7, *Using Tables to Add Structure*. You can use a table to organize data within its orderly rows and columns. You also learn how to take advantage of the structure of a table as a valuable page layout and design tool.

Skill 8, *Displaying Images in Your Pages*, covers another important feature in any Web site: the images it displays. You'll learn the differences between GIF and JPEG image files, and you'll learn how to convert images to other formats. You'll see how to insert images and video clips into a page and how to change their size and appearance. Skill 9, *Getting Graphic with Image Composer*, takes you on a grand tour through Microsoft Image Composer, the dramatically redesigned image-editing program that comes with the stand-alone version of FrontPage.

Skill 10, *Creating a Consistent Look for Your Web*, shows you how to create new pages in FrontPage using templates or wizards, and apply themes that provide backgrounds, colors, and buttons for all the pages of your web. One of the newest HTML features, cascading style sheets, is introduced in this Skill, in addition to information on how to import and export files between webs.

Skill 11, *Automating Your Web with FrontPage Components*, covers some of the exciting new dynamic HTML and other automated features incorporated into FrontPage 2000. You learn how to create hover buttons, banner ads, and scrolling marquees, and how to add automated features such as a table of contents and hit counter to your web pages.

Skill 12, *Letting Users Interact with Forms*, introduces you to building forms in web pages. You'll see how easy it is to create text fields, check boxes, radio buttons, drop-down menus, and other form controls. In Skill 13, *Getting Fancier with Frames*, you'll learn about a frames page, which is a single page that displays other pages, each within a separate frame, or window. You'll also examine the question of when to use frames most effectively and when not to use them.

Finally, Skill 14, *Publishing Your Web Site*, covers some of the Web administration tasks you can perform in FrontPage, such as assigning access rights to a Web site when the site is hosted by a Web server. Following this Skill is Appendix A, *Installing and Starting FrontPage*, which discusses the issues you need to consider when installing FrontPage.

You'll find plain language whenever possible in this book, which was a pretty daunting task considering that acronyms and jargon are rampant in the language of the Internet. You'll also find these special features, which serve as adjuncts to the main body of text:

NOTE NOTE NOTE NOTE NOTE NOTE NOTE NOTE NOTE NOTE NOTE NOTE NOTE NOTE
Notes emphasize important information about a topic.

TIP TIP TIP TIP TIP TIP TIP TIP TIP TIP TIP TIP TIP TIP TIP TIP TIP TIP TIP TIP TIP TIP
Tips provide shortcuts and easy-to-use techniques.

WARNING WARNING WARNING WARNING WARNING WARNING WARNING WARNING
Warnings inform you about potential problems and pitfalls.

All the sample web pages and examples of HTML features in this book are simple, uncluttered, and to the point. You won't have any trouble following along with the exercises and explanations.

This book utilizes some typographical elements you'll find useful to help distinguish certain aspects of the text. Text you enter with your keyboard is in **boldface**, while filenames and URLs are in a monospaced `program font`.

I hope you find *Microsoft FrontPage 2000: No Experience Required* to be helpful as well as enjoyable to read, and that it becomes a valuable tutorial and reference guide as you build your web pages and sites. If you have any comments about this book, please send them to me in care of Sybex; they will be much appreciated.

Web Publishing with FrontPage 2000

- ➔ **Understanding the Internet**
- ➔ **Accessing the World Wide Web (WWW)**
- ➔ **Using an intranet as an in-house Web site**
- ➔ **Understanding Web publishing**
- ➔ **Using FrontPage as your Web site publishing solution**

T he explosive growth of the Internet in the past few years is ample evidence of how a simple concept—a network that can connect every computer on Earth—can fulfill countless needs. This Skill first introduces you to the Internet, the World Wide Web, and subsets of the Internet called *intranets*. Then you'll see how Microsoft FrontPage 2000 offers the tools you need to set up and manage a site on the Web, create web pages, and leap over many of the hurdles you'll encounter while publishing on the Web.

If you are already familiar with the World Wide Web and want to get right to work creating web pages with FrontPage's fully integrated WYSIWYG (what you see is what you get) HTML editor, you can skip ahead to Skill 2. Skill 5 shows you how to access the files and hyperlinks in an existing site using FrontPage's web management views and tools. If you want to focus on creating and editing graphics, Skill 9 describes how to work with the Microsoft Image Composer. For help installing FrontPage, turn to Appendix A, *Installing and Starting FrontPage*. And if you're brand new to the role of Web designer, follow right along and you'll soon be a pro.

Understanding the Internet, the Web, and Intranets

The *Internet* was originally conceived, designed, and implemented in the 1960s as a United States Defense Department strategy to protect lines of communication and access to vital databases in the event of a nuclear attack. The early version of the Internet, called ARPAnet, connected computers in military installations and universities in the United States; this network was then expanded to Canada and Western Europe. It was only in the 1990s, however, that the Internet moved out of university research centers and into the homes and businesses of millions of people around the world. This phenomenon is the result of the *World Wide Web (WWW)*—an amazing development that transformed a boring, text-based communications system into a dynamic, colorful, multimedia-rich environment.

One of the strengths of the Internet has always been that it is platform-independent: regardless of the type of computer and operating system you have, you can connect to the Internet. This means that a Macintosh user living in Great Britain can post information on a computer in London that runs the Windows NT operating system. Then, someone in Framingham using a PC running Windows 3.1 can connect to a computer in Boston that runs the UNIX operating system, have that computer connect to the computer in London, and receive the information they need. In a matter of seconds, information is literally transported halfway around the world.

Of course, the original designers of the Internet did not envision the innumerable uses that people of the '90s have found for this incredible communications tool. But the need to make any sort of file available to remote users, regardless of which computer they use, is exactly why the Internet was created.

Clients, Servers, and Networks

The Internet consists of three fundamental elements:

Servers   Computers and software that make data available to other programs on the same or other computers, also called *hosts*.

Clients   Computers that request data from servers.

Networks   Groups of computers that can communicate with each other, such as clients requesting and receiving data from a server. The communication can be over copper wire, coaxial cable, fiber-optic cable, microwave relay, satellite transmission, and so on.

NOTE NOTE NOTE NOTE NOTE NOTE NOTE NOTE NOTE NOTE NOTE NOTE NOTE NOTE NOTE NOTE

When you connect to a server halfway around the world, you might use any or all of these network communication methods. Of course, it doesn't really matter to you; the system simply follows the most advantageous route over the network until it reaches the computer you want to access.

Internet Protocols

Although the Internet is a network, you shouldn't think of it as a single network. It's really a collection of countless smaller networks, all of which agree to send and receive data according to a set of standards called *protocols* to communicate across the Internet.

Transmission Control Protocol/Internet Protocol (TCP/IP) is the means by which these computer networks communicate. *TCP* specifies how messages should be split up into packets for transmission. *IP* addresses the packets and routes them to their destination. It's the combined TCP/IP protocol that makes the Internet the Internet, because it allows any computer or network using TCP/IP to access and exchange information with other TCP/IP computers.

There are many ways to get data from the Internet. For example, *File Transfer Protocol (FTP)*, a program that transfers files from one computer to another, is one of the original Internet services; mailing lists for users who were interested in specific topics were another early Internet tool. But there's one Internet access method that has taken the world by storm: It allows companies and individuals to publish newspapers and magazines, open online retail stores, offer online catalogs and reference material, and even broadcast live audio and video from around the world. This latest addition to the Internet family is called the World Wide Web.

The World Wide Web

The rocket fuel for the Internet's dizzying rise is the World Wide Web (WWW, or simply, the Web). Tim Berners-Lee created the graphical-based Web in 1992 to make it easier to search for documents. The rapid international adoption of the Web has vastly improved the way you access data on the Internet.

NOTE NOTE NOTE NOTE NOTE NOTE NOTE NOTE NOTE NOTE NOTE NOTE NOTE NOTE NOTE

In this book, you'll see the word *web* used frequently in different contexts. The word Web (capitalized) refers to the World Wide Web; the term Web site, or just plain site, refers to a collection of files on the Web that you access with a browser. A FrontPage web (lowercase), or simply a web, is a Web site that you've created in FrontPage. Realize that it's not always easy, or even necessary, to distinguish between a Web site and the Web because the network and the computers connected to it must all function together.

Understanding Internet Addresses

Each file, or resource, on the Web is identified by its *Uniform Resource Locator (URL)*, which is its address or location on the Web. URLs begin with the name of the protocol used by the URL's server. *Hypertext Transfer Protocol*, or *HTTP*, is the protocol designed for the World Wide Web. The protocol is followed by a colon, two slashes, and the site type. The site type is usually World Wide Web (www), but could be File Transfer Protocol (ftp) or Gopher (gopher). The site type is followed by the address of the host computer, called a *domain address*. The domain address includes the site name, followed by the *domain*, which indicates the type of organization that owns the server. The URL for the HTTP server owned by Sybex looks like this:

```
http://www.sybex.com
```

http is the server protocol; *www* is the site type; *sybex* is the site name; and *com* is the domain.

NOTE NOTE NOTE NOTE NOTE NOTE NOTE NOTE NOTE NOTE NOTE NOTE NOTE NOTE NOTE

Don't confuse URL (Uniform Resource Locator) with IRL, which is online short-hand for "In Real Life."

Domain Names

Until recently, there were only six root (top level) domain names used in the United States:

com For commercial companies, like Sybex in the URL listed above

edu For schools, colleges, and universities

gov For federal, state, and local government entities

mil Reserved for the military

net For companies that administer or provide access to the Internet

org For noncommercial organizations, like nonprofits

Countries outside the United States use a two letter country code as the domain name: for example, uk for the United Kingdom and jp for Japan. Due to the rapid expansion of the World Wide Web, seven new domains have been approved for use on the Web:

firm For commercial businesses

store For retail and mail order businesses

web For organizations that deal with the World Wide Web

arts For cultural and entertainment organizations

rec For organizations emphasizing recreation/entertainment activities

info For companies that provide information services, like information brokers and libraries

nom (as in *nomenclature*) For individuals who want their own Web server

Accessing Resources on the Internet

The software you use to access data on the Web is the *browser,* which is essentially a file viewer that can use HTTP to communicate with servers. There are several popular browsers available, including Microsoft Internet Explorer (which is included with FrontPage in the Office 2000 suite) and Netscape Navigator.

Here's the overview of how you open a resource (file) on the Web:

1. In your browser, you specify the complete URL of the Web resource you want to access.

2. The browser sends your request to the server with which you're communicating.

3. Your server forwards the request to the server you specified in the URL.

4. That server locates the resource and sends it back to your server.

5. Finally, your server sends the resource to your browser.

It may sound complicated, but all this usually happens in a matter of seconds, no matter where on the Internet the resource may be located. It's really no different (at least, from your perspective) than picking up the telephone, dialing a phone number, and having the phone system make the connection.

Once you open a resource in your browser, you can view it, print it, or save it on a disk. Basically, it's yours to play with. Note that when a Web browser receives a file it can't handle, such as an audio or video file, it may ask you if you'd like to save that file on a disk so you can work with it later on. Otherwise, it passes the file along to the computer's operating system, which then opens the appropriate program (assuming there is one) for that file.

Web Sites, Pages, and Links

When you want to create documents, or pages, that Web browsers can read, you use the *Hypertext Markup Language (HTML),* the language used to format Web pages. You use HTML to create the content and specify the structure and format of the Web page. HTML files are always plain text files, so you can send a page to virtually any type of computer in the world (as long as it's connected to the Internet, of course).

Each user's browser interprets the HTML code and displays the page. A page may not appear exactly the same when displayed in different browsers. This is because the precise appearance of a page is not explicitly included in the HTML code. Rather, the page's appearance is broadly described and the browser is responsible for coming up with a suitable representation. This may sound like a weakness of the Web, but it's actually a great strength—browsers on completely dissimilar computers can present reasonable renditions of the same page.

A *Web site* is a collection of Web pages and other resources that have something in common, and can be considered as one body of information, like a set of encyclopedias. The resources in a Web site are often all located on one server, but they don't need to be. The Web site's *home page* is the initial page that you see when you access a Web site without specifying the name of a specific file at that location. For example, `www.sybex.com` is the URL (address) of Sybex's home page, shown in Figure 1.1. The home page usually serves as a welcome mat or a table of contents, and may give instructions for accessing the other resources in the site.

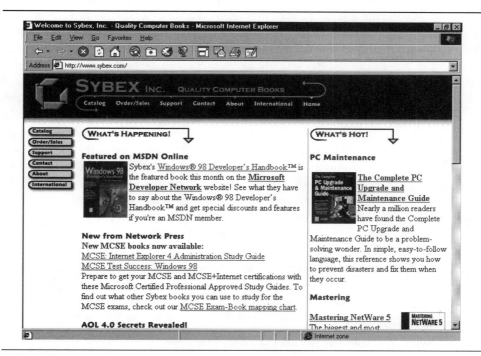

FIGURE 1.1: The Sybex home page has hotspots for user navigation.

The best aspect of the Web is the ability to embed links within pages so users can move easily between pages in a Web site, or jump to another related site with a single click. A *hyperlink,* or link, is text (usually underlined and in a different color) or a graphic image called a *hotspot* that you can click to access the target resource of that link anywhere on the Web. In Figure 1.1, the home page includes links that take the user to Catalog, Order/Sales, and several other areas on the Sybex Web site, as well as to pages for specific books promoted on the home page. Text hyperlinks and hotspots are a quick, easy, and very effective way to let you jump from one URL to another.

The Internet and Intranets

All the issues discussed in the previous sections relate to the global Internet and the World Wide Web. However, you can also set up a local TCP/IP network that takes advantage of HTML pages, links, URLs, Web sites, and the rest, but isn't necessarily connected to the global Internet. Such a network is called an *intranet,* and differs from the Internet only because it is not accessible to every Internet-connected computer in the world. The term *I*net* refers to both the Internet and intranets.

Thousands of businesses are realizing the low costs and numerous benefits of using an intranet to distribute information within an organization. Even older computers can run some type of browser, and it's quite likely that the computers on a local network already have Web-browsing software installed, so there's no additional investment needed on the client end. Many users of those computers are probably already familiar with browsing the Web and can browse an intranet with little or no additional training. Once you've set up an intranet, it's easy to publish just part of it to the Internet at large because all the resources on the intranet are already in a Web-ready format.

NOTE NOTE NOTE NOTE NOTE NOTE NOTE NOTE NOTE NOTE NOTE NOTE NOTE NOTE NOTE

The trick is making sure that outside users can't access your company's intranet through the public pages that you open to the Internet. Companies use a variety of software packages called *firewalls* to prevent unauthorized access from the Internet to an intranet—or to keep employees from surfing the Internet on company time.

Finally, the browsing and linking concept of the Web effectively allows multiple users at client computers to share the same server resources via their browsers. And it works just as well for interoffice communications within a company as it does between countries on separate continents. For more information and examples

of intranets created with FrontPage, visit the Site Developer Network at
`http://www.microsoft.com`.

The FrontPage Solution to Web Publishing

You can create a Web site from scratch using any text editor. However, this makes
the job of creating and running a Web site difficult and time consuming. Enter the
Web-smart components of FrontPage 2000:

Server Extensions   Add-on programs for Web server software that make
the server "FrontPage-aware" and able to interact more closely with Front-
Page webs.

FrontPage Views   Different views of your web that allow you to add,
remove, and rename resources, keep all the hyperlinks up to date, edit web
pages in a powerful yet easy to use HTML editor, and much more. They are:

- Page view (for editing web pages)
- Folders view
- Reports view
- Navigation view
- Hyperlinks view
- Tasks view

Image Composer   An image editor that lets you create images for any
Web site, import them, modify them, adjust them, embellish them, and
otherwise slop paint on the old electronic canvas.

In the sections that follow, we'll take a short look at these FrontPage components
so you can see how each one simplifies your task of creating and running a web.

NOTE NOTE NOTE NOTE NOTE NOTE NOTE NOTE NOTE NOTE NOTE NOTE NOTE NOTE

**Earlier versions of FrontPage included the Microsoft Personal Web Server, a
"personal-sized" Web server that allowed you to create, test, revise, and host
a Web site. It was required for developing FrontPage webs, but is no longer
needed in FrontPage 2000. However, if you would still like to use this afford-
able (free) server to host your web on your intranet or the Internet, you'll find
the Personal Web Server included with Windows 98, or you can download it
for free from Microsoft's Web site at** `www.microsoft.com`**.**

The FrontPage Server Extensions

You'll get the most out of your FrontPage webs when your Web server is set up to work with the special features FrontPage has to offer. There are many servers on the market, but most of them are not FrontPage-ready.

If you want to take advantage of all of FrontPage's features with other servers, you need to install the FrontPage Server Extensions on the server. FrontPage includes these server extensions for widely used servers like the Microsoft Internet Information Server (IIS), Apache, O'Reilly WebSite, and Netscape Communications Server, and you can download more extensions from Microsoft's Web site free of charge:

```
http://www.microsoft.com/frontpage/
```

If you can't find server extensions for the server you need, don't worry. Your web will run fine under the server if you don't include those features that are unique to FrontPage (Skill 14 discusses those features and how to enable or disable them in your FrontPage webs).

The FrontPage Views

The FrontPage views allow you to create, revise, and manage an entire web, as well as write, edit, and format individual web pages. We'll look at the Hyperlinks view first as a typical example.

NOTE NOTE NOTE NOTE NOTE NOTE NOTE NOTE NOTE NOTE NOTE NOTE NOTE NOTE NOTE

Web management is covered in detail in Skills 5, 10, and 14; web page editing is covered in Skills 2 through 4, 6 through 8, and 11 through 13.

Figure 1.2 shows FrontPage in the Hyperlinks view with an open web. Notice the Microsoft Office-like menu bar and toolbars at the top, and the status bar at the bottom. FrontPage shares many of the design features and tools that are found in Microsoft Office 2000.

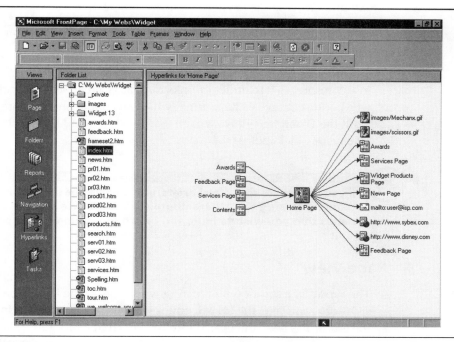

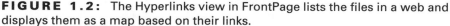

FIGURE 1.2: The Hyperlinks view in FrontPage lists the files in a web and displays them as a map based on their links.

The FrontPage window consists of three vertical panes when you're working in the Page, Folders, Navigation, or Hyperlinks views. The pane on the left is the Views bar, which displays a button for each view; simply click a button to display that view (the Hyperlinks button was selected in the example in Figure 1.2). You can instead select a view command from the View menu. To change the size of the buttons, right-click in the Views bar and choose Small Icons or Large Icons from the shortcut menu.

The pane in the middle is the Folder List, which displays all the web pages and other files that make up the resources of the current web. You can manipulate the list of resources in the usual Windows Explorer manner—click the plus sign to expand a level of the list to show more detail (show the contents of a folder), or click the minus sign to hide the detail. Right-click a file or folder to display its shortcut menu.

The pane on the right displays the body or content of the view. In Hyperlinks view (see Figure 1.2), it displays a model of the web, with lines connecting a page to any resources it includes or links to. This is a real peek behind the scenes of your web because it reveals the normally hidden relationships among its resources.

All the FrontPage views will be discussed in detail later in this book, but we'll take just a quick look at them now.

NOTE NOTE NOTE NOTE NOTE NOTE NOTE NOTE NOTE NOTE NOTE NOTE NOTE NOTE NOTE

If you need more screen real estate, you can give the entire window to any single pane by closing the others. Simply go to the View menu and select those panes that you wish to hide, and return to that menu to display them again.

Page View

The FrontPage solution for creating web pages is the Page view. In previous versions of FrontPage, the HTML editor was a separate module; in FrontPage 2000, the editor has been integrated into the FrontPage program as the Page view. If you double-click a web page filename in the Folder List, FrontPage will open the file for editing in Page view, as shown in Figure 1.3.

The page editing pane is essentially a WYSIWYG word processor that is designed to work specifically with HTML pages, and offers you all the common page layout options that are available in the most recent version of HTML. Many of the tools and features are the same that you would expect to find in a Windows word processor. For example, you can open multiple documents and copy and paste data between them in the usual ways.

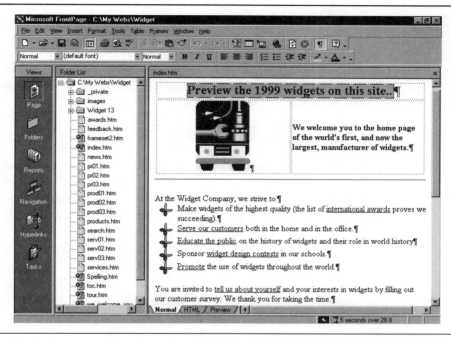

FIGURE 1.3: Editing a web page in FrontPage is like working in a Windows word processor.

NOTE NOTE NOTE NOTE NOTE NOTE NOTE NOTE NOTE NOTE NOTE NOTE NOTE NOTE
If you use Microsoft Word or other programs in Microsoft Office, you'll find that the Page view's HTML editor is carved from the same block of granite. The Office spelling dictionary and thesaurus are shared with FrontPage. You'll recognize many other features and commands, and you should find it a comfortable place to work.

Folders View

You can click the Folders button to display the files and folders that make up the contents of your web. These are displayed in the Folder List as usual, but details about each one are displayed in the right-hand pane: the page title (for HTML web pages), file size, the date and time it was last modified, the person who modified it, its URL, and any comments that have been attached to it.

As in Windows Explorer, you can sort a list of files by clicking a column title, move a file to a new folder by dragging its icon, select one or more files, rename a file, or delete a file. You can use the commands on the menu bar, or right-click a file or folder to display its shortcut menu. The Folders List is discussed later in Skill 5.

Reports View

FrontPage helps you maintain, manage, and keep track of your web in many ways. The Reports view offers a variety of detailed reports about your web that you can display at any time. You can choose one of the reports from the Reporting toolbar, or pick one from the View ➤ Reports menu. As in the Folders view, simply click a column title to sort the items in each report.

For example, the Broken Hyperlinks report lists all pages in which a hypertext link no longer points to a valid target, such as when the target file has been moved, renamed, or deleted outside the influence of FrontPage. The maintenance of your web becomes a lot easier with important information such as this at your fingertips. The Reports view is discussed later in Skill 5.

Navigation View

FrontPage allows you to define the structure of your web by arranging the pages in a graphical map-like view, the Navigation view. You can also add navigation buttons to one or more pages in your web. For example, FrontPage makes it easy for you to place navigation buttons on each page, so that users of your site can, for example, just click a button to display the previous or next page, or return to the home page.

When you click the Navigation button in FrontPage, you'll see the navigation path for your web, as shown in Figure 1.4. Simply drag and drop file icons in the right-hand pane to change or expand the path defined in the navigation buttons. You'll read more about the Navigation view in Skill 5.

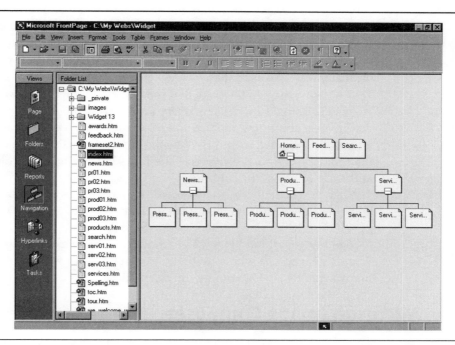

FIGURE 1.4: In the Navigation view, changing the path that can be followed in a web is as easy as dragging and dropping file icons.

Tasks View

Creating and maintaining a Web site is no small feat, at least not if you want to do the job well. You need to attend to countless web-related assignments, large and small. To help you keep track of these jobs, FrontPage offers the Tasks view, which is discussed further in Skill 5 and shown in Figure 1.5.

Status	Task	Assigned To	Priority	Associated With	Modified Date	Description
Not Started	Customize home page	Gene	Medium	Home Page	3/18/99 4:35:17...	Replace the generic text with spe
Not Started	Press releases	Gordon	Medium	News Page	3/18/99 4:36:12...	Get a list of press releases from th
Not Started	Update products list	Gordon	High	Products Page	3/18/99 4:37:15...	When Gordon returns, he needs t
Not Started	Add instructions	Cheryl	Medium	Search Page	3/18/99 4:37:59...	We need to add some basic instru
Not Started	Pricing policy	Gene	High	Services Page	3/18/99 4:39:42...	We need to revise the pricing poli
Not Started	Fine-tune ToC	Gordon	Low	Contents	3/18/99 4:40:25...	The final job is to add descriptive

FIGURE 1.5: The FrontPage Tasks view helps you manage web-related tasks.

When you've selected a filename or icon, or when you're editing a web page in the Page view, you can invoke the Edit ➤ Task ➤ Add Task command to create a description of a task that is automatically linked to the chosen file. When you later display the Tasks view, you'll see the task description you created, along with any other tasks that are in the list. You can select a task and choose Edit ➤ Task ➤ Start to open the page that is associated with that task.

There is a single Tasks list in every FrontPage web. Anyone working on the site can create a new entry and include information such as a name for the task, to whom it's assigned, its priority, the file to which it's linked, and a description of the task. You can sort the items in the Tasks list by clicking a column title button at the top of any of the columns.

When you actually finish a task, you can mark it as completed in the Tasks list, and either delete it from the list or retain that task as part of a history of jobs completed. The Tasks view is discussed in Skill 5.

Together, the different views in FrontPage let you examine and manipulate the FrontPage web as a whole, so that you don't have to work with and keep track of many separate and seemingly unrelated files.

Microsoft Image Composer

The World Wide Web would not be the exciting place that it is if it weren't for the rich and varied use of graphical images in the millions of pages on the Web.

Because images play such a crucial role in bringing a Web site to life, the stand-alone version of FrontPage 2000 comes with Microsoft Image Composer. With the Image Composer, you can create images, add clip art and photos, open many different image file formats, and add a wide range of special effects to your work. You'll find it discussed in Skill 9.

Now that you've had an introduction to the Internet, the World Wide Web, Web sites, and FrontPage 2000, we'll look at how you can create a web and add content to a web page.

Are You Experienced?

Now you can:

- ☑ Speak the language of the Internet
- ☑ Describe the process for creating a web page
- ☑ Outline the functions of Web servers
- ☑ Identify the different views in FrontPage

Creating a Web and Web Pages

- ➔ Creating a new web
- ➔ Viewing a web
- ➔ Creating a new page
- ➔ Editing your page
- ➔ Working with HTML code
- ➔ Previewing a page in a browser
- ➔ Spell-checking a page or web
- ➔ Finding and replacing text in a page or web

FrontPage is your web navigation center, the place where you start and finish your work on a web. This Skill shows you how to create a web and use the Page view to design exciting web pages. The overview of the editing process and the features presented in this Skill pave the way for the Skills that follow, where you'll learn about a wide variety of HTML elements you can create in your pages.

The Standard toolbar (shown below) contains many of the tools you'll use to manage and edit your web.

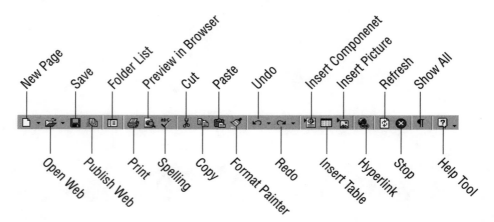

Creating a New Web

We'll call the web you are viewing or modifying in FrontPage the *current* or *active* web. When you create and save individual pages for that web using FrontPage's built-in editor, they become part of the active web unless you specify otherwise.

Because creating or revising web pages is probably the job you'll perform most often in FrontPage, when you start the program you'll normally see just two panes: the Views bar and the Page view with a blank web page, ready for editing. You can instead open an existing page or an entire FrontPage web, or create a brand new FrontPage web.

TIP TIP TIP TIP TIP TIP TIP TIP TIP TIP TIP TIP TIP TIP TIP TIP TIP TIP TIP TIP TIP TIP TIP

You can also choose to have the last web you worked on open automatically when you start FrontPage. Choose Tools ➢ Options, and select Open Last Web Automatically from the General tab in the Options dialog box.

There are two primary steps required to create a new web: select the type of web you want to create, and specify a location for it. First choose File ➢ New ➢ Web, or select Web from the drop-down list in the New Page button (on the Standard toolbar). This opens the New dialog box, which is shown in Figure 2.1.

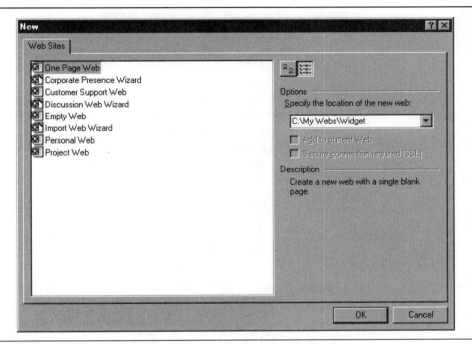

FIGURE 2.1: The New dialog box lets you create a new FrontPage web from a web template or wizard.

In this dialog box, select one of the web templates or wizards listed on the Web Sites tab. For example, if you are new to FrontPage, you may want to start out by creating just a one-page web from the template of that name. This way you can get comfortable working with web pages before moving on to more complex projects. If you are already familiar with FrontPage and want to import an existing web or create a web with a wizard or one of the more richly populated templates, you may want to skip to Skill 10, *Creating a Consistent Look for Your Web*, before returning to this Skill.

You also specify a name and location for the new web in the New dialog box. You can give your web any name you want using spaces, upper- and lowercase letters, numbers, and any other characters that are acceptable in filenames.

You may want to avoid spaces in your web names, because some Web servers won't accept them. You should also stick with just lowercase letters, because some servers are case-sensitive and will distinguish between the file or folder name "my web site" and "My Web Site." It's easier for visitors to enter all lowercase letters in their browsers to access your site, and not have to remember the case of the name exactly.

When you are creating a local web (as opposed to a web on a server), the default location for your web is generally the My Webs folder. When you are ready to publish your web for all the world to see, you can transfer the web from your local drive to its permanent location (see "Publishing a Web to a Server" in Skill 14).

A FrontPage web contains not only the files you create, but several other folders and files that are created by FrontPage and used to manage and run your web. The names of these folders begin with an underscore, such as _borders, and are not normally displayed within the Folders List in FrontPage because they are strictly for FrontPage's own use. You can, however, view these folders by enabling the Show Documents in Hidden Directories option, which you'll find on the Advanced tab for the Tools ➣ Web Settings command. You can also view them within Windows Explorer, although you definitely should not change or delete them. There are two FrontPage folders that you are free to use as you need them:

images   This is a convenient folder in which to store image files, such as GIF and JPEG files.

_private   This folder is not visible to browsers when your FrontPage web is hosted by a FrontPage-aware server, so any files in it are invisible as well. Once your site is up and running under a server for the public to see, this might be a place to keep pages that are under construction, reference files, and other documents you want to be available for your use only. Unlike the other FrontPage folders that begin with the underscore character, the contents of this folder are visible to you while you're working in FrontPage.

When you create a new web, it is ready for you to enhance and expand it.

One bonus of FrontPage is that you don't have to worry about periodically saving your web. When you make changes, such as renaming pages or importing new files, those changes are saved automatically. When you are editing pages, however, there is a File ➢ Save command for you to use, just as you would in any word processor.

SKILL
2

Opening an Existing Web

To open an existing FrontPage web that you've recently worked on, use the File ➢ Recent Webs command, which lists the webs you've opened in the recent past. Otherwise, use File ➢ Open Web, or click the Open Web button on the Standard toolbar. (If that button is displayed as the Open button, for opening a file not a web, click the down arrow next to it and select Open Web).

The Open Web dialog box is similar to a typical files dialog box, except in this case you are not selecting a file but an entire folder—the folder that contains a FrontPage web. Select the one you want and click OK to open that web. If you already had a web open in FrontPage, a new FrontPage program window will be started for the web you're opening. You will then have two FrontPage windows open, each displaying a different web.

If the web you open has security controls placed on it, you may have to enter your username and password before you can open the web. See Skill 14, *Publishing Your Web Site*, for more information about security.

To open a different web in the same window, choose File ➢ Close Web first. You can choose File ➢ Exit at any time to close FrontPage. If you have been editing one or more web pages and have not saved your work, you will first be asked if you wish to do so. Note that if you have multiple FrontPage windows running, each displaying a separate web, you can close any of them while leaving the others open.

Creating, Opening, and Saving Web Pages

You normally use the Page view's built-in HTML editor to create and revise web pages. If you are familiar with an earlier version of FrontPage, you'll most likely be pleased that the HTML editor is now an integral part of FrontPage, and not a separate application. You don't need to switch back and forth between the page you are editing and your web in FrontPage.

Creating a New Page

To create a new blank web page, simply click the New Page button on the Standard toolbar, and the new page will appear in the right-hand pane. You can have multiple pages open at the same time, switching between them as needed by choosing one from the Windows menu.

You can also create a new page from a FrontPage template, which is a ready-built page that serves as the basis for the new page. You choose a template when you use the File ➤ New ➤ Page command (Ctrl+N), or you can right-click a folder in the Folders List and choose New Page from the shortcut menu. The Normal Page template is the standard blank page that opens when you click the New Page button. Templates are discussed in Skill 10.

To close the active document, choose File ➤ Close. If you have not saved the document since making changes to it, you will be prompted to save it to avoid losing that work.

Opening an Existing Page

There are several ways to open an existing page for editing in FrontPage. You can use File ➤ Open (Ctrl+O) and choose a file from the Open File dialog box, or click the Open button on the Standard toolbar. You can also double-click a page name or icon from the Folder List or the Hyperlinks view, or right-click the filename or icon and choose Open from the shortcut menu.

Saving Your Work

Just as in your word processor, you must save your work to keep it. Normally, you will save a web page within the active web in FrontPage, but you can choose to save it elsewhere as a separate file, independent of your web. Use the File ➤ Save command (Ctrl+S), or click the Save button on the Standard toolbar. If the page is a new one that you have not yet saved, you will see the Save As dialog box, shown in Figure 2.2, which will always be displayed when you choose File ➤ Save As.

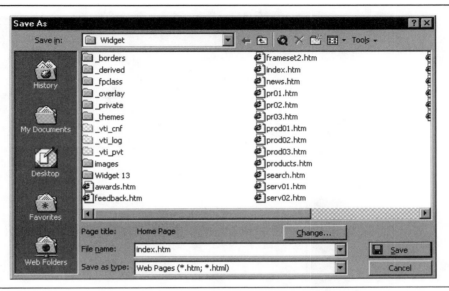

FIGURE 2.2: The first time you save a web page, or when you choose File ➤ Save As, you specify the filename, location, and page title in the Save As dialog box.

In the Save As dialog box, you pick a location for the file (normally one of the folders in your web), enter a name for the file and, optionally, click the Change button and specify a page title (you can also specify a title while editing the page).

TIP TIP TIP TIP TIP TIP TIP TIP TIP TIP TIP TIP TIP TIP TIP TIP TIP TIP TIP TIP TIP TIP TIP

You can create folders in your FrontPage web to organize its files. For example, you can save or move files to them, just as you do with the normal folders and documents you create on your computer. When you insert a hyperlink into a page in your web, the location of its target is automatically specified in the link.

Entering and Editing Text

Editing a page in the Page view is very much like working in a typical WYSIWYG word processor, where "what you see is what you get." In this case, what you see is pretty much what the rest of the world sees in their Web browsers when they view that page on your Web site (see Figure 2.3).

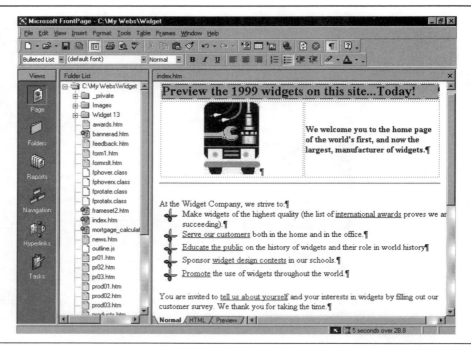

FIGURE 2.3: You create web pages in FrontPage in much the same way that you create documents in a word processor.

If you are a Microsoft Word user, you may notice that the process of editing an HTML document in FrontPage looks suspiciously similar to Word. The similarities are not accidental. Microsoft has worked very hard to have all its Office products—Word, Excel, PowerPoint, and FrontPage—share the same look and even the same program resources. For example, you'll find the same toolbar buttons for commands such as New, Open, Save, Cut, and Paste. Those commands also appear in the same menus, so if you're already familiar with Microsoft Word, you won't have any trouble getting started in FrontPage.

TIP TIP TIP TIP TIP TIP TIP TIP TIP TIP TIP TIP TIP TIP TIP TIP TIP TIP TIP TIP TIP TIP TIP

Paste Special is also available, so you can insert text with or without formatting that copied from within FrontPage or from other applications. For example, when you copy a paragraph from a Word document, FrontPage will convert the formatting into an equivalent look in HTML (as best it can). If you want the text without any formatting, choose Paste Special ➤ Normal Paragraphs.

Let's take a quick look at some of the features of the Page view in Figure 2.3:

- At the top of the screen, beneath the title bar, is the menu bar, the Standard toolbar, and the Formatting toolbar. Several other toolbars are available as well. You can turn the display of a toolbar on or off by selecting it from the View ➤ Toolbars menu.

- At the bottom of the screen is the status bar, which displays useful information as you work on your web page. For example, the left side of the status bar displays the target address of a hyperlink when you point to a link in the page.

- Just above the status bar are three tabs that switch you between views of your document: Normal, HTML, and Preview (more about those later).

- The web page you're editing appears in the window beneath the toolbars and to the right of the Views bar and Folder List (unless you have closed those panes to provide more room for the page you're editing). You can open multiple web pages and switch between them with the Windows menu.

- The horizontal and vertical scroll bars offer one way to scroll through your document; you can also use the usual keyboard keys, such as PgUp and PgDn. If your mouse has a scrolling wheel, such as Microsoft's IntelliMouse, you can use the wheel to scroll up or down through the page.

Basic Editing Procedures

The best way to familiarize yourself with the process of editing pages in the Page view is to start typing. Most of the basic procedures you've already learned in your word processor are applicable in FrontPage:

- You can have multiple documents open at the same time, but only one is active. The active page receives the text you enter and is the target of any commands you issue.

- In the active document, enter text just as you would in your word processor; FrontPage wraps text automatically, so press Enter only to create a new paragraph.

- Press Del to delete the character to the right of the insertion point; press Backspace to delete the character to its left. Press Ctrl+Del to delete the word to the right of the insertion point, and press Ctrl+Backspace to delete the word to its left.

- Press Home to go to the beginning of the current line and End to go to its end. Press Ctrl+Home to go to the top of the document and Ctrl+End to go to the bottom.

- When you have opened multiple documents, their windows are stacked one on top of the other in the Page view pane; you can't reduce their size or minimize them.

- Select text by dragging over it with your mouse or by pressing the Shift key while you use a keyboard arrow key to select the material.

- Once you select a portion of the document, you can act on the selection by making choices from the menu, a toolbar, or a shortcut menu. For example, choose Edit ➢ Cut from the menu, click the Cut button on the toolbar, or right-click and choose Cut from the shortcut menu to remove the selection from the document and send it to the Windows Clipboard.

- You can transfer text or images between FrontPage and other programs in the usual ways by using Copy or Cut and Paste with the Clipboard.

- Choose Edit ➢ Undo from the menu, click the Undo button on the Standard toolbar, or press Ctrl+Z to undo your most recent action in the document. You can "undo an undo" by choosing Edit ➢ Redo or by clicking the Redo button.

You can add comments in a page by selecting Insert ➢ Comment from the menu. The text you enter is displayed in the page you're editing, but not when the page is viewed in a browser. A comment can explain an area in the page or serve as a reminder to you or another author. (Comments are discussed in the "Inserting a FrontPage Component for Your Comments" section in Skill 11.)

Inserting Paragraphs and Line Breaks

When you want to create a new paragraph in a document, simply press Enter, just as you would in your word processor. Behind the scenes, this inserts new <P> and </P> opening and closing tags in the underlying HTML code, defining the beginning and end of the new paragraph.

A new paragraph not only begins on a new line, it also has its own formatting, just as in Word. For example, if you press Enter at the end of a left-aligned paragraph (the default alignment), you can center the new paragraph, right align it, or add other paragraph formatting without changing the formatting for the previous line.

NOTE NOTE NOTE NOTE NOTE NOTE NOTE NOTE NOTE NOTE NOTE NOTE NOTE NOTE NOTE

When you press Enter but do not enter any text in the new paragraph, Front-Page places the HTML code for a non-breaking space (Ctrl+Shift+Space) between the two paragraph tags, so the code created looks like this: <P> </P>. The non-breaking space on a line by itself forces a browser to display a blank line, where it might otherwise ignore the "empty" paragraph.

You can force a line to break without creating a new paragraph by pressing Shift+Enter instead of Enter. This inserts the line break tag,
 (you can also choose Normal Line Break from the dialog box of the Insert ➤ Break command). The text that follows the line break appears on a new line, but is otherwise still a part of the current paragraph and carries all of its formatting.

Most browsers insert some extra space between two paragraphs of text, so there are instances when you'd rather use the <BR> tag than the <P> tag to create a new line. For example, when you display your name and address in a page, you don't want extra space between each line of the address.

The next graphic shows two addresses in a table in a page being edited in FrontPage. In the address on the left, Enter was pressed at the end of each line to insert a line break. In the address on the right, Shift+Enter was pressed.

John and Joan Doe¶	John and Joan Doe ↵
	Widgets, Inc. ↵
Widgets, Inc.¶	123 S Proton Dr ↵
	Hanford, WA 98765 ¶
123 S Proton Dr ¶	
Hanford, WA 98765 ¶	

Notice that FrontPage displays a right-angle arrow for the line break and a paragraph mark between regular paragraphs. You can turn the display of line breaks and some other on-screen marks on or off by clicking the Show All button on the Standard toolbar.

Inserting Special Characters

Your computer's keyboard is limited to a standard set of letters, numbers, and punctuation. But there are a lot of other characters that simply are not included on your keyboard. For example, there's the degree symbol (100°), the copyright symbol (©1999), and the fraction symbol for one-half (½).

In FrontPage, you insert symbols into your page just as you do in Word: with the Insert ≻ Symbol command, which displays the Symbol dialog box (see Figure 2.4). Select the symbol you want and click the Insert button to place that symbol into your document at the insertion point. You can continue to select other symbols in the dialog box and click the Insert button. When you are finished, click the Close button.

FIGURE 2.4: The Insert ≻ Symbol command lets you pick a symbol to include in your page.

HTML and Browsers—The Start and End of Your Work

All of the pages that you edit are built from HTML code. However, FrontPage does such a good job of displaying the page and letting you manipulate it that you often just work along without even thinking about the underlying code that is being created.

Nonetheless, HTML is there and waiting if you need it, and the more you work with web pages, the more often you may want to take a peek at the HTML code. The Page view gives you several ways to interact with a page's HTML code:

- You can view the code at any time, making changes to it as though you're working on the page in a text editor.

- You can display the HTML tags within your document while still viewing your document in the WYSIWYG format.

- You can insert HTML tags that FrontPage doesn't support.

- You can view your page in any available Web browser, so you can see exactly how the HTML in the page will be interpreted by various browsers.

Seeing the HTML Source Code

When you want to see the HTML code behind the active page, click the HTML tab on the bottom left of the editing pane. The display switches to show the actual HTML code for your page—the same code that is saved on disk when you save your page.

Figure 2.5 shows the HTML view for the page that was displayed in Figure 2.3. If you're just viewing the code and do not want to make any changes to it, you can return to the page by clicking the Normal tab.

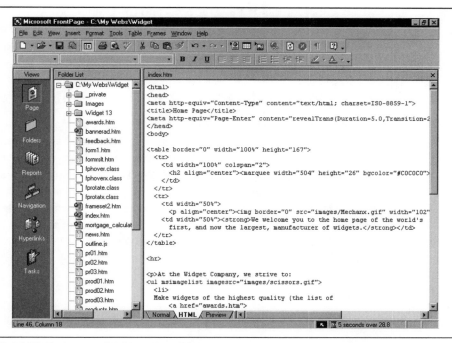

FIGURE 2.5: Clicking the HTML tab lets you view or edit the underlying HTML code for a page.

The HTML view is just another way to display your web page. Use caution when making changes to the HTML code, as they're reflected in the page when you return to Normal view. If, for example, you accidentally delete one of the angle brackets for an HTML tag, you'll see the result reflected on the page when you switch back to Normal view.

NOTE NOTE NOTE NOTE NOTE NOTE NOTE NOTE NOTE NOTE NOTE NOTE NOTE NOTE

Many, but not all, of the menu choices are available while you are in HTML view. For example, you can use Cut, Copy, and Paste to move or copy text; insert a horizontal line or graphic image; and create a data-entry form.

HTML view not only displays the underlying HTML for the active page, it also helps you interpret it by color-coding it. For example, text you enter is shown in the normal black, while HTML tags are shown in blue. To adjust the colors that are used, choose Tools ➤ Page Options and the Color Coding tab in the dialog box.

The different colors make it a lot easier to make sense of the code as you scroll through it. Viewing the underlying code is always a good exercise to help you get a feel for the ins and outs of HTML.

Displaying HTML Tags in Your Document

Another way to get a sense of the HTML code that makes up a page is to display just the tags—choose View ➤ Reveal Tags (choose it again to turn off the display of the tags). Your page will still be shown in the Normal view, but the HTML tags for paragraphs and text will be displayed as well. Figure 2.6 shows the same page from Figure 2.3 after the Reveal Tags option was turned on.

The tags can help you differentiate between the various codes, and you can delete a tag to eliminate that code from your document. Point to a tag and its definition will be displayed in a pop-up screen tip. On the other hand, the tags tend to clutter the screen and slow down screen scrolling, so you will generally want to leave them turned off.

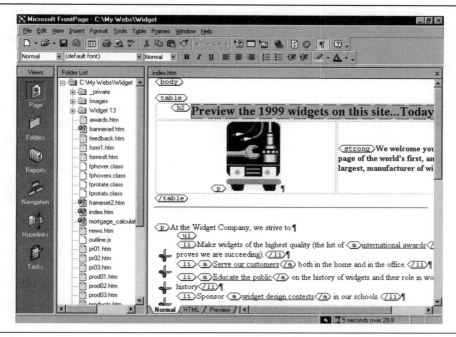

FIGURE 2.6: Choosing View ➣ Reveal Tags displays the basic HTML paragraph and text formatting tags within your WYSIWYG page.

Inserting Unsupported HTML Code

The fast-paced development of HTML means that there will always be some tags that some browsers accept even though those tags have not been incorporated into the official HTML specification.

Even if it is not supported by FrontPage, you can still add HTML code to your web pages by using the Insert ➣ Advanced ➣ HTML command. This displays the HTML Markup dialog box, in which you enter the HTML code you want to include in the page.

WARNING WARNING WARNING WARNING WARNING WARNING WARNING WARNING
FrontPage basically ignores the HTML code you enter in the HTML Markup dialog box, and does not check it for accuracy. So it's up to you to enter the code with no mistakes and ensure that it will be interpreted correctly by a browser.

When you click OK to close the HTML Markup dialog box, you'll see a small icon in your page (as shown here) that represents the code you added. Even though you won't be able to see how the page lays out around this new material in Page view, the code you added will be interpreted and displayed (assuming you entered it correctly) when you preview the page in a browser, as discussed in the next section.

Previewing Your Work in a Browser

The ultimate outcome for a page is to be viewed within a Web browser. Although FrontPage does a very good job of showing you how a page will appear within a browser, it can never offer the final and absolutely definitive view of a page. No editor can.

The primary reason for this is that HTML is designed to be very flexible in the way its pages are formatted. The same HTML code can be interpreted somewhat differently in different browsers.

On top of that inherent flexibility is the fact there are just too many variables that affect the ultimate appearance of a page within a browser. For example, a browser running within a screen resolution of 800×600 pixels displays over 50 percent more of a page than a browser running within a screen resolution of 640×480.

The only way to be sure how your web looks is to view it within a browser or, preferably, in several of the more popular browsers. You can also view a single page, right from within FrontPage, to see how that page looks in Internet Explorer. Click the Preview tab at the bottom of the editing pane to view the page. (This requires that you have Microsoft Internet Explorer 3.0 or higher installed on your system. If you do not, you won't have a Preview tab.)

To open an actual browser such as Microsoft Internet Explorer or Netscape Navigator, choose File ➢ Preview in Browser. The Preview in Browser dialog box, shown in Figure 2.7, opens so you can choose which browser you want to use.

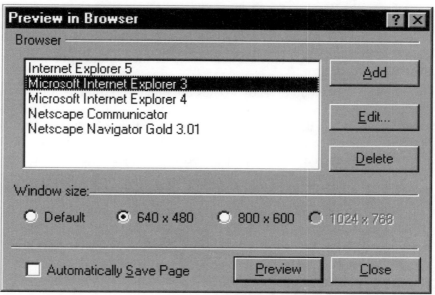

FIGURE 2.7: The Preview in Browser dialog box lets you choose a browser to view your page.

When you initially install FrontPage, it searches for browsers on your computer and automatically adds installed browsers to the list in the Preview in Browser dialog box. If you add other browsers after you install FrontPage, you can add them to the list by clicking the Add button. You enter a name for the browser, which appears in the list of browsers, then enter the command that opens that browser. Use the Browse button to select the program from a typical Windows files dialog box.

Once the new browser appears in the list, you can select it to preview the page you're editing. Use the Edit or Delete buttons in the Preview in Browser dialog box to revise the settings for a browser or to remove a browser from the list.

If you have not saved the page you want to view, click the Automatically Save Page check box. (If you don't, you'll be told that you can't view the page until you save it.) FrontPage opens a Save As dialog box if you haven't saved the page. If you've previously saved the page, it just goes ahead and saves it again before displaying it in the browser.

Before clicking the Preview button, select a size for the browser's window in the Window Size group of options. For example, if your monitor's resolution is 800 × 600 or higher, you can choose the 640 × 480 option to see how the page looks in a browser that has been maximized to full-screen size on a monitor whose screen resolution is only 640 × 480. Choose the Default option to open the browser without specifying a size.

Now you're ready to click the Preview button. If you've already saved your page, this action takes you directly to the browser you selected.

When the page opens in the designated browser, you can see how your page actually looks when others view it on the Web. Review how the page looks when displayed within the specified window size and how the features within the page compare to the way they appear in FrontPage. When you're ready to go back to work on the page, switch back to FrontPage in one of the usual Windows ways: press Alt+Tab, click its icon on the Taskbar, minimize the browser, or close the browser completely. When you are ready to view the page again in the same browser, all you have to do is click the Preview in Browser button on the toolbar.

Printing Your Page

You can print the active page of the Page view in the same way you print a document in your word processor. Of course, the need to print rarely arises, since a page is meant to reside on a Web site and be viewed by a browser. Nonetheless, you may wish to print pages to proof them for accuracy, hang them on your refrigerator, or show them to others when you can't access a computer.

To print the active page using the current print settings, choose File ➤ Print or click the Print button on the toolbar. This displays the standard Print dialog box, in which you can specify the number of copies to print, the range of pages to print, and the printer to which the job should be sent.

Previewing the Printout

Before you print a page, take a few seconds to preview what your printout will look like on paper by choosing File ➤ Print Preview. The buttons on the Preview toolbar perform the following tasks:

Print   Closes the preview but opens the Print dialog box, where you can print as usual to a printer.

Next Page   Displays the next page of a multi-page printout; you can also use PgDn. The left side of the status bar shows the current page number.

Previous Page   Displays the previous page; you can also use PgUp.

Two Page/One Page   Toggles between displaying a single page or two pages of the printout.

Zoom In   Magnifies the preview so you can see more detail on the page, but less of the entire page.

Zoom Out   Shows you more of the page but shrinks the size of the characters on it.

Close   Closes the preview and returns to the active page; you can also press Esc.

Again, your pages are meant to be viewed within your Web site by a browser, so you'll probably print pages only if you're developing the web and want input from others, or if you want to lay it all out and see how the pages fit together.

Spell-Checking

When you create a web, you should make sure that all the text is spelled correctly in each page. After you publish the web, you still need to provide periodic maintenance as new pages are added and existing pages require editing. It's all too easy to introduce a misspelling, even if you only spend 30 seconds on a page.

You probably use the spell-checker in your word processor every day as a quick and easy way to check the spelling of all the words in a document. FrontPage offers you the same tool, and it's even more powerful than you might suspect, because you can check the spelling in every page of your entire web in one operation. This is yet another example of how FrontPage condenses huge web management tasks into simple, one-step operations.

NOTE NOTE NOTE NOTE NOTE NOTE NOTE NOTE NOTE NOTE NOTE NOTE NOTE NOTE NOTE

FrontPage only checks the spelling of text that you can edit from the Normal tab of the Page view. Generally, that's the text that a visitor to your site will see. FrontPage doesn't check the underlying HTML code, such as the page title or hyperlink target names, nor the text in any included pages in the active page. These are pages that appear as the result of the Include Page component, which is discussed in "Including Another Web Page Automatically" in Skill 11, *Automating Your Web with FrontPage Components*. You must open these pages separately to check their spelling.

Spell-Checking the Active Page

To check the spelling of the active page in the Page view, choose Tools ➤ Spelling (F7), or click the Spelling button on the Standard toolbar. If you have experience with any of the applications in Microsoft Office, this routine is quite familiar.

If the spell-checker finds no misspelled words in the page, a dialog box notifies you of the success. If it finds a misspelled word (or rather, a word not in the spelling dictionary), you see the Spelling dialog box (shown in Figure 2.8) with the suspect word displayed in the Not in Dictionary field.

TIP TIP TIP TIP TIP TIP TIP TIP TIP TIP TIP TIP TIP TIP TIP TIP TIP TIP TIP TIP TIP TIP TIP

FrontPage can check your spelling while you work and underline those words that it can't find in the spelling dictionary. To turn this feature off or on, choose Tools ➤ Page Options, select the Spelling tab, and select or deselect the Check Spelling As You Type option.

If the Word Is Spelled Correctly

The spell-checker flags many words that are actually correct, especially proper names and technical or medical terms. When the suspect word is correct, you can do any of the following:

- Click the Ignore button to bypass this word and continue to check the spelling; if the suspect word appears again, it's flagged again.

- Click the Ignore All button, bypassing all occurrences of the suspect word during this spell-checking session.

- Click the Add button to add this word to the custom dictionary. In the future, FrontPage will recognize that the word is spelled correctly.

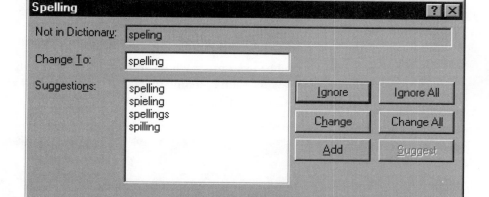

FIGURE 2.8: The Spelling dialog box displays a suspected misspelled word and offers a list of suggested replacements.

If the Word Is Misspelled

If the word in question is not correct, you can either type the correct spelling into the Change To field or select one of the words from the Suggestions list (which then appears in the Change To field). At this point you have some options:

- Click the Change button to replace the misspelled word with the word in the Change To field.

- Click Change All to change all occurrences of the misspelled word in the active page.

You can also click the Cancel button at any time to end the spell-checking session.

Spell-Checking an Entire Web

To check the spelling of all or selected pages in the active web, first save all open web pages in the Page view to ensure that they are up to date on disk. Then display your web in Folders view, Navigation view, or Hyperlinks view. If you want to check the spelling of only some files, select the files in the Folders view. Then choose Tools ➢ Spelling (F7), or click the Spelling button. This displays the web-wide Spelling dialog box, shown in Figure 2.9, which offers two options for web-wide spell-checking:

- Choose to check all pages in the web or just those you had selected.

- Choose whether to fix misspellings immediately, or simply to add a task to the Tasks view for each filename that contains misspelled words so you can return at your convenience to correct the misspellings.

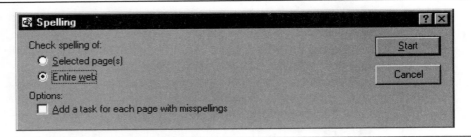

FIGURE 2.9: The Spelling dialog box allows you to check the spelling in selected pages or the entire web.

When you click the Start button to begin the spellcheck, the dialog box expands to list all the pages in which misspelled words have been found, as shown in Figure 2.10. You can click the Cancel button at any time to stop the spell-checking.

When the process is finished, you can double-click a page to open it, at which point the spell-checking continues as described earlier for a single page. When you're finished with one page, you're given the option to open the next one and continue.

You can also choose to return to a page later by selecting the page in the list and clicking the Add Task button. A new task will be added to the Tasks list that reminds you to check the spelling on that page.

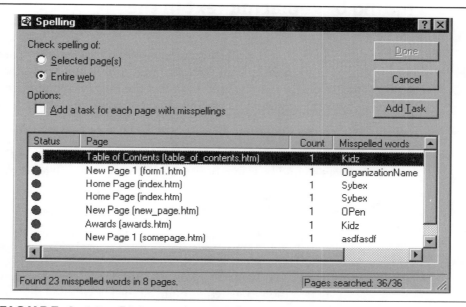

FIGURE 2.10: Each page that contains a suspected misspelling is listed in the Spelling dialog box; you can either fix each one immediately or add a task so you can fix it later on.

Finding or Replacing Text

Suppose the Widget Company decides to change its business focus and create a new image, including changing its name to the Technical Tools Company. Even though you redesign the web to reflect the company's new image, you also want to make sure that the company's online presence is maintained through the transition so that visitors to the web aren't disappointed. You need to find every occurrence of *Widget* in every page in the web, and replace it with *Technical Tools*.

Once again, FrontPage can come to your assistance by providing another set of tools that you undoubtedly already use on a regular basis in your word processor—the Find and Replace commands. You use these commands to seek out a word, sentence, or just a few characters in the document, and to replace text with other text. Like the spell-checker in FrontPage, the Find and Replace commands can act on the active page of the Page view or on every page in your entire web.

Finding or Replacing Text in the Active Page

Select Edit ➤ Find to find all occurrences of text you specify in either the active page or in all pages in your web (that procedure will be discussed a little later). Enter the characters you want to find in the Find What field of the Find dialog box (shown in Figure 2.11). There are several options you can use to refine your search:

- You can find those characters in the current page or in all pages in the web.

- You can select the Find Whole Word Only option to specify that the characters should be found only when they are a complete word.

- You can select the Match Case option to specify that the case (UPPER or lower) exactly matches the case of the text you entered.

- You can also choose to search up or down the page, starting from the insertion point.

- When you're displaying a page in the HTML view, you can use the Find in HTML option to search through all the HTML code that underlies your page, allowing you to find, for example, all occurrences of a <B> or <HR> tag.

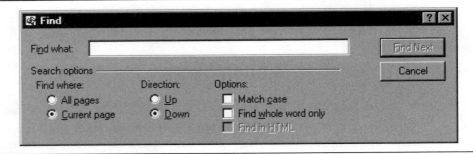

FIGURE 2.11: While in Page view, the Find dialog box lets you search for text in the current page or in all pages in the web.

To begin the search in the active page, click the Find Next button. The first occurrence of the specified text is selected in the page. At this point you can:

- Click Find Next to find the next occurrence.

- Click Cancel to close the Find dialog box.

- Click on the page so you can continue to work in it, perhaps to edit the text that was found. The Find dialog box remains open.

Select Edit ➤ Replace command to specify the text to search for as well as the text with which to replace it. If you leave the Replace With field empty, the text that is found is deleted. You perform the Replace operation with three buttons in the Replace dialog box:

- Click Find Next to find the next occurrence of the specified text.

- Click Replace to replace the current occurrence, then move on to find the next occurrence.

- Click Replace All to replace every occurrence of the text.

TIP TIP TIP TIP TIP TIP TIP TIP TIP TIP TIP TIP TIP TIP TIP TIP TIP TIP TIP TIP TIP TIP TIP TIP

Practice safe computing by saving the page before using the Replace All command on the entire page.

When you're finished finding and replacing text, you can click on the page to leave the dialog box open and continue working on the page, or click the Cancel button to close the dialog box and return to the page.

Finding or Replacing Text in the Entire Web

The process of finding or replacing text in all or selected pages is very much like the spell-checking process described earlier in "Spell-Checking an Entire Web." If you want to check just a few pages, first select them in Folders view. Then choose Edit ➤ Find or Edit ➤ Replace, and choose either the Selected Pages or All Pages option.

This time, instead of seeing the matching text that is found, you'll see a list of all the pages that contain that text. As with the web-wide spell-checking (look back at Figure 2.10), you have two options. You can double-click a page to open it and then decide whether or not to replace each occurrence of the text in that file, or click the Add Task button to create a reminder task for a page so you can return to it later on.

NOTE NOTE NOTE NOTE NOTE NOTE NOTE NOTE NOTE NOTE NOTE NOTE NOTE NOTE NOTE NOTE

When you double-click a page to replace text within it, the Replace command does not automatically replace the text it finds; you can verify each change within the page itself so you can confirm the changes.

Are You Experienced?

Now you can...

- ☑ Create a new web
- ☑ Open, close, and save a web
- ☑ Open a web page for editing
- ☑ Save a web page
- ☑ Add content to a web page
- ☑ Add special characters
- ☑ View the underlying HTML code
- ☑ Preview a web page in a browser
- ☑ Print a page you are working on
- ☑ Check the spelling of a page or the entire web
- ☑ Find and replace text in a single page or the entire web

Working with Lists and Headings

- → Dividing a page with a horizontal line
- → Changing the properties of a line
- → Creating an outline structure with headings
- → Creating and working with bulleted and numbered lists
- → Changing the look of a list, including using Picture Bullets
- → Nesting lists
- → Creating collapsible lists
- → Creating other types of lists

In this Skill, you learn how FrontPage lets you organize a page into logical sections with horizontal lines, headings, and lists. These features can make your web page more attractive and easier for users to browse.

Creating Sections with Horizontal Lines

Perhaps the simplest way to add definition to a web page is by inserting a horizontal line with the Insert ➤ Horizontal Line command. This adds the HTML tag <HR>, and is often referred to as a horizontal rule. By default, the line spans the entire width of the page in FrontPage or in a browser. It is a simple but very effective way to delineate one section from another, as shown in Figure 3.1.

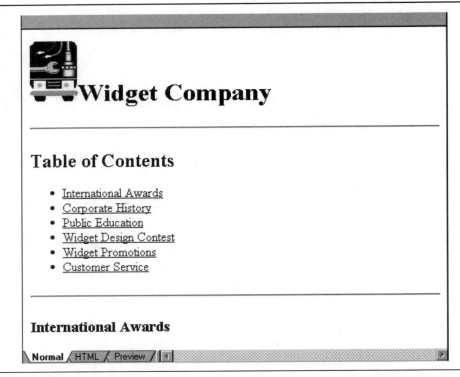

FIGURE 3.1: You can use horizontal lines to divide sections within a page.

In this case, the page has a banner headline and graphic across the top, with a horizontal line separating the banner and graphic from a hyperlinked table of contents. Beneath the table of contents is another line, followed by the main body of the page (which you cannot see in Figure 3.1). The lines create obvious divisions between logical sections of the page.

Changing the Look of a Line

The default horizontal line is thin. To modify the look of a horizontal line, open its Properties dialog box (shown here) by right-clicking on the line and choosing Horizontal Line Properties from the shortcut menu. You can change the width, height, alignment, and color of the line.

SKILL 3

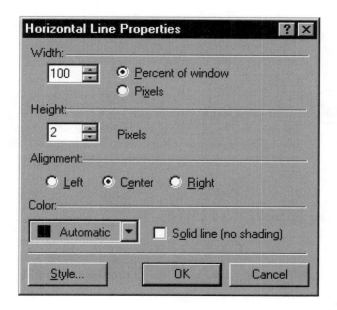

Width   The width of a default line is 100 percent of the width of the FrontPage or browser window, so it always spans the page. Change the percentage to 50 for a line half the width of the window, which is centered by default. Choose Pixels to specify an exact width for the line, no matter how wide the window may be. If the resulting line is longer than the width of window, the portion that extends beyond the edge of the window is simply hidden from view.

NOTE NOTE NOTE NOTE NOTE NOTE NOTE NOTE NOTE NOTE NOTE NOTE NOTE NOTE NOTE

A *pixel* is an individual display element on a screen. For example, if your monitor's display *resolution* is 640 × 480, there are 640 pixels across and 480 pixels down the screen. If you need a graphic element like a line to span the screen, you shouldn't specify its width in pixels because some users may have their display set at a different resolution.

Height   The default height, or thickness, of the line is two pixels; increase or decrease the height as needed.

Alignment   If you specify a width other than 100 percent for the line, you can align the line to the left or right side of the window or center it within the window. You can choose different alignments even if the line is set to 100 percent, but the effect won't be noticeable.

Color   Select a color for the line; you can also choose to have the line displayed with a shadow effect or as a solid line.

NOTE NOTE NOTE NOTE NOTE NOTE NOTE NOTE NOTE NOTE NOTE NOTE NOTE NOTE NOTE

The Style button on the Horizontal Line Properties dialog box, and numerous other dialog boxes, takes you to the Cascading Style Sheet Properties dialog box, one of the more recent features to be introduced into HTML. For more about cascading style sheets, see Skill 10, *Creating a Consistent Look for Your Web*.

Using Images as Lines

Another common way to create a dividing line in a page is to use a graphic image as a line. Lines and horizontal images both serve the same purpose, but the image can include multiple colors, patterns, or a picture.

NOTE NOTE NOTE NOTE NOTE NOTE NOTE NOTE NOTE NOTE NOTE NOTE NOTE NOTE NOTE

One small disadvantage of a graphic image is that it takes time for an image to download, while horizontal lines are quickly created "on site" by the browser's interpretation of the HTML <HR> tag. However, most line image files are small, and if you reuse the image elsewhere in the page or in the site, the browser only needs to download it once.

FrontPage comes with a collection of clip art images, several of which are suitable for horizontal lines. You'll read more about using clip art images within your pages in Skill 8, *Displaying Images in Your Pages*.

Creating a Hierarchy with Headings

A very common and quite efficient way to add structure to a web page is through the use of headings. Just take a look at the table of contents of this book to see headings in action; a Skill is divided into several main headings, each of which may contain several subheadings. Those subheadings may contain yet other sub-subheadings. It's essentially the structure of an outline, only with a lot of text and graphics between the headings.

A web page can have up to six levels of headings, which you create by applying paragraph formats. Because headings are paragraph styles, they're applied to an entire paragraph, not just selected text. The HTML tags that FrontPage creates for the six different headings are easy to remember: <H1> for heading 1, <H2> for heading 2, and so on.

To make a heading, first click within the paragraph of text you want as the heading, and then choose one of the six headings from the Style list on the Formatting toolbar, as shown here.

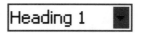

If you look back at Figure 3.1, you'll see examples of three different headings. The Widget Company heading at the top of the page is level 1, the Table of Contents is a level 2 heading, and the International Awards heading is level 3. If you ignore the graphic at the top of the page and the items under the Table of Contents heading (other than International Awards), the HTML code for the headings and the horizontal lines between them looks like this:

```
<H1>Widget Company</H1>
<HR>
<H2>Table of Contents</H2>
<HR>
<H3>International Awards</H3>
```

As with all HTML codes, there is no built-in style for headings—different Web browsers might interpret the look of a heading in a different way. In general, a level 1 heading is in a larger, bolder font than a lower-level heading and may have a blank line above and below it. In the FrontPage Page view, the headings look the same way they do in Microsoft's Internet Explorer Web browser. A sample of the six headings within that browser is shown here.

Heading 1

Heading 2

Heading 3

Heading 4

Heading 5

Although headings help organize a page, FrontPage has no rules about how you use them. You are free to turn any text into a heading and use the various levels of headings in any order you choose. For example, you could choose to use level 5 headings for titles and level 1 headings for subtitles. But, it makes very good sense to use them as you would in an outline, relying on the fact that all browsers make higher level headings look "more important" than lower level headings.

For example, the first heading you use on a page should usually be the highest level that appears in that page, although you don't have to start with level 1 (you may choose to start with level 2 and go on from there). Once you pick the highest level for a particular page, you'll probably want to continue using lower levels for subsequent headings.

Organizing Data within Lists

A very practical way to organize groups of items on a page is to arrange them in a list. There are several built-in lists in HTML. The two most useful are:

Bulleted list   Prefaces each item (paragraph) in the list with a bullet. Bulleted lists begin with the <UL> tag because they are also called *unordered lists.*

Numbered list   Numbers each item in the list. The <OL> tag begins the list, which is also called an *ordered list.* The browser applies the appropriate number to each line when it opens the page, so you can add or delete items from the list while you create the page without having to worry about updating the numbering.

You can create a list before or after you enter the items. Each item in the list is a separate paragraph.

Creating a List from Existing Text

Suppose you have text that you've already entered on a page, and you want to turn it into a bulleted list. For example, the left side of Figure 3.2 shows the table of contents from Figure 3.1 before it was changed to a bulleted list.

Table of Contents	Table of Contents	Table of Contents
International Awards	• International Awards	1. International Awards
Corporate History	• Corporate History	2. Corporate History
Public Education	• Public Education	3. Public Education
Widget Design Contests	• Widget Design Contests	4. Widget Design Contests
Widget Promotions	• Widget Promotions	5. Widget Promotions
Customer Survey	• Customer Survey	6. Customer Survey

FIGURE 3.2: You can turn multiple paragraphs into a bulleted list.

To turn paragraphs like these into a bulleted list, simply select them all and click the Bullets button on the Formatting toolbar, or select Bulleted List from the Style drop-down list on the Formatting toolbar. The resulting bulleted list is shown in the middle of Figure 3.2.

It's just as easy to turn existing text into a numbered list. With the text selected, click the Numbering button on the Formatting toolbar, or choose Numbered List from the Style drop-down list. The result is shown on the right side of Figure 3.2. You can switch back and forth between the two list styles at any time.

In both examples shown in Figure 3.2, the six selected paragraphs are reduced to a single paragraph when they are converted to a list. List styles, like headings, are paragraph styles, so you don't have to select all the entries in a list to switch to the other type of list. Just click anywhere in the list before clicking the Numbering or Bullets button.

Here's the HTML code for the bulleted list in Figure 3.2. (The list in Figure 3.2 includes hyperlinks, but they're left out of this code so that you just see the code for the list.)

```
<H2>Table of Contents</H2>
<UL>
    <LI>International Awards</LI>
    <LI>Corporate History</LI>
    <LI>Public Education</LI>
    <LI>Widget Design Contests</LI>
    <LI>Widget Promotions</LI>
    <LI>Customer Survey</LI>
</UL>
```

The code for the numbered list is the same, except that the beginning and ending tags for the unordered list are replaced with those for an ordered list: <OL> and </OL> appear in place of the <UL> and </UL> tags, respectively. As always with HTML, the way a browser formats the list, such as the amount of indentation and the style of the bullets, varies from browser to browser. On the other hand, graphics look the same in every browser, although there may be differences caused by individual video cards and monitors. Later in this Skill, you'll find out how to use graphic images as bullets.

Creating a List As You Type

You can also create a list as you type the items into the list. Here's how to create the table of contents bulleted list shown in the center of Figure 3.2:

1.   On a new blank line in the page, click the Bullets button. You'll see a bullet appear next to this line, which is now the first line in the list.

2. Type the text you want to appear on this line; in the list shown in Figure 3.2, the first entry is **International Awards**.

3. Press Enter to move to the second line in the bulleted list. Type the item text and press Enter. Continue with each new line in the list.

4. When you have typed the last item in the list, either press Enter twice or press Ctrl+Enter to finish the list.

The first new line following the list is in the Normal style.

Working in a List

Let's look at how to perform some typical tasks in a bulleted or numbered list:

- To add an item within a list, place the insertion point at the beginning of a line and begin typing. The text you type is inserted in front of the existing text. Press Enter to move the existing text to the next line.

- To add an item to the end of a list, place the insertion point at the end of the last item in the list and press Enter to create a new list item.

- To select one item in the list, move the mouse pointer to the left of the item's bullet or number and click.

- To delete an item, select it, then press Delete or choose Edit ➤ Delete.

- To change a list to another list type, select the entire list and either click a list button on the Formatting toolbar, choose a different list style from the Style drop-down list, or choose a list style in the Bullets and Numbering dialog box (Format ➤ Bullets and Numbering).

Changing the Look of a Bulleted or Numbered List

The Bullets and Numbering buttons on the Formatting toolbar create lists in the default style, but you can choose other types of bullets or numbering for lists. The easiest way to see the effects of changing the list style is by selecting an existing list, and then choosing Format ➤ Bullets and Numbering, or by right-clicking on the list and choosing List Properties from the shortcut menu.

The List Properties dialog box contains four tabs:

Picture Bullets   Use an existing image as the bullet character (see dialog box below). Click the Browse button to locate the file. In FrontPage, you can even use animated images as bullets. If you have a theme applied to the page, you can click the Use Images from Current Theme button. For more about themes, see Skill 10, *Creating a Consistent Look for Your Web*.

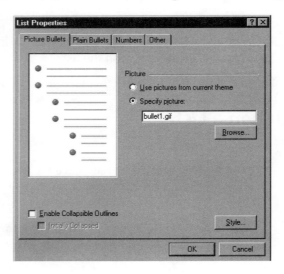

Plain Bullets   Choose the style of bullets you want to use in the list, such as solid or hollow round bullets. The first choice, which shows no bullets, removes the HTML list tags and returns the list to normal text.

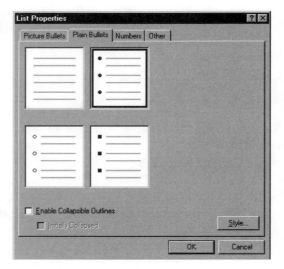

Numbers   Choose the numbering style for a numbered list, such as Arabic or Roman numeral numbering, or uppercase or lowercase lettering. The first choice, which shows no numbering, returns the list to normal text. In the option labeled Start At, you can specify the starting number for the list (the default is 1).

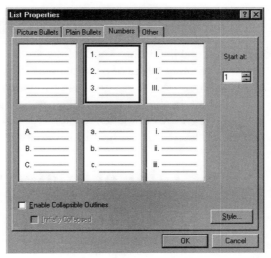

Other   Choose a list style, such as Bulleted, Numbered, or Definition (see "Creating Other Types of Lists" later in this Skill). Choose (None) to turn a list back into normal text.

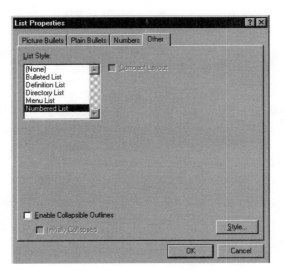

Changing the List properties from the default adds attributes to the HTML tag for the list. For example, if you select the Roman numeral numbering list and set the Start At property at V (5), the HTML tag that marks the beginning of the list looks like this:

```
<OL TYPE="I" START="5">
```

Creating a Nested List within a List

You can nest one list within another so that the second is a subordinate of the first. This lets you create tables of contents with chapter titles and section titles, or display lists of inventory items grouped by category or employee e-mail addresses by department. In short, nested lists provide a good way to display information that has to be *grouped* to make it easier to use or understand. Shown here is the original bulleted list from Figure 3.2 with a second list nested within it.

Table of Contents

- International Awards
- Corporate History
- Public Education
    - Kidz Widget Magazine
    - Public Television Widget Night
    - Widgets at Home Pamphlet
- Widget Design Contests
- Widget Promotions
- Customer Survey

NOTE NOTE NOTE NOTE NOTE NOTE NOTE NOTE NOTE NOTE NOTE NOTE NOTE NOTE NOTE
Although FrontPage uses different types of bullets for the main list and nested list, some browsers do not.

Here is how you create the nested list shown in the previous example:

1. At the end of the Public Education line, press Enter to create a new item in the primary list.

2. With the insertion point still on the new line, click the Increase Indent button on the Formatting toolbar. Click it a second time to make this item an indented, nested list.

3. Enter the text for the line and press Enter to create the next item in the nested list.

4. Continue to create new items until you're finished with the nested list. Then simply move the insertion point to another location in the page.

Collapsible Outlines

On each List Properties page there is a check box called Enable Collapsible Outlines. If you're familiar with the Outline view in Microsoft Word, or use Windows Explorer to view files and folders, you understand the basic concept of collapsible outlines. Users can click a bullet and the items underneath will collapse to show only the heading, or expand to display all of its subpoints.

Collapsible outlines require a Web browser that supports Dynamic HTML, such as Microsoft Internet Explorer 4 or later. In FrontPage, if you attempt to preview a page that has Dynamic HTML elements without a supporting browser, you receive a warning like the one shown below:

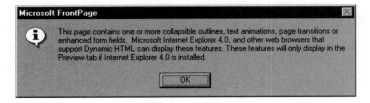

You can include collapsible outlines on your pages even if you're using a browser that doesn't support Dynamic HTML, but you won't be able to see how the outlines affect your overall design.

NOTE NOTE NOTE NOTE NOTE NOTE NOTE NOTE NOTE NOTE NOTE NOTE NOTE NOTE NOTE

It doesn't make sense to rely on collapsible outlines for Web sites until more browsers support Dynamic HTML. However, some companies that include Internet Explorer 4.0 in their standard desktop configuration are already using Dynamic HTML features on their intranets.

Creating Other Types of Lists

There are several other types of HTML lists you can create in FrontPage, although they're used only rarely in Web sites. The Menu and Directory lists made early appearances in the HTML standard, but added little functionality to the basic unordered (bulleted) list and have essentially fallen into disuse. They look just like the bulleted list in FrontPage, as well as in the most popular browsers. Instead of the <OL> tag, they use the <MENU> and <DIR> tags, respectively.

You can use the Definition list to create a glossary of terms, such as the sample shown here. This type of list is a bit different from the ones we've discussed so far, because it actually consists of two different types of elements—terms and definitions.

> bookmark
> > Named text in a page that can be the target of a hyperlink.
> browser
> > A client-side program that can request files over the WWW
> > or an intranet, and display HTML Web pages.
> CGI
> > The Common Gateway Interface is a standard for programs
> > on a server that process requests or data from browsers.

Web browsers usually display the defined term as normal text, with the definition for the term indented from it. Here's how you create a Definition list:

1. On the line where the first defined term appears, choose Defined Term from the Style list on the Formatting toolbar either before or after you type the term.

2. Press Enter; FrontPage assumes that the next text you enter is the definition for the term.

3. Type the definition for the term and press Enter. When you press Enter following a definition, FrontPage assumes the next entry is a new term.

4. Continue to type terms and definitions, pressing Enter after each. When you're finished with the list of terms and definitions, press Ctrl+Enter or press Enter twice to end the Definition list.

Here's the HTML code for the Definition list shown on the previous page:

```
<DL>
    <DT>bookmark</DT>
    <DD>Named text in a page that...</DD>
    <DT>browser</DT>
```

```
        <DD>A client-side program that...</DD>
        <DT>CGI</DT>
        <DD>The Common Gateway Interface is a...</DD>
    </DL>
```

Are You Experienced?

Now you can...

- ☑ Organize a page with horizontal lines
- ☑ Use styles to add various heading levels to paragraphs
- ☑ Create bulleted and numbered lists
- ☑ Modify lists and use images as bullets
- ☑ Create collapsible outlines
- ☑ Create other types of lists, such as definition lists

Formatting Your Pages

- ➔ **Changing fonts**
- ➔ **Changing paragraph styles**
- ➔ **Aligning paragraphs**
- ➔ **Indenting paragraphs**
- ➔ **Changing character and line spacing**
- ➔ **Changing page titles**
- ➔ **Setting the background color**
- ➔ **Specifying a background picture**
- ➔ **Defining a background-definition page**
- ➔ **Assigning pages to categories and authors**
- ➔ **Animating text and images with DHTML**

This Skill deals with the overall appearance of a page: the way text is displayed, and the background behind the text. You will learn how to change the format of text, paragraphs, and the page itself to make your page stand out from the crowd.

Setting Text Properties

The first thing to remember about formatting your pages is that it's the browser that determines how the HTML tags in your pages are displayed. You can play with the formatting of a page all you want, but once it's out on your Web site, all your design work and artistry may be lost when viewed on a one- or two-year-old browser that can't support the features you've included.

You could, of course, choose not to spend much time on page layout—but that would be a mistake. High quality Web browsers that render HTML beautifully are cheap or free, and many users upgrade their browsers several times a year. If a visitor to your Web site is using any recently released browser, for the most part your page should come through as you intended. The exceptions to this rule are the Dynamic HTML (DHTML) features such as collapsible lists (Skill 3), and text animation and page transitions, described in this Skill, which are only supported by the latest versions of top-of-the-line browsers.

Most of the formatting you can apply to text can be found in the Font dialog box (choose Format ➤ Font from the menu). There are also equivalent buttons for many of the same features on the Formatting toolbar. Text properties, or attributes, include familiar ones such as bold, italic, underline, subscript, and superscript, but also other, less familiar properties like strikethrough and typewriter.

You can also apply styles to paragraphs and pages, which often changes the default font properties for a page or paragraph. You'll read about these in the "Setting Paragraph Properties" and "Setting Page Properties" sections later in this Skill.

Here's a tip for quickly copying the formatting from one block of text to another. It's the same method you use in other Office applications—the Format Painter button on the toolbar. You can copy the formatting either from individual characters or from an entire paragraph.

To copy the formatting from one block of text to another (but not the paragraph formatting), select at least one character within the source text (don't just click within it) and then click the Format Painter button. Now select the text to which you want to duplicate that formatting, and the job is done.

To duplicate only the paragraph formatting, select the entire source paragraph, such as by double-clicking to its left, click the Format Painter button, and then click once within the target paragraph.

If you want to apply the same formatting to multiple targets, double-click the Format Painter button. When you're finished applying the format, click the button once more.

Choosing the Text to Format

To change the format of existing text, first select the text in any of the usual Windows ways:

- Drag the cursor over text with your mouse.

- Click at the beginning of the text you want to select, hold down the Shift key, and click on the end of the selection.

- Hold down the Shift key and make the selection using the keyboard arrow keys.

- Double-click to select a single word.

- Move the mouse pointer to the left of a paragraph (the pointer will change to an arrow instead of an I-beam) and double-click to select the entire paragraph.

- Choose Edit ➤ Select All (Ctrl+A) to select the entire document. Once you select text, you are free to modify its format. You can also move or copy it, realign it, or if all else fails, delete it.

Changing Font Properties

Select the text you want to format, then open the Font dialog box in any of the following ways:

- Choose Format ➤ Font from the menu.

- Right-click the selected text and choose Font from the shortcut menu.

- Press Alt+Enter.

Of course, you can also change the formatting of selected text with the buttons and tools on the Formatting toolbar, shown below. For example, select text and click the Bold button.

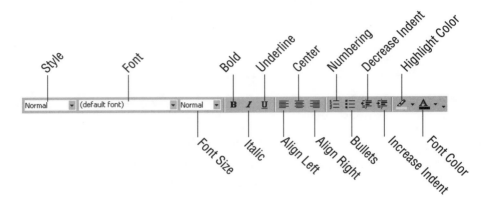

NOTE NOTE NOTE NOTE NOTE NOTE NOTE NOTE NOTE NOTE NOTE NOTE NOTE NOTE NOTE

You can return selected text to its default paragraph style by choosing Format ➤ Remove Formatting, or by pressing Ctrl+Spacebar or Ctrl+Shift+Z. This is a quick way to eliminate any changes you've applied to that text, such as a font, font size, or font attribute.

The default settings for the Font tab of the Font dialog box are shown in Figure 4.1. The default font settings lack any special formatting, so each browser displays the text using the browser's default settings. For example, the default FrontPage settings for the regular text on a page are Default font, Normal size, Regular style, Automatic color, with no font effects specified (such as Underline, Superscript, and so on). With most browsers, this results in a 12-point Times Roman font.

NOTE NOTE NOTE NOTE NOTE NOTE NOTE NOTE NOTE NOTE NOTE NOTE NOTE NOTE NOTE

Point is a typesetting measurement. One point is ½", so 12-point type is ⅙" high.

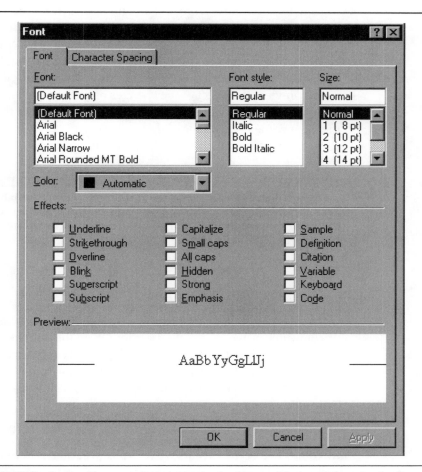

FIGURE 4.1: You can change the look of text with the options in the Font dialog box.

Can you assume, then, that in most browsers, unstyled text is some version of Times Roman characters about ⅛" tall? No. All but the lowliest browsers allow users to change their default font setting. Screen resolution, which users can also change, determines how large text and images appear when displayed on-screen. Therefore, you can't know whether everyone who views the page sees it exactly the same way. Part of web design is making good choices about the elements you *can* control, and learning to let go of the rest, as you'll see in the following section.

To change Font properties for selected text, make your selections in the dialog box, and preview the effect of the changes on the sample text in the dialog box. When you're finished, either click the Apply button to see the changes take effect in the page while keeping the dialog box open, or click OK to accept the changes and close the dialog box. Let's look at the font options.

NOTE NOTE NOTE NOTE NOTE NOTE NOTE NOTE NOTE NOTE NOTE NOTE NOTE NOTE NOTE

If you are creating webs that are displayed in different languages (Japanese, French, etc.), you can open the Page Options dialog box (Tools ➤ Page Options) and use the Default Font tab to specify the default fonts that are used for different character sets.

Font

You can select a specific font from the list of all the fonts available to Windows on your computer. You can also choose a font from the Font list on the Formatting toolbar. Again, when using the Font dialog box, keep your eye on the Preview pane to see the effect of the font change on the sample text.

The font you choose appears in the FACE attribute for the <FONT> tag in the HTML code, such as:

```
<FONT FACE="Arial">This is not the default font.</FONT>
```

Now comes one of the caveats we referred to earlier: Although you can apply any font you might have on your own computer, browsers display fonts by loading them from their local machine. If the font you choose isn't installed on the browser's computer, the browser displays the text in its default font. (You remember, Times Roman, 12 point—boring.) The trick is to shoot for the majority of users by choosing the more common (albeit less exciting) fonts like Times New Roman and Arial that are installed on almost every computer.

When you become more confident as a FrontPage user and want to dabble in HTML, you can click the HTML tab at the bottom of the Page view, then edit the code to include multiple font names in the FACE attribute. If a browser doesn't have the first font, it tries the second, and so on until it finds one it does have. If none of the fonts listed are installed locally, it uses the default font. Here's how the previous code looks with alternate fonts included:

```
<FONT FACE="Arial,Helvetica,Humana">This is…</FONT>
```

Font Style

The Font Style list in the Font dialog box includes the standard font style options: Regular (no bold or italic), Bold, Italic, and Bold Italic. You can also press Ctrl+B and Ctrl+I to apply or remove these styles from selected text, or use the Bold and Italic buttons on the Formatting toolbar to toggle text styles on or off.

> NOTE NOTE NOTE NOTE NOTE NOTE NOTE NOTE NOTE NOTE NOTE NOTE NOTE NOTE NOTE
>
> **The HTML code for the text you make bold is enclosed in the <B> tag, which generally has the same effect on text in a browser as the <STRONG> tag. The <I> tag italicizes text, as does the <EM> (emphasis) tag.**

Font Size

To change the size of the font, select one of the sizes from the Size list in the Font dialog box, or from the Font Size list on the Formatting toolbar. The default choice, Normal, doesn't specify a size, so a browser uses the default font size, whatever that might be.

The choices in the Size list range from 1 through 7. FrontPage shows a point size in parentheses next to each of those numbers, but you should only use the point sizes as a guide. Font sizes are (you guessed it) interpreted by the browser.

Size 3 is the default font size. If you choose size 4, the browser displays the text in a font one size larger than the default font. If you choose size 1, the text is displayed in a font two sizes smaller than the default. When you look at the Size list, you'll notice that the sizes change on a sliding scale, with two points between the smaller fonts (sizes 1 and 2), and up to 12 points between sizes 6 and 7. When you specify a size, the HTML code created by FrontPage looks like the code below for a font two sizes larger than the default font:

```
<FONT SIZE="5">
```

Font Effects

Use the Effects options in the Font dialog box (see Figure 4.1) to apply different effects to text. For example, Underline <U> places a single underline under the text; Strikethrough <STRIKE> draws a line through the text; Superscript <SUP> reduces and elevates the text; and Keyboard <KBD> displays the text in a non-proportional font like those used on manual typewriters. (Before you get nostalgic, or curious, read "The Formatted Paragraph Style" section later in this Skill.)

NOTE NOTE NOTE NOTE NOTE NOTE NOTE NOTE NOTE NOTE NOTE NOTE NOTE NOTE

Don't forget that most browsers designate hyperlinks by underlining them. Therefore, most visitors to your Web site expect that clicking on underlined text takes them somewhere else. Unless you're creating an entry for the "Most Annoying Web Page" contest, don't underline regular text.

If you have used earlier versions of FrontPage, you'll notice that the font effects are now all combined in this one Effects list, instead of being split between two different tabs in the Font dialog box. You'll find that some of these effects essentially duplicate others in the list. This is due to the evolution of the HTML standard, as newer tags supplant older ones. For example, the Strong effect produces exactly the same results as Bold text in just about all browsers, and Emphasis is virtually the same as Italics.

Font Color

Another way to add interest to a web page is by making effective use of different colors for text. There are several ways to choose a new color for selected text in the Color drop-down list in the Font dialog box:

- Choose Automatic to apply no specific color to the text; each browser uses its own default color to display the text.

- Choose one of the 16 colors in the Standard Colors group.

- Choose one of the colors in the Document's Colors group, which offers each of the colors that are already in use on the current page. This makes it easy to duplicate a color.

If none of these colors suits you, choose More Colors in the Color list to create your own color in the Colors dialog box. The palette of colors it offers are "browser safe," meaning that most browsers can display these colors without having to guess at a "close match." If the color you want to use isn't in the palette, you have several options:

- Click the Select button and the mouse pointer will change to the eye-dropper tool. Then click a color anywhere on the screen, such as from a picture or drawing, to use that color.

- Click the Select button and drag a box around a region of the screen to create a color that is the average of all the colors in that region.

- Enter a hexadecimal color value in the Value field, in the format HEX={nn,nn,nn}, where n is a valid hex value. You'll see a number appear here when you click one of the colors in the palette, which you can then simply edit as needed.

- Click the Custom button to open the Color dialog box (shown below) where you can mix your own color. Click Add to Custom Colors to add the color you mixed to the palette in the Color dialog box so you can apply it to the selected text.

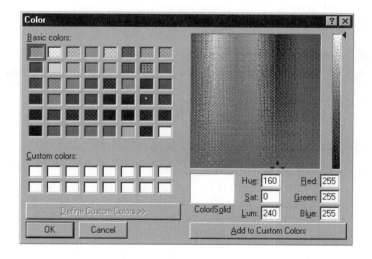

NOTE NOTE NOTE NOTE NOTE NOTE NOTE NOTE NOTE NOTE NOTE NOTE NOTE NOTE

If you create a color that is not one of the browser-safe colors, the result may appear somewhat "off" in different browsers or on different computers. There are numerous sites on the Internet that list the 216 browser-safe colors and why you should try to stick with them.

SKILL
4

If the only text property you want to change is color, it's faster to click the down-arrow to the right of the Font Color button on the Formatting toolbar, which displays the same color list that you saw in the Font dialog box. Select a color from the ones that are offered, or choose More Colors to display the Colors dialog box. The color you choose will then be the default for the Font Color button, so you can apply that color to more selected text simply by clicking the button.

Character Spacing

You can adjust the horizontal spacing and the vertical alignment of text with the options in the Character Spacing tab in the Font dialog box. The Spacing option lets you expand or condense the spacing between each character, something you might want to do for a title that you want to fill a particular space on the page.

The Position option lets you increase or decrease the height and size of text; in other words, create superscripts or subscripts. The difference between using this option and the Superscript and Subscript options in the Effects list is that you can specify how much the text should be raised or lowered. The choices are 1 through 10, each of which simply adds another <SUP> or <SUB> tag to the HTML code to raise or lower the text.

WARNING WARNING WARNING WARNING WARNING WARNING WARNING WARNING

Be prudent in your use of the Position option, since most browsers simply ignore any height changes greater than 2.

Formatting Text as You Enter It

If you want to establish the format of text before you type it, change the properties first and then start typing—any text you type after that reflects the changes you made.

However, the default formats are still there, just beyond the insertion point. If you examine the HTML code while entering text, you see the tag to end the current format just past the insertion point, like </B> to end boldface. If you reach the end of a line and press Enter, the next text you type is still bold, because pressing Enter moves the HTML tag to the next line. If you use the down arrow to move to a new line, however, the HTML tag remains in place on the line above, and the next text you enter is in the default, unbolded style.

If you want to quit typing formatted text and enter text in the default style, press the down arrow to move to the next line, or right arrow to move past the

HTML tag on the same line. To keep entering text in the current style, make sure you press Enter.

Setting Paragraph Properties

FrontPage has a variety of styles that affect entire paragraphs, not just selected text within a paragraph. You've already seen some of these styles, like headings and bulleted and numbered lists. When you apply a paragraph style anywhere in a paragraph, the entire paragraph gets formatted. If you want to change multiple paragraphs, select them all first, then apply the style.

You access the paragraph styles from the Style list on the Formatting toolbar. Remember that the Normal style removes all paragraph formatting and resets the paragraph back to its default style.

NOTE NOTE NOTE NOTE NOTE NOTE NOTE NOTE NOTE NOTE NOTE NOTE NOTE NOTE NOTE NOTE

Paragraphs are normally preceded by the <P> tag. When you apply a style to a paragraph, however, the style tags precede and follow the paragraph (for example, the <OL> tag appears before a numbered list and at the end), so the default paragraph tag <P> is no longer required.

When you press Enter at the end of a paragraph, paragraph styles (like headings) are automatically turned off. (The exceptions are the list styles, where you must press Enter twice to turn them off.) Any text formats you applied independent of the character style (bold, underline, font size) stay on. The new paragraph returns to the default paragraph format.

To split a paragraph into two that both have the same formatting, position the insertion point where you want the split and press Enter.

The Formatted Paragraph Style

You can select the Formatted style from the Style list on the Formatting toolbar. It is particularly useful because a browser displays text in this style in a monospaced font like Courier, where each character takes up exactly the same amount of space. It is the one instance in HTML when multiple spaces are displayed exactly as they appear in the code.

This style uses the <PRE> tag (for preformatted), and lets you use spaces to align text in columns or with indentations, having the characters fall exactly where you expect them to. Before the HTML language included tables (see Skill 7), the Formatted style was the only way to align columns of text on a page.

For example, Figure 4.2 shows a web page that uses the Formatted style. It was quite easy to align the form fields with one another just by pressing the Spacebar.

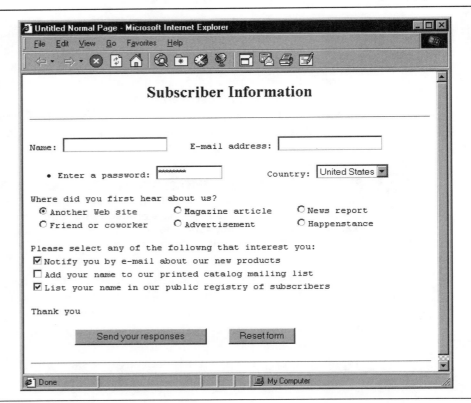

FIGURE 4.2: The Formatted style makes it easy to align the fields in this form page.

Setting Paragraph Alignment

By default, paragraphs are aligned along the left side of the Page view in Front-Page or in a browser window. You change the alignment of the current paragraph or selected paragraphs by clicking the appropriate button on the Formatting tool-bar: Align Left, Center, or Align Right.

If you prefer, you can select Format ➤ Paragraph and choose an alignment from the Alignment drop-down list in the Paragraph dialog box (see Figure 4.3). You can also right-click in the selection and choose Paragraph Properties to open the dialog box. Choosing Default removes any other alignment setting. The default for most browsers is left-aligned.

The alignment setting in the HTML code appears as an attribute of the paragraph tag, such as:

```
<P ALIGN="center">This paragraph is centered</P>
```

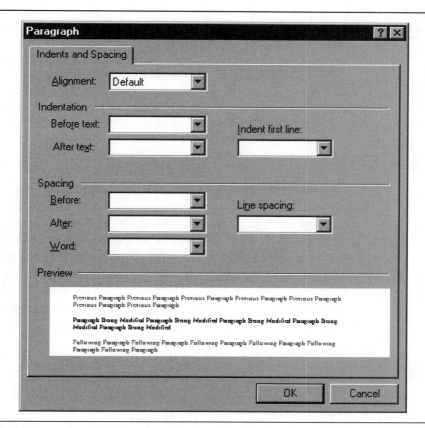

FIGURE 4.3: The Paragraph dialog box lets you fine tune paragraph alignment, indentation, and spacing.

Indenting Paragraphs

The quickest way to indent the current or selected paragraphs is to click the Increase Indent button on the Formatting toolbar. FrontPage adds the <BLOCK-QUOTE> tag, which indents both the left and right margins of the text, as you might want for a block indent used to set off a long quote from other text. Each time you click the Increase Indent button, the indentation is increased. A few browsers automatically italicize <BLOCKQUOTE> text, but indention alone is the norm.

To remove indentation one level at a time, click the Decrease Indent button. As described in Skill 3, you can also use the Decrease Indent button to change a selected bulleted or numbered list back to normal text.

If you want more control over paragraph indentation, use the Format ➤ Paragraph command. You'll see the Paragraph dialog box shown in Figure 4.3. You can specify the amount of indentation for the left and right sides, the amount of space that precedes and follows the text, and the line spacing for the entire paragraph.

Adding Borders and Shading

Another way to change the look of a paragraph is to add a border or shading to the text. Choose Format ➤ Borders and Shading, which displays the dialog box of that name. Its Borders tab is shown in Figure 4.4. When you specify a border, you choose the style of box that will surround the text, its color and thickness, and the amount of space (padding) between the text and the border.

Click the Shading tab in the dialog box to define the look of the shading for the paragraph (you can define both a border and shading if you want). Choose a color for the background and foreground (the text), or select a picture to display behind the text. The picture will be tiled to fill the space behind the paragraph, just as a picture in the page's background will do.

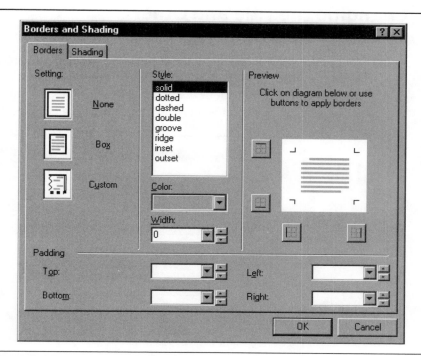

FIGURE 4.4: You choose the type of border or shading to apply to a paragraph in the Borders and Shading dialog box (shown is the Borders tab).

Setting Page Properties

Each web page has its own set of properties that you can access by choosing File ➤ Properties (when no page elements are selected), or by right-clicking anywhere on the page and choosing Page Properties from the shortcut menu. The Page Properties dialog box has six tabs: General, Background, Margins, Custom, Language, and Workgroup. Each is described in the sections that follow.

Changing the Title and Other General Options

We'll take a quick look at all the settings for the General tab. You might choose to change some of these settings now; others you'll probably want to leave as is until you learn more about them in later Skills. The General tab of the Page Properties dialog box contains the following settings (see Figure 4.5).

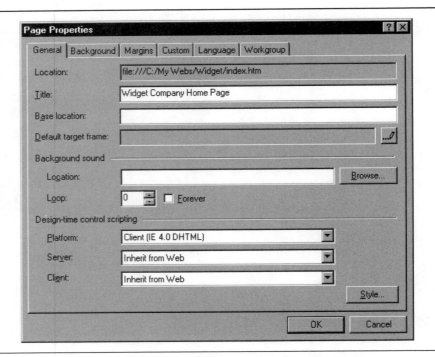

FIGURE 4.5: The General tab of the Page Properties dialog box

Location Displays the page's complete URL or filename and path. You can't change a page's location in this dialog box. To move the page to a new location, use the File ➤ Save As command or rename/move the page in the Folder List or in Folders view.

Title Displays and lets you revise the page's title. You usually create a title the first time you save a page (see "Saving Your Work" in Skill 2). In the HTML view, you'll find the <TITLE> tag within the <HEAD> tag near the top of the page. Giving your web a good title is critical, because the title is used by Web search engines. A poorly titled page is very frustrating for users because the page may show up in search results when it shouldn't. It's also frustrating for you, because users whom you wish to attract to your page won't be able to locate it by searching. The title should accurately and briefly describe the contents of your page. Web browsers display the page's title in their title bar, and offer the title as the default name when you save the page's URL as a favorite or bookmarked location, so the title needs to remind users about the contents of the page.

Base Location   If you enter an absolute URL here, you ensure that any hyperlinks on this page that use relative URLs always point to the correct target. (Absolute URLs are discussed in "Understanding Links" in Skill 6.)

Default Target Frame   If your page is displayed within a frame set, you can specify the name of the frame that serves as the default frame for all hyperlinks in this page that do not otherwise specify a frame. (Frame sets are discussed in Skill 13.)

Background Sound   To pique a visitor's interest, you may want to specify the name of a sound file, such as a WAV or MIDI file, that a browser plays when it opens the page (such as Ta Da!!!!). By default, the sound file plays once. If you want it to repeat, increase the Loop number. Select the Forever check box, and the sound loops continuously while the page is open in a browser.

WARNING WARNING WARNING WARNING WARNING WARNING WARNING WARNING

Playing a short, welcoming sound when a page is opened can be a nice feature. Using an annoying sound file even once can be an absolute turnoff. So use discretion with background sounds—a little goes a long way.

Changing Background Settings

To set page background properties, move to the Background tab of the Page Properties dialog box (see Figure 4.6). You can also open this tab by choosing Format ➤ Background from the menu. Changes you make on this page are added as attributes to the page's <BODY> tag.

You can specify a color or an image file that a browser displays as a page's background. FrontPage also includes a trick that lets you change the background for many pages in a web in one operation; it's a real time-saver (see "Getting Background Options from Another Page" later in this Skill).

You have two possibilities: you can choose the colors you want to use for background and text, or use the settings from an existing page. The default choice is for you to specify the background and colors yourself. The defaults are both set to Automatic, which in Internet Explorer produces black text on a white background. If this seems rather boring, you can, for example, change the screen to white text on a blue background.

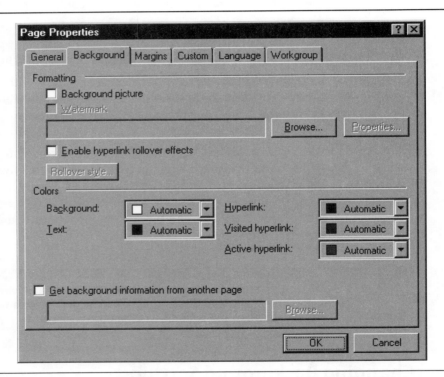

FIGURE 4.6: The Background tab of the Page Properties dialog box.

NOTE NOTE NOTE NOTE NOTE NOTE NOTE NOTE NOTE NOTE NOTE NOTE NOTE NOTE NOTE

You can also change the colors used for hyperlinks, visited hyperlinks, and active hyperlinks. However, it's easier to recognize hyperlinks when you use standard colors for them throughout your web. You should probably avoid changing their colors for an individual page unless the default colors conflict with the color you've chosen for that page's background.

Specifying a Background Image

Just as you can paint or wallpaper a wall in your office or on the Windows desktop, you can add color to a page's background, or "wallpaper" it with an image file. A browser normally tiles a small picture to fill the background completely, so there's no need to use a large picture. In fact, the smaller the image file, the faster it loads into a browser. Speed is always an important consideration, because visitors to your Web site may skip over a page if it takes too long to load.

Not all pictures are meant to be backgrounds. For example, dropping in a stunning M.C. Escher picture or a detailed graphic of the starship Enterprise may make the page almost leap out of the screen, but also makes all but the largest, boldest text unreadable.

Effective background images are small and textured and can be easily tiled together into a seamless background. They provide a muted and comfortable backdrop that does not dominate the page.

To specify a picture for a page's background, select the Background Picture option. Then, click the Browse button to select an image file from the current FrontPage web (such as in the web's Images folder) in the Select Background Picture dialog box, shown in Figure 4.7.

 To locate a file outside the current web, click the Use Your Web Browser to Select a Page button for web pages, or the Select a File on Your Computer button to locate a file on a local or network drive. Both of these icons are next to the URL text box. If the image isn't in the current web, but is part of another web page, you can type a URL for the image in the URL text box.

SKILL
4

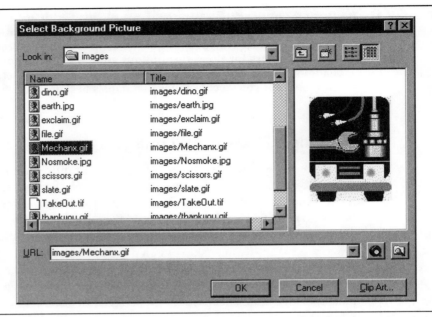

FIGURE 4.7: Choosing a Background Image from the Select Background Picture dialog box

You can access images from the Microsoft Clip Art Gallery (shown in Figure 4.8) by clicking the Clip Art button. This may look familiar, because FrontPage uses the same clip art gallery as Microsoft Office. Click one of the picture categories to display the images it contains. Click the piece of clip art you want to use, and then click the Insert button on the pop-up menu (you'll read more about clip art in Skill 8).

Whether you choose clip art or another image file, the file's name appears on the Background page of the Page Properties dialog box. When you're finished specifying page properties and you close the dialog box, you'll find the background image you selected, tiled to completely fill the page's background in FrontPage's Preview and Page views, just as it would in a browser.

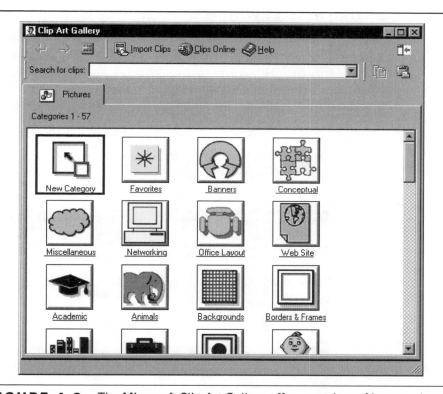

FIGURE 4.8: The Microsoft Clip Art Gallery offers a variety of images that are suitable page backgrounds.

NOTE NOTE NOTE NOTE NOTE NOTE NOTE NOTE NOTE NOTE NOTE NOTE NOTE NOTE NOTE

When a background image is tiled to fill a page, a browser scrolls the background as you scroll the page. If you choose the Watermark option in the Background options, browsers that support this feature leave the background image stationary while you scroll the page.

Once you specify a background image file and save it as part of your web, you can return to the Page Properties dialog box and click Properties to view or modify the properties of this image. These and other image-editing issues are discussed in "Setting Image Properties" in Skill 8.

Saving Images with Your Page

If you include an image file from outside of your web, you should save a copy of the image with the page so that it's always available. FrontPage makes this extraordinarily easy. When you save a web page that includes images or other files that came from outside the current web, the Save Embedded Files dialog box opens (see Figure 4.9) , listing all the embedded files on the page. You can rename the embedded files, choose a different folder (Images is a good choice), set the action (Save or Don't Save), then click OK. If you can't remember what a particular image looks like, you can click the image name, and a thumbnail of the image appears in the Picture Preview pane.

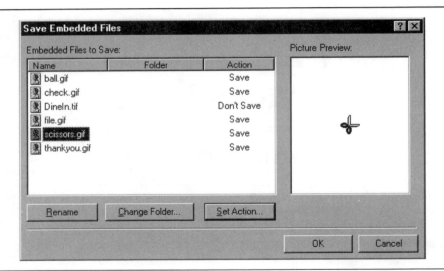

FIGURE 4.9: Setting the options for saving embedded files

Getting Background Options from Another Page

Imagine that your Web site has dozens of pages, and you'd like them to share a consistent look. One of the site's most noticeable features is the pale yellow background that includes a rendition of your company's logo. It's a real beauty—understated, yet attention grabbing.

Now imagine that a special someone who signs your paycheck has suggested that perhaps a soft, very light green would make a better background for these pages. This is simple enough to try if your Web site is only a one- or two-pager. Changing the look of your 50-page work of art, however, is a daunting task.

Happily, FrontPage has a feature that can help you brush off this project single-handedly and in record time: the Get Background Information from Another Page option.

Select this option (shown below) from the Background tab of the Page Properties dialog box, then specify a page in your web that you want to copy the Background settings from for use on the current page. There's nothing more to it. Each time the current page is opened in a browser or in FrontPage, the settings for its Background options are read from the other page. Therefore, if you simply change the background settings in the former page, you will effectively change those settings in all the pages that refer to it.

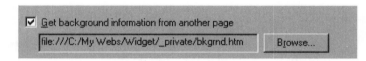

To really take advantage of this feature, of course, you should use it from the very beginning when building your web. Right now, you're working with a single page web. If each new page you create refers back to this page (or, perhaps, one of just a couple pages) for its colors and background, it's a snap to modify the colors and backgrounds of all the pages in your web just by modifying the few pages that all pages are based on. To find out more ways to standardize your design and make future site maintenance easy, see "Adding Pages Using Templates" in Skill 10.

Setting Hyperlink Rollover Effects

Some of the newer HTML features supported by FrontPage are the special effects that appear when a visitor to your web page passes the mouse pointer over a text hyperlink. For example, you can choose to have a link change its font style or color when triggered by the mouse pointer passing over it.

You adjust these effects in the Background page of the Page Properties dialog box by clicking the Enable Hyperlink Rollover Effects check box (refer back to Figure 4.6). Once selected, click the Rollover Style button, which displays the Font dialog box. Here you choose the effects you want for all hyperlinks on this page. You can specify a different font style, size, and color, as well as the various font effects. The Rollover Effects affect all text links on the page, but doesn't affect links embedded in images.

Setting Page Margins

To specify a top or left margin for the page, select the Margins tab of the Page Properties dialog box. By default, both margins are set to zero, so no margins are specified.

You can only define the margin in pixels, so the actual width of the blank area at the top or left side of the page in a browser depends on the screen resolution on the users' computers. For this reason (and the fact that not all browsers support the TOPMARGIN and LEFTMARGIN attributes for the <BODY> tag), you should use caution when setting margins for your pages. If you are creating pages for a company intranet and there are company standards for browser software and screen resolution, you should be relatively safe adjusting margins.

Creating Meta Page Information

HTML includes the <META> tag as a way for a page's author to supply information about the page to both the server that processes the page and browsers that open the page. For example, an author can include a list of keywords in a <META> tag that the server uses to index that page for Web-wide searching. A browser checks the <META> tag to find out which character set should be used to display the page, or at what interval it should automatically reload the page. When included in a page, the <META> tag appears within the page's <HEAD> tag.

In the Custom tab in the Page Properties dialog box, you add, modify, or remove what FrontPage refers to as *variables*, which appear within the <META> tag for a page. It's unlikely you'll need to work with variables, but it's good to know where you can access them.

By default, FrontPage creates several variables for a page. The single system variable, which isn't displayed on the Custom tab, tells a browser or server what type of document this is and the character set that should be used for it. The user variables simply let the world know which program generated this page. Each variable consists of a name, such as Generator, and a value, such as Microsoft FrontPage 4.0. If you enter variables on the Custom tab, the system variables you create appear as part of the HTTP-EQUIV attribute for the <META> tag, and user variables appear as their own attributes of that tag.

NOTE NOTE NOTE NOTE NOTE NOTE NOTE NOTE NOTE NOTE NOTE NOTE NOTE NOTE NOTE

If this sounds a little technical, then it's probably not yet time for you to create your own system or user variables. As you can see, though, the process of entering the variable name and value is pretty straightforward. So when the need arrives and you know the variable that should be used, entering the variable will be a snap.

Specifying the Page's Language

One of the problems with using the Internet is that there are simply too many languages in the world—if only we could all agree to use just one and get on with our lives! In the meantime, you can localize your web pages by specifying their base language in the Language tab of the Page Properties dialog box.

The options in this tab allow you to create web pages in whatever language your Windows installation supports. For example, if you're using an English-language version of Windows, its character set allows you to create web pages in German. You can also specify which language the spell-checker should use when you check the spelling in this page.

Setting Workgroup Properties

The process of building or maintaining a web can quickly become a large, complex job. Pages and images are added, material must be revised and updated, multiple authors might be working on the same web, and so on. In other words, you not only need tools for creating web content, you also need tools for managing the web while you are building it and later when you are maintaining it.

One of the management tools that FrontPage offers can be found on the Workgroup tab of the pages Properties dialog box, shown in Figure 4.10 (this tab is only available when a page is part of a FrontPage web). The Workgroup tab offers three ways to organize and track pages:

Available Categories   Assign the page to one or more categories by selecting them in the list. You can click the Categories button to add or remove categories to the list.

Assigned To   Assign the page to an author by selecting a name from the drop-down menu. Click the Names button to add or remove names.

Review Status   Specify the status of the page by selecting a status from the drop-down menu. Click the Statuses button to add or remove statuses.

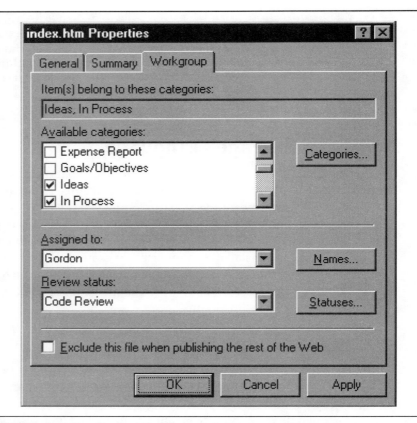

FIGURE 4.10: On the Workgroup tab you can assign a page to one or more categories, identify the author, and specify its current status.

As you assign pages to categories and authors, and give them each a status, you create a framework for tracking the progress of your web. You can view these elements in the Reports view with the Categories, Assigned To, and Review Status reports. These list all the files in your web, with columns for the various assignments.

TIP TIP TIP TIP TIP TIP TIP TIP TIP TIP TIP TIP TIP TIP TIP TIP TIP TIP TIP TIP TIP TIP TIP TIP TIP

You can quickly change the Workgroup settings for multiple files by selecting them in Folders or Reports view, right-clicking one of them and choosing Properties from the shortcut menu, and then changing its Workgroup properties. The change will affect all the selected files.

As changes are made to pages and the entire web, you can adjust these properties as needed. For example, if one of the authors assigned to pages in your web leaves the project, you can remove that name from the pages. Or, as pages are created but not finished, you might assign them to the category named In Process. When you complete a page, you could remove it from that category.

Animating Your Pages with Dynamic HTML

As Web designers develop more exciting Web sites by adding objects that move on the page, it becomes harder to find pages that load within a reasonable amount of time. No matter how amazing a page, if visitors get tired of waiting, they can always move on to another location. Dynamic HTML (DHTML) is a way to add movement to a page without compromising loading speed. (Of course, visitors to your site must have a browser, such as Microsoft Internet Explorer 4 or later, that can handle Dynamic HTML.) FrontPage allows you to add Dynamic HTML features to elements in your pages via the DHTML Effects toolbar. You can animate an entire page when it is opened in a browser via the Format ➤ Page Transitions command.

Animating Page Elements

To animate text or another page element such as a graphic image, first select it. Then, choose Format ➤ Dynamic HTML Effects, which displays the DHTML Effects toolbar (shown below). You can also choose this toolbar from the View ➤ Toolbars menu.

The choices on the toolbar will vary, depending on the type of object you have selected. For example, when you have selected an image, you can choose to have a second image replace it when a user passes the mouse pointer over the image. With text, you can define the font that will be used when a user points at the text or clicks on it (much like the page-wide Rollover Effect discussed earlier in "Setting Hyperlink Rollover Effects "). Let's add some Dynamic HTML to text so that the text is enclosed in a border when a user passes the mouse over it.

1. Select the text you want to include in the effect and then display the DHTML Effects toolbar.

2. In the DHTML Effects toolbar, choose Mouse Over from the On drop-down list.

3. Now choose Formatting from the Apply list on the toolbar.

4. In the effects lists on the toolbar, select Choose Border.

5. In the Borders and Shading dialog box that appears (the same one you see with the Format ➤ Borders and Shading command), select the style of border that you want to see displayed around this text when a user points to the text.

6. Click OK to close the dialog box.

7. You're done, so click anywhere in the page outside of the text you just formatted.

To see the effects of the DHTML, click the Preview tab to preview the page, or save the page and preview it in a browser. When you point to the text, a border appears around it; when you move the mouse pointer off the text, the border disappears. If a user's browser doesn't support Dynamic HTML, the text appears in its regular style and position on the page. You can remove DHTML effects from text by selecting the text and clicking the Remove Effect button on the DHTML toolbar.

Once you've defined an animation, you can copy it to another element in the same way that you copy any formatting—with the Format Painter button on the toolbar. For example, click within the animated text, click the Format Painter button, and then select the target text.

 NOTE NOTE NOTE NOTE NOTE NOTE NOTE NOTE NOTE NOTE NOTE NOTE NOTE NOTE NOTE
If you work with Microsoft PowerPoint, you're probably already familiar with animation, called a "build" in older versions.

Animating Page Transitions

Now that you've seen how you can create animated text similar to the builds in PowerPoint, you'll learn how to create page transitions, just like PowerPoint's slide transitions. As with page element DHTML, page transitions are visible in browsers that support Dynamic HTML.

To access page transitions, in Page view choose Format ➤ Page Transitions. The dialog box, shown here, has only a few options you need to set.

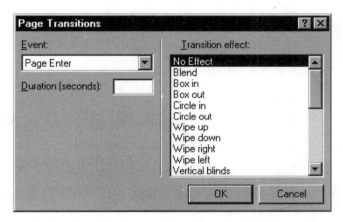

First, in the Event drop-down list, choose the event you want to tie the transition to:

Page Enter   Displays when a user opens the page

Page Exit   Displays when a user leaves the page

Site Enter   Displays when a user initially enters the site

Site Exit   Displays when a user leaves the site

Next, choose the transition you want from the Transition Effect list, which offers more than two dozen choices. You should probably test a few of them out to see how they affect your pages.

Finally, in the Duration field, indicate how long you want the transition effect to last. More than a few seconds is typically too long—fewer than two or three seconds is often too short. It depends on the contents of the page, so try different lengths and see how they work.

Once you've set the transition, click OK and save the page. Preview the page in a browser that supports Dynamic HTML, and remember—the transition is tied to entering or exiting. It's easiest to see the transition if you follow a hyperlink in or out of your page or site.

SKILL
4

Are You Experienced?

Now you can...

- ☑ Select text using a number of different methods
- ☑ Change text fonts and apply text formatting
- ☑ Change paragraph styles
- ☑ Align and indent paragraphs
- ☑ Change character and line spacing on a page
- ☑ Change the properties of a page
- ☑ Specify a background picture or color
- ☑ Organize your pages with categories and author assignments
- ☑ Add animation to pages and text and other page elements with Dynamic HTML

Managing Webs in FrontPage

- → **Adding and rearranging pages with the Navigation view**
- → **Working in the Hyperlinks and Folders views**
- → **Updating links when you rename or move a file**
- → **Working with file properties**
- → **Keeping tabs on your web with the Reports view**
- → **Associating files with editors or viewers**
- → **Organizing chores with the Tasks view**

Up to this point, you've been working with a single-page web. Now it's time to add pages to your web and link them together so visitors can move around your site easily. The best developers lay out the entire design for the web first, create the various pages and relationships (links) between the pages, and design the consistent elements that appear on every page before entering the actual content for each page. This process ensures consistency between different sections of the web and correct connections between the pages.

Although you can create individual pages in the Page view and then link them together, it is better to create the structure of your web first in FrontPage and allow it to automatically build links between the pages for you. FrontPage also gives you an inside look at your web and reveals the relationships among its files. Because FrontPage can update hyperlinks automatically, you are free to add, move, or rename files in your web without worrying about tracking and updating individual links.

In this Skill, you learn how to create additional pages that are automatically linked to your home page; how to move pages; and how to keep track of the myriad tasks that a web designer must manage while developing a web.

Working in Navigation View

With FrontPage, there are several ways to view a web, depending on what it is you want to do to it: Navigation view, Hyperlinks view, Folders view, Reports view, and Tasks view. When you create a new web that contains at least one page you'll generally find it most helpful to open the Navigation view, where you can see your web in its entirety. Figure 5.1 shows a fully developed version of the Widget Company's web in Navigation view. In the right-hand pane, you see an organizational chart of the web called a *site map*. The home page, also called a *parent page*, is on the top level and the additional pages are shown underneath. In this example, News, Products, and Services are *child pages* to the home page, but each is also a parent page to other, subordinate pages.

The Folder List, to the left of the Navigation pane, lists the files and folders contained in the web. Drag the vertical divider right or left to change the relative size of the panes.

TIP TIP TIP TIP TIP TIP TIP TIP TIP TIP TIP TIP TIP TIP TIP TIP TIP TIP TIP TIP TIP TIP

Click any of the icons in the Views bar on the left side of the FrontPage window to switch between the different views of your web. Changing views does not change the contents of the current web.

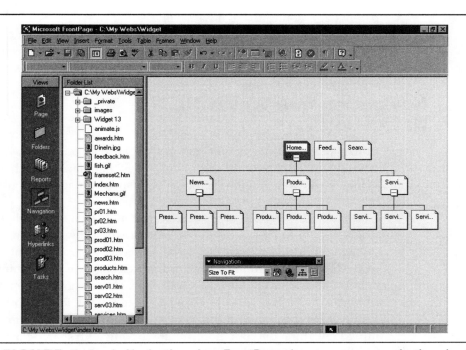

FIGURE 5.1: In Navigation view, FrontPage shows you an organization chart of your web based on the relationship between pages in the web.

NOTE NOTE NOTE NOTE NOTE NOTE NOTE NOTE NOTE NOTE NOTE NOTE NOTE NOTE NOTE

To follow along with the activities in this Skill, use the one-page web you worked on in previous Skills, or create a new one by choosing File ➤ New ➤ Web, and select One Page Web. Enter a name for the web, a new location (if you wish), and click OK.

When you've created a new web (other than the Empty Web) or opened an existing one, you can add a new page to the web by right-clicking the page in the Navigation view site map that will serve as parent to the new page. In a one-page web, that's the home page. (You can create a page on the same level as the home page by not selecting a page, but you'd rarely want to do this.) On the shortcut menu, choose New Page, and the new page will appear as an icon beneath its parent page, connected to it with a line.

You can continue to create new pages in this way, filling out the structure of your web as your plans dictate. Of course, each new page is completely empty, but serves as a placeholder that you can later edit in Page view.

Navigating Your Web with Navigation Bars

When you're working in Navigation view, at some point you will likely want to take advantage of two features in FrontPage that make it much easier for you to manage your web and for visitors to your site to navigate through it—shared borders and navigation bars.

Navigation bars are sets of buttons located on each page that allow visitors to move to another page in the current web. They are typically placed in a section of a page called a *shared border*, a page area that displays the same content on each page in the web. If you're familiar with word processing, you might think of shared borders as the headers or footers of a web page. There is one difference: Shared borders can appear on any or all edges of a page—left, right, top, or bottom. Figure 5.2 shows a web page in FrontPage's Page view that has all four shared borders turned on. You'll find out more about working with shared borders and navigation bars in "Using and Modifying Navigation Bars" in Skill 6.

When you tell FrontPage to create navigation bars in Navigation view, it automatically adds hyperlinks where appropriate in the current web. Even if you move, delete, or add pages in Navigation view, FrontPage updates the links it created in the navigation bars. If you create links yourself, however, you are responsible for updating them when you change the parent/child relationship. For this reason, if you want to create the hierarchical web structure so well-illustrated in Navigation view, it is best to add pages while in that view and let FrontPage add and update the links in the navigation bars.

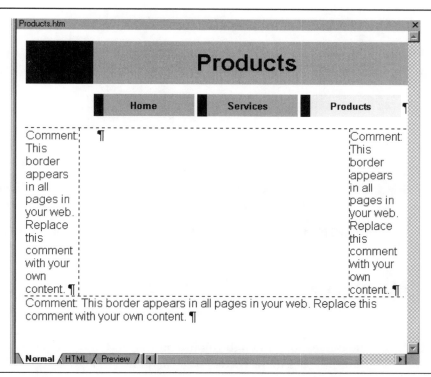

FIGURE 5.2: Shared borders on the top, bottom, left, and right sides of a page share content with other pages in the current web.

Renaming Pages in Navigation View

When you add a new page to your web, it is called New Page *n*, where *n* is the number of new pages you've created in this session, just as new Word documents are called Document *n* and new Excel workbooks are called Book *n*. You can easily change this riveting, sequence-oriented name to something more descriptive by right-clicking the page icon and choosing Rename from the shortcut menu. Or, select the icon and press F2. The background around the name in the Navigation diagram turns blue to indicate that it is selected and you can type in the new name.

SKILL
5

 NOTE NOTE NOTE NOTE NOTE NOTE NOTE NOTE NOTE NOTE NOTE NOTE NOTE NOTE NOTE
The name displayed for each page icon in Navigation view is the page title of the file, *not* its filename. Changing an icon's name will therefore also update its HTML title. To change the filename of a page, do so in the Folder List.

Moving Pages within a Web

Once you create a page, you can change how it relates to other pages by dragging and dropping it into a new position. In Navigation view, click the page you want to move, hold down the mouse button, and drag the page until the connecting line attaches to the correct page, as shown in Figure 5.3.

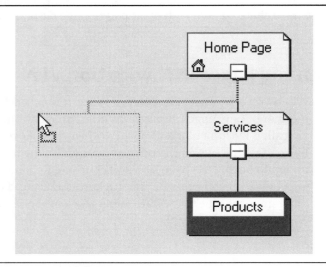

FIGURE 5.3: Change the relationship between pages by dragging and dropping a page into a new position.

If the page you want to reposition has child pages under it, moving the parent moves all the children with it. In other words, you can't break up a family unit by moving the parent—all the kids tag along.

Deleting Pages in Navigation View

There are two options for deleting pages from the Navigation view structure. If you select the page you want to delete and press the Delete key on the keyboard, a dialog box like the one shown here appears with the possible options.

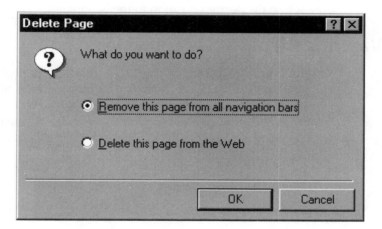

You may then choose to:

- Remove this page from all navigation bars.

- Delete the page from the web entirely, which means the page itself and all links to the page are deleted.

Removing a page from all navigation bars is more like hiding the page than deleting the page. FrontPage removes the page and all links to the page from the active web, but keeps the page available for future use. For example, if you have a page you want to work on or have revisions you want to make to a page on a published web, you can remove the page from navigation bars so that visitors can't access the page while it's under construction. When your work is complete, you can add the page back into the web, as you'll see in the next section.

If you only want to remove a page from the navigation bars, right-click the page's icon in Navigation view and choose Included in Navigation Bars so that this

SKILL
5

option is no longer enabled. You can also select the icon and click the Included in Navigation Bars button on the Navigation toolbar.

Inserting an Existing Page in Navigation View

You can add existing pages from your web to the Navigation view so that Front-Page can add navigation bars and appropriate links to them. To add an existing page to the Navigation view site map, select the page in the Folder List pane and drag it into the desired position in the Navigation view site map.

Viewing All or Parts of Your Web

As your web gets bigger, you'll probably want to see just one branch of the site map at a time, so you won't have to scroll through the entire map. In Navigation view, each parent page includes a Collapse button with a minus sign. Click that button, as shown in the next graphic, to hide the child pages under the parent page (and any child pages subordinate to those child pages).

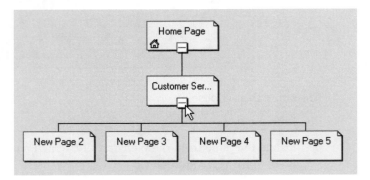

The minus sign changes to a plus sign, called the Expand button. Click this button to display the children of the branch. While you're working on your web, use the Expand and Collapse buttons to display the parts of the web that are relevant.

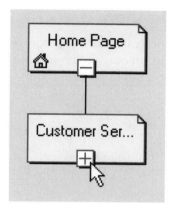

Displaying All of Your Web's Structure

When your web is fully expanded, you may not be able to see the entire site map within your screen display. However, you can easily move around the site map. Click and hold down the mouse button any place on the display, and when the pointer changes to a hand, drag the site map to move the portion you wish to view into the window. Or, for a fast tour, you can pan back and forth across the site map. This gives you a quick view of hidden parts of the web.

If you really want to see the entire web at once, FrontPage gives you a way to do this, too. On the Navigation toolbar, select the Size To Fit option from the pull-down list of scaling factors. FrontPage reduces the web to fit into the Navigation pane. However, if the web is too big, Front Page truncates or simply doesn't display page names.

You can choose any of the other scaling factors on the Navigation toolbar to size the Navigation pane accordingly. For example, select 50% to reduce the size of the icons by half, or 150% to increase their size by half. To return to the normal size, choose 100%.

Rotating the View

Depending on your web's structure, you may find that you can see more of your web if you turn it over on its side, as shown in Figure 5.4.

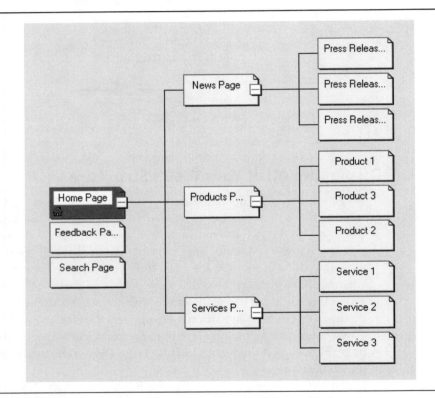

FIGURE 5.4: Rotating the web may make it easier to view.

Click the Portrait/Landscape button on the Navigation toolbar to rotate the orientation. Click it again to return to a vertical (portrait) orientation. You can also right-click the background of the Navigation view and choose Rotate.

Printing the Navigation View

As you design your web, you'll find times when it's helpful to have a hard copy available to share with other team members, clients, or supervisors. While you are working in the Navigation view, choose File ➤ Print to print a copy of the Navigation view site map.

If you'd rather see how the site map looks before printing it, choose File ➤ Print Preview. Navigation view is the only view you can print in FrontPage, although you can print a copy of a web page from the Page view.

Displaying Your Web in Hyperlinks View

The Hyperlinks view allows you to examine your web's underlying structure and see how your pages connect to each other. When you choose View ➤ Hyperlinks, or click the Hyperlinks icon in the Views bar, the web is displayed according to the hyperlinks in its pages. The Hyperlinks pane (see Figure 5.5) displays a graphical representation of the web—a model that uses the selected file in the Folder List as its starting point. Pages and other items, like URLs and images, are shown as icons in this model, with arrows connecting a page to the links it contains and the files it includes.

SKILL
5

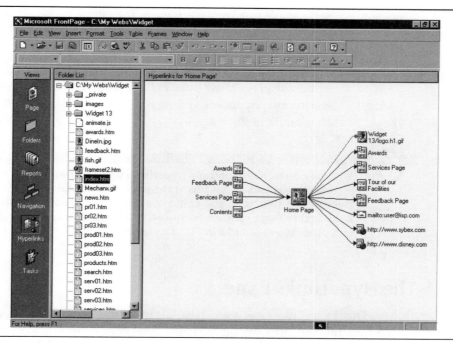

FIGURE 5.5: In Hyperlinks view, FrontPage displays the links between pages.

Expanding the Hyperlinks View

FrontPage allows you to expand or contract the scope of the Hyperlinks view. Right-click the background of this view to display the shortcut menu and the options that change the scope of the view. Remember that you can turn these view options on or off at any time, either to see more of the details of your site or to simplify the display. All are turned off by default.

Show Page Titles   Displays each page's title instead of its filename.

Hyperlinks to Pictures   Displays the icons of image files that are the target of links. If a site contains many image files, you can turn off this option so you get a better view of other types of files in the web.

Repeated Hyperlinks   Displays multiple links from one web page to another page, file, or URL. The default setting in FrontPage is to display only a single link; enabling repeated hyperlinks shows each link to a file or page, even if there are several from the same page. Keep in mind that it's not unusual to use the same image for seven different buttons on a page. Working with Repeated Hyperlinks turned off makes sure that you only see a single link from the page to the image, rather than having six extra links cluttering up the Hyperlinks pane.

Hyperlinks Inside Page   Displays links in a target page that target the original source page. In other words, if Page A has links to Page B, this option displays those links in Page B that target Page A. You should hide the internal hyperlinks when you're checking the links between pages so they aren't in the way.

 NOTE NOTE NOTE NOTE NOTE NOTE NOTE NOTE NOTE NOTE NOTE NOTE NOTE NOTE NOTE

You may often have multiple hyperlinks within a page, such as when you have a table of contents at the top of the page that contains links to locations within the page. In this case, you could use both the Repeated Hyperlinks and Hyperlinks Inside Page options to see all the links. You can read about bookmarks and other types of links in "Understanding Links" in Skill 6.

The Hyperlinks Pane

The Hyperlinks view, as seen earlier in Figure 5.5, is a model of the underlying link relationships among the pages and other items in a web. Each page or file is represented by an icon as well as its title, file name, or URL.

Both the Hyperlinks and Navigation views show you the underlying structure of your web and the relationships among its files. The Hyperlinks view relates one file to another based on the hyperlinks in the first file that target the second. If no hyperlinks target that second file, then the two will not be connected in the Hyperlinks view. The Navigation view, however, is of your own making. You determine the parent/child relationship by actually moving one file beneath another.

The item you select in the Folder List becomes the center of focus in the Hyperlinks pane. To change the focus of the model, right-click an icon in the Hyperlinks pane and choose Move to Center from the shortcut menu, which shifts the center of focus to the item represented by the icon.

Figure 5.6 shows another example of the Hyperlinks view. The Product 2 page is selected in the Folder List, so it is the focus in the center in the Hyperlinks pane.

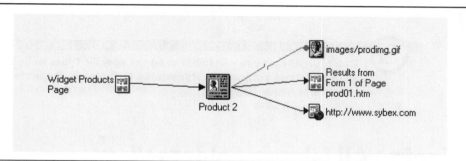

FIGURE 5.6: The Hyperlinks pane shows you the chain of links among the pages and resources in the web.

The Hyperlinks pane shows you a vast amount of information at a glance—information that's very difficult to glean and organize by combing through each page in the web. Here's what you can see in the Hyperlinks pane in Figure 5.6:

- When you're looking at links, read the Hyperlinks pane from left to right. Pages that contain hyperlinks to the page selected in the Folder List are shown at the left, with arrows pointing to that page's icon. In Figure 5.6, the Widget Products Page contains hyperlinks to the Product 2 page.

- The Product 2 page contains hyperlinks to other pages, which are represented by arrows that run from the page's icon to target icons on the right.

- A link arrow that ends in a bullet indicates that the target is included in the page. The Product 2 page has one link to an included resource, the image file `prodimg.gif` that appears in the page.

- A link arrow that is broken indicates the link is broken (invalid), such as the link to the image file in Figure 5.6. In this case, that file might have been deleted in FrontPage, but the reference to it in the page has not yet been removed, or someone working outside FrontPage might have moved, deleted, or renamed that target file so that FrontPage can no longer find it.

- A link arrow that ends in an arrowhead indicates a hyperlink that opens the link's target. The Product 2 page has two hyperlinks that open other resources. One link is to a page within the current web (an *internal link*), and one is a link to a URL outside of the current web (an *external link*).

- Icons for pages that contain links (other than the one at the center of focus) include a plus sign. Click a plus sign to expand the links, and the plus changes to a minus sign. Click the minus sign to collapse the links.

NOTE NOTE NOTE NOTE NOTE NOTE NOTE NOTE NOTE NOTE NOTE NOTE NOTE NOTE NOTE

Don't forget that you can focus in on the specific types of links you want to see with the three commands Hyperlinks to Pictures, Repeated Hyperlinks, and Hyperlinks Inside Page.

Seeing All Files in Folders View

To view your web's folders and files in FrontPage, choose View ➤ Folders or click the Folders icon in the Views bar. The Folder List displays the folders contained in the web, and the right pane displays all the files in the selected folder, along with various file details such as the date and time they were created, the titles of pages, and so on. Figure 5.7 shows the Folders view of the Widget web used in earlier examples.

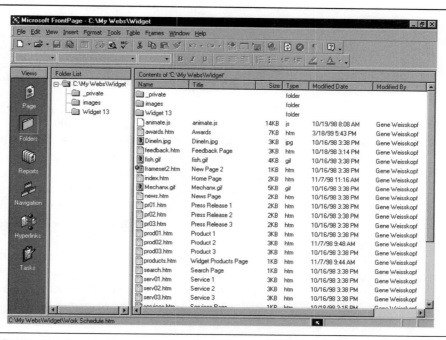

FIGURE 5.7: The Folders view provides a detailed list of all the files in your web.

Folders view is very much like the Windows Explorer view of a disk or network. The contents of the folder selected in the Folder List are displayed in the pane on the right. In the Folder List, click the plus sign on a folder to expand it and display the folders it contains. To hide the folders within a folder, click the folder's minus sign.

The Files pane displays columns of information for each file in the web: name, page title, size, type, date and time modified, modifier, and comments. The Title and Comments columns display the same information you can view and modify in the item's properties, as you'll see in the next section.

You can manipulate the list of files just as you would in Windows Explorer:

- Click a column heading to sort the file list by that column. For example, click the Modified Date column title to see the most recently edited files at the top of the list.

- Click the column heading again to reverse the sort order.

- Resize a column by dragging the right edge of the column heading to the left or right.

- Select multiple contiguous files by selecting the first file, then holding Shift and clicking the last file you want to select. Select multiple non-contiguous files by selecting the first file, then holding Ctrl while selecting each additional file.

To create new folders in Folders view, just select the folder in which you want to create the new subfolder and choose File ➣ New ➣ Folder, or click the New Folder button on the toolbar (click the down-arrow for the New button and select Folder). In the Folder List, you can right-click a folder to create a new folder. If you're working under the auspices of a Web server, you'll need administrator level permission (see Skill 14, *Publishing Your Web Site* for more about permissions).

Use subfolders to organize a web the same way you organize files within folders and subfolders on your hard drive. For example, by default FrontPage creates a folder called Images within a new web, in which you can conveniently store all image files. Suppose your web includes many pages and images that make up a reference manual. You can put those files out of the way by placing them all in subfolders, such as /MyWeb/Manual and /MyWeb/Manual/Images.

Now let's look at the many ways you can manipulate files in the Hyperlinks and Folder views.

NOTE NOTE NOTE NOTE NOTE NOTE NOTE NOTE NOTE NOTE NOTE NOTE NOTE NOTE NOTE

If you include a file named with the default home page name for the web (like INDEX.HTM) in a subfolder, you create a "nested" subweb. When a user browses the subfolder, the server sends the browser the file INDEX.HTM from that folder. This means you can have different "home pages" in a web.

Manipulating Files and Their Properties

Each file has its own set of properties, some of which you can modify directly. For example, you can rename a file or edit the comments about the file. Other properties are updated automatically when the file is modified, such as file size, modification date, and modifier name.

When a team is working on a web, other team members' changes are not automatically displayed in your copy of FrontPage. Choose View ➤ Refresh from the menu to have FrontPage read the web from the server and update your view of the web.

Regardless of the view you choose, there are a number of commands you'll use to work with files. You can either select a file or icon and choose a command from the menu, or right-click the selected file and choose a command from the shortcut menu. A few of the choices are only available in some views, and with particular types of files. The following commands are available from the shortcut menu or the File or Edit menu.

Open   Opens a page in the Page view; opens other items in their associated application. For example, you can open and edit a GIF or JPEG image file in Microsoft Image Composer, or a MIDI sound file in the Windows Sound Recorder.

Open With   Lets you choose the editor or viewer in which to open the selected file. (See "Specifying Web File Editors" later in this Skill.)

Delete   Removes the file from your web and deletes it (except for external files, which are outside your control). You're prompted to confirm the deletion. In Navigation view only, you are given the option to delete navigation links but retain the file itself in the web.

Properties   Displays the file's Properties dialog box.

Cut/Copy/Paste   The Cut command removes the resource from the web and copies it to the Windows Clipboard. The Copy command copies the resource to the Clipboard, and the Paste command places the contents of the Clipboard into the selected folder in the active web. In Folders view, these commands let you copy or move a file to a different folder. In Navigation view, use Cut and Paste to relocate a selected page or branch, including a parent page and its child pages, to a different position in the view. Use Copy and Paste to duplicate a portion of the web.

Rename   Allows you to change the filename of the selected folder or file. You can also select the file and press F2, or click the name of a file twice with a pause between clicks and edit the name. If the file is already selected, just click once on the filename. (Don't double-click or you'll open the file!) In Navigation view, renaming an icon changes its page title, not its filename.

SKILL
▼ 5

Add Task   Creates a new entry in the Tasks view that is linked to the selected file (see "Keeping Track with the Task View" later in this Skill).

Renaming or Moving a File

Before you rename or move a file, be sure that the file is not open in another application like an editor or the Image Composer. This avoids conflicts that can occur when two programs try to access the same file, or when a file that is open is moved from its original location.

In the Folders view, move a file to another folder simply by dragging it there, or by using Cut and Paste. For example, you can move all the images for a particular section of the web into a subfolder in the Images folder.

To copy a file or a folder, hold down the Ctrl key while you drag it, or use Copy and Paste. You can also drag a file or a folder with the right mouse button instead of the left, and then choose Copy Here, Move Here, or Cancel from the shortcut menu, just as you do in the Windows Explorer.

 WARNING WARNING WARNING WARNING WARNING WARNING WARNING WARNING
Never change a file extension (the characters following the period) unless you know exactly why you need to do so. The extension identifies the file's type, and links it to the appropriate application.

When you rename a file that is the target of one or more hyperlinks in other files, you see the Rename dialog box, shown here.

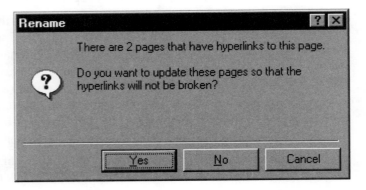

The dialog box lets you know that FrontPage is on the job, watching over your web. It tells you how many other resources are linked to the file whose name you are changing, and asks whether you want to update those links to reflect the new name. At this point, you can do any of the following:

- Click Yes to have FrontPage automatically revise the links to this file so they refer to the new name.

- Click No if, for some reason, you want to rename the file without having the links to it revised; this "breaks" the links to the page or file.

- Click Cancel to cancel the renaming operation.

 NOTE NOTE NOTE NOTE NOTE NOTE NOTE NOTE NOTE NOTE NOTE NOTE NOTE NOTE NOTE

Renaming a page file does not change the page's title. To change the title, switch to Navigation view and rename the page in the Navigation site map, or edit the page and change its title in the Page Properties dialog box.

You can read more about the Explorer's link-maintenance abilities in the "Fixing and Verifying Links" section in Skill 6.

Viewing and Revising File Properties

You can view or modify the properties of a file by right-clicking the file's name or icon and choosing Properties from the shortcut menu (or choosing File ➤ Properties from the menu). Figure 5.8 shows the General and Summary tabs of the Properties dialog box.

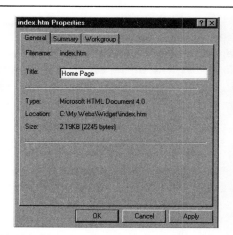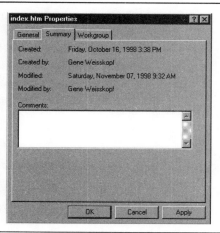

FIGURE 5.8: The General and Summary tabs of the Properties dialog box

The General and Summary tabs display the file's name, type, size, and the date and time it was last modified. These are the same properties that you see in the columns in the Folders view. You can change two of the properties:

Comments   Enter comments about the file, such as its purpose in the web or when it should be updated.

Title   Revise a page's HTML title, the same title that you can revise while editing the page. For files that are not HTML pages, such as image files, you can enter a more descriptive title here that only FrontPage uses to identify the resource. By default, a file's title will be the same as its filename, such as bh10-01.gif. You could change this file's title to "Home Page Button Image" to make it more descriptive. Note that this changes only the title that FrontPage uses, not the actual filename.

You also see a Location field in the General page that displays the resource's URL, such as:

```
C:\My Webs\Widget\index.htm
```

Reporting on Your FrontPage Web

The Navigation and Hyperlinks views in FrontPage lay out your web like a map of a city. When you want some good hard statistics on your web, however, turn to the Reports view. This powerful feature lets you see the details of your web in plain and simple columnar reports—nothing fancy, colorful, or dazzling, just numbers and facts about your web that you'll find invaluable.

Click the Reports icon in the Views bar, and a report will appear in the right-hand pane of the FrontPage window. You can also choose a specific report from the View ➤ Reports menu. Either way, the report and the Reporting toolbar will be displayed, as shown in Figure 5.9. (You can also access the Reporting toolbar from the View ➤ Toolbars menu.)

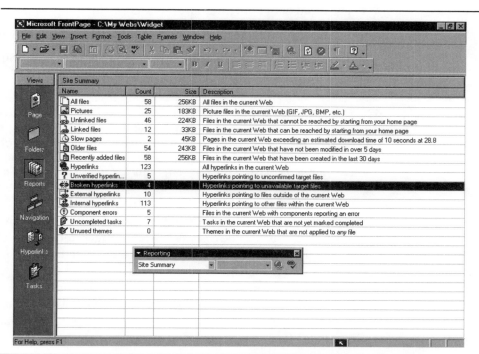

FIGURE 5.9: The Reports view offers a variety of columnar reports about your FrontPage web.

The reports cover a wide range of web-related statistics. Try each one in a web you're already somewhat familiar with and you'll see how much more you can learn about that web. The Site Summary report, the one shown in Figure 5.9, is probably the first one you'll want to inspect. It gives you a great deal of information, including:

- The total number of files in your web

- The number of image files

- The number of files that are targets of hyperlinks in your home page

- The number of files that are *not* reachable via links in your home page

- The total number of hyperlinks in the entire web

- The number of both internal and external links

- The number of links that are broken (no longer point to a valid target)

- The number of pages that are slow to download (where you choose what amount of time is considered "slow")

NOTE NOTE NOTE NOTE NOTE NOTE NOTE NOTE NOTE NOTE NOTE NOTE NOTE NOTE NOTE

Several reports have parameters that you can adjust, such as the number of seconds it takes to download a "slow" page, and the number of days for a file to be considered "old." You can adjust each of these in the Reporting toolbar when you're displaying the relevant report. You can adjust any or all of them in the Reports View tab of the dialog box for the Tools ➤ Options command.

Some items in the Site Summary report are simply the totals from other, more detailed reports. Such is the case for the Slow Pages item. If you choose that report from the Reporting toolbar, or just double-click that item in the Site Summary report, you'll get a list of all the pages in the web that will take longer to download than the time you specify. You can set that time in the Reporting toolbar, as shown below. You can also specify the download rate that will be used in the speed equation; you'll find this setting in the Reports View tab of the Tools ➤ Options dialog box.

Another handy tool is the All Files report. Like the Folders view, it lists files in your web. In this case, however, it lists *all* files, no matter in what folder they reside. This is a good way to check for duplicate files or simply to find a file—just sort the list by whatever column will help you locate the file.

You can display just one report at a time, but while a report is displayed you can:

- Click a column title to sort by that column; click it again to sort in the opposite order (ascending or descending).

- Change a column's width by dragging its right-hand edge.

- Print the report.

- Open a more detailed report by double-clicking a summary item.

- Open a file that is listed in a report by double-clicking it; inspect its properties by right-clicking it and choosing Properties from the shortcut menu.

- Select another report from the pull-down list in the Reporting toolbar, or from the View ➢ Reports menu.

Specifying Web File Editors

By default, a page is opened in the Page view in FrontPage, but you can choose to use a different editor if you prefer. You can also specify the editor or viewer you want to use to open file types other than HTML pages.

A file type is defined by its file extension, so FrontPage opens files in whatever program is associated with the file's extension. By default, several FrontPage file types are already associated with editors. For example, files with either .htm or .html extensions are assigned to FrontPage; files with no extension are assigned to Notepad, the Windows text editor; and image files with .gif and .jpg extensions are assigned to Microsoft Image Composer, the graphics-editing program that comes with the stand-alone version of FrontPage (if you installed it along with FrontPage).

You can add or change file and editor associations at any time in FrontPage. For example, you can specify that files with the .wav extension should be opened by your favorite sound editor, or that files with no extension should be opened in a text editor other than Notepad.

NOTE NOTE NOTE NOTE NOTE NOTE NOTE NOTE NOTE NOTE NOTE NOTE NOTE NOTE

If a file type is not associated with an editor in FrontPage, you may still be able to open that file if there is an application associated with the file's extension in Windows.

Let's create an association for sound files with a WAV extension. In a typical Windows installation, this file type is already associated with the Sound Recorder (filename sndrec32.exe), so we shouldn't have any problems creating the same association in this exercise in FrontPage:

1. Choose Tools ➢ Options.

2. In the Options dialog box, select the Configure Editors tab. This displays the current list of file and editor associations, which is shown in Figure 5.10.

SKILL
5

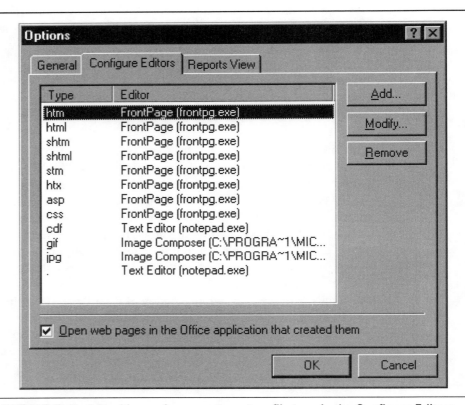

FIGURE 5.10: You assign a program to a file type in the Configure Editors tab of the Options dialog box.

3. Click the Add button, which displays the Add Editor Association dialog box.

4. In the File Type field, enter the file name extension **WAV**.

5. In the Editor Name field, enter a descriptive name like **Windows Sound Recorder**.

6. In the Command field, enter the path and program name, such as `c:\windows\sndrec32.exe` or click the Browse button and select the program in the Browse dialog box.

7. Click OK when you are finished to close the Add Editor Association dialog box. Click OK again to close the Options dialog box.

Now when you double-click a file with the .wav extension in FrontPage, the file is opened in the Windows Sound Recorder.

If you have Office 2000 installed on your system, you can choose to open any Office Web page documents in the application that created them. Select the option of that name in the Configure Editors page of the Options dialog box (see Figure 5.10).

You can remove a file association from the Configure Editors list by selecting it and clicking the Remove button. To change an association, select it in the list and click Modify. Because the width of the Options dialog box does not always allow for a display of the complete command for an associated application, you can also click the Modify button to see the entire command. Click Cancel if you don't want to make any changes.

To open a file that is not associated with an application, right-click the file and select Open With from the shortcut menu. This displays the Open With Editor dialog box, which lists all the current associated programs in FrontPage. Just pick the program you want to use to open this file and click OK.

The Open With Editor dialog box only includes the editors that have been configured in FrontPage. If, for example, you want to open an embedded video clip, there may not be an appropriate editor already configured in FrontPage. In that case, you need to follow the steps listed above to find and configure an editor before you can open the file from within FrontPage.

Keeping Track with the Tasks View

The number of files and links in a web can grow astoundingly large, so getting the site ready may require many tasks, both large and small. The fact that multiple authors can work on the same web means that you need a method to track who is responsible for completing specific tasks related to each page, link, or file.

A good web grows and changes, and someone needs to manage the tasks related to keeping the information up to date and meaningful for users. In print media, publishing something—a book, magazine, or newspaper—means that you are absolutely and completely done with it, at least until the next edition. But

SKILL
5

when you publish electronically on the Web, there's just no such thing as a final draft. What you finish and publish on Friday afternoon may be fodder for your Monday morning projects.

The FrontPage Tasks view will help you keep track of the myriad and ever-changing jobs associated with building and maintaining a web.

Opening the Tasks View

The FrontPage Tasks view, shown in Figure 5.11, is just what its name implies—a convenient way for you to keep a list of things that need to be done in the current web. You can add tasks to the list, remove tasks, sort the list, and mark tasks as completed. Because you can assign tasks to various individuals, departments, or teams working on a web, tasks should be self-contained units that you or someone else can make progress on in a single work session. For example, "Check links on home page" or "Create drop-down list of states" are better task descriptions than "Finish home page" or "Make drop-downs for all pages."

To open the Tasks view, click the Tasks icon in the Views bar or choose View ➤ Tasks from the menu.

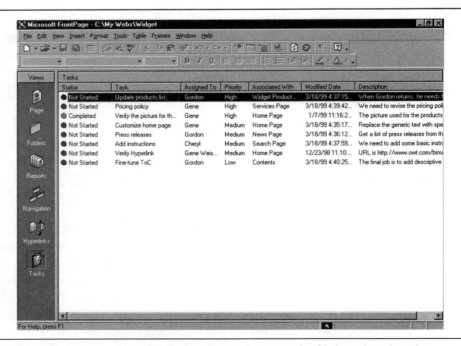

FIGURE 5.11: Use the Tasks view to keep track of jobs related to the current web.

Viewing Tasks

There are seven fields that define a task in the Tasks view, four of which you can modify when you create or revise a task. Each field is a column in the Tasks view:

Status   Shows whether a task is Not Started or Completed

Task   Your name for the task

Assigned To   The person or team responsible for completing the task

Priority   The importance of the task: Low, Medium, or High

Associated With   The page, image, or file to which this task applies

Modified Date   The date on which the task was modified or completed

Description   Your comments about the task

TIP TIP TIP TIP TIP TIP TIP TIP TIP TIP TIP TIP TIP TIP TIP TIP TIP TIP TIP TIP TIP TIP TIP

You can sort the items in the Tasks view by clicking a column-title button at the top of a column. For example, click the Associated With button to sort the list by the web resources to which the tasks are linked. Or click the Priority button to put all of the highest priority tasks at the top of the list.

SKILL
5

To see all the tasks related to a web, including those that have been completed, right-click a blank area of the Tasks view and choose Task History from the shortcut menu. Scanning the history of your site provides a good dose of reality about halfway through development, when you have a lot of unfinished items in the Tasks view.

Working with Tasks

Right-click any task in the list to choose from among the following options on the shortcut menu:

Edit Task   Opens the Task Details dialog box, shown in Figure 5.12, where you can view or modify any of the task's items, such as its name or priority.

Start Task   Opens the page, image, or other file that is linked to this task in the associated editor so you can go to work.

Mark as Completed   Marks the task as completed and changes the Modified Date to today's date.

Delete   Deletes the task from the list.

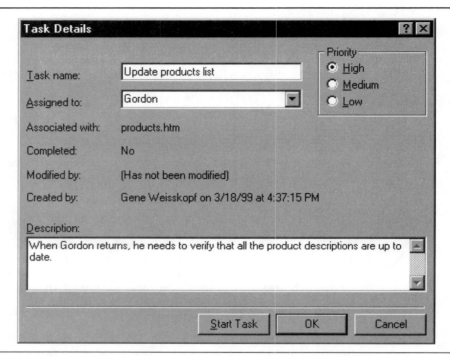

FIGURE 5.12: You can view or modify the elements of a task in the Task Details dialog box.

Adding a Task

If you want to add a task that is specific to a page, image, or other file, right-click the file in one of the views and choose Add Task from the shortcut menu. This opens the New Task dialog box, which is essentially the same as the Task Details dialog box shown in Figure 5.12. The new task is automatically linked to the selected page or file. If you are working on a page in the Page view, choose Edit ➢ Task ➢ Add Task to create a new task related to the active page.

In the New Task dialog box, you can enter a name and priority for a task, revise the person responsible for the task (the default is the task's creator), and enter descriptive comments to help those responsible understand the task. Other task information, such as the date the task was created and the page, image, or file to which it is linked, is not editable.

NOTE NOTE NOTE NOTE NOTE NOTE NOTE NOTE NOTE NOTE NOTE NOTE NOTE NOTE NOTE

Be sure you enter names in the Assigned To field consistently. There's a drop-down list in the dialog box exactly for that purpose, which lists any names that have already been assigned to tasks. Otherwise, sorting the Tasks view by the Assigned To field won't be very useful.

When you are finished, click the OK button and the new task is added to the Tasks view.

Completing and Removing Tasks

When you finish the job that is described in a task, right-click the task in the Tasks view and choose Mark as Completed. The red ball icon to the left of the task changes to green, the Status field indicates Completed, and the Modified Date field changes to the current date. If the Task History is turned off, the task no longer appears on the list after it is refreshed.

NOTE NOTE NOTE NOTE NOTE NOTE NOTE NOTE NOTE NOTE NOTE NOTE NOTE NOTE NOTE

When you mark a task as being completed, FrontPage doesn't check to see that you actually did the work described by the task. You're on the honor system!

SKILL 5

Are You Experienced?

Now you can...

- ☑ **Add pages to your web with the Explorer's Navigation view**
- ☑ **Rearrange pages in Navigation view**
- ☑ **Work with links in Hyperlinks view**
- ☑ **Copy, move, and delete files in the Folders view**
- ☑ **Work with file properties**
- ☑ **Use reports to understand your web**
- ☑ **Associate files with editors or viewers**
- ☑ **Organize jobs with the Tasks view**

Linking Your Pages to the Web

- → **Learning about hyperlinks**
- → **Creating a hyperlink**
- → **Changing or deleting a hyperlink**
- → **Creating bookmarks**
- → **Linking to a bookmark**
- → **Modifying navigation bars**
- → **Keeping links up to date**

This Skill describes what is perhaps the distinguishing characteristic of Web sites—hyperlinks. You'll learn about the different kinds of hyperlinks you can place in a page, how to create bookmarks and hyperlinks, how to modify navigation bars, and how to let FrontPage keep your links up to date.

Understanding Links

The feature that puts the "Web" into "World Wide Web" is the *hyperlink* (or *link*), first discussed in Skill 1. A hyperlink is a connection from one file to another. In the case of a Web site, for example, the link could be from a page on the World Wide Web to another page, image, e-mail address, or file at another location on the Web. A hyperlink can connect internally to a location within the current web or externally to a location halfway around the world through the World Wide Web or other network connection.

There are several types of hyperlinks you can include in a page, and many different ways to create them, but every hyperlink consists of two primary parts:

Hyperlink   The text or image in a page that you define as a hyperlink; clicking the hyperlink in a browser opens the link's target.

Target   The page or file that opens when a user clicks a hyperlink; a target is usually defined by its URL.

NOTE NOTE NOTE NOTE NOTE NOTE NOTE NOTE NOTE NOTE NOTE NOTE NOTE NOTE NOTE

The hyperlinks you create in your Office documents consist of these same two components. If you include linked documents in a FrontPage web, their hyperlinks appear just like the hyperlinks in HTML pages.

Text or Image Hyperlinks

A *text hyperlink* is probably the most common type of hyperlink, and can be from one word to several lines long. However, the fact that link text *can* be several lines long doesn't mean it usually is, or should be. The hyperlink text should be just enough to let users know what they'll find when they click the link, not a five hundred word description of every item they'll find when they arrive.

You can see two examples of hyperlinks displayed in Internet Explorer in Figure 6.1. The first hyperlink is a text hyperlink. Like most popular browsers,

Internet Explorer employs several different ways to indicate that text is a hyperlink. For instance, the link text is underlined and displayed in a different color, making it stand out on the page.

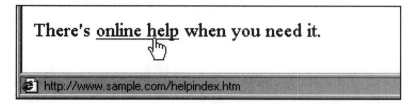

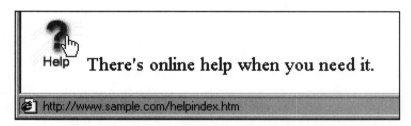

FIGURE 6.1: Many browsers display the URL of a text or graphic hyperlink in the status bar when you point to the link.

As you can see in Figure 6.1, when you move your mouse pointer over a link, the pointer changes to a hand and the name of the link's target appears on the status bar in the lower-left corner of the screen. (This also happens in FrontPage, so you can see what it looks like.) This cue not only tells you this text is a hyperlink, but it also lets you know what URL you access by clicking the link.

Hyperlinks aren't limited to text; any image or part of an image (called a "hotspot") in a page can be used as a hyperlink, so clicking the image or hotspot activates a link. An image not only livens up a page but, when used well, can be very descriptive. The bottom of Figure 6.1 shows an *image hyperlink*. In this case, the text next to the image merely describes the link. As with a text link, when you point to an image hyperlink in Internet Explorer, the pointer changes to a hand and the status bar displays the hyperlink's target. In this example, the target URL is the same for both the text link on the top and the image link on the bottom. You'll read more about images and their use as hyperlinks in Skill 8, *Displaying Images in Your Pages*.

Target Files and Bookmarks

You specify the target file of a hyperlink with its URL or filename, such as:

```
http://default/myweb/helpindex.htm
```

The file you list as the target is the file that a browser opens when a user activates the link by clicking it.

The target can be any type of file. For example, the browser might open a web page, a graphic image, a sound file, or a video file. The target can also be a program file that the target server runs, such as a CGI (Common Gateway Interface) script that might, for example, calculate the total number of accesses to the current Web site and then return the result to the browser. The target file doesn't have to be on the World Wide Web. For example, the target file might be located on the browser's local hard disk, a network drive, or on a local server.

When you specify a page as the target of a hyperlink, you can also include the name of a *bookmark*, or named location, within that page. The browser displays that location at the top of the reader's screen when the page is opened. (This allows you to create a link to a specific entry in the middle of a list, rather than forcing the user to scroll down the list after they arrive on the page.)

The HTML anchor tag, <A>, defines a link. It includes the source of the link (the text or image hyperlink) and the target file. Here is the code for the top text link shown in Figure 6.1:

```
There's <A HREF="helpindex.htm">online help</A> when you need it.
```

Now look at the code for the image link shown on the bottom of Figure 6.1:

```
<A HREF="helpindex.htm"><IMG SRC="images/help.gif" border="0"
width="46" height="51"></A> There's online help when you need it.
```

In each case, the target of the hyperlink is specified as an attribute of the <A> tag. However, you don't have to enter the HTML code; FrontPage creates it for you.

Absolute and Relative URLs

When you create a hyperlink (or otherwise refer to another file in a web page), you can define the target (reference) in one of two ways: as an absolute reference or a relative reference. An *absolute reference* uses the complete URL to specify the exact location of the file. Here are four examples of absolute URLs:

```
http://www.widget.com/
http://www.widget.com/hist-toc.htm
```

```
http://www.widget.com/images/logo.gif
file:///c:/mywebs/homepage.htm
```

As always, if a URL does not include a specific filename ending in `.htm` or `.html`, (see the first example), the server at that location sends the default file, such as `Index.htm`, or may simply send a list of all the files in the specified folder.

A *relative reference* specifies the location of a file in relation to the location of the page that contains the hyperlink. For example, if a link in the `hist-toc.htm` page (see the second example) refers simply to:

```
history1-1.htm
```

the implication is that `history1-1.htm` is stored in the same folder as the source of the reference, `hist-toc.htm`. If `hist-toc.htm` also includes a relative reference to the file:

```
images/logo.gif
```

this means the Images folder is a subfolder of the folder that `hist-toc.htm` is stored in.

In general, you should use a relative reference when the target of a hyperlink is stored in the active FrontPage web (an internal reference). In many cases, you use an absolute reference only when the target is stored outside of the web (an external reference). If you use relative references, you're free to move the entire web without penalty. For example, if you rename the Widget Web site *Technical Tools*, you would have to spend hours revising absolute references to files on the former Widget site, like:

```
http://www.techtools.com/images/logo.gif
```

But you could ignore relative addresses to files, such as:

```
images/logo.gif
```

The relative URL still points to the Images folder within the source page's folder, which now happens to be TechTools instead of Widget. It's not unusual for designers to move a Web site to a new and improved server or different service provider. You can save yourself needless effort later by avoiding absolute references when relative references suffice.

Because a relative URL is based on the source page's URL, you can't create a relative hyperlink in a page until it has been saved. For example, if you're working on a new page, hyperlinks you create have absolute references. Once you save the page, however, FrontPage updates the links and makes all the internal links relative.

SKILL
6

Creating a Hyperlink

As you have learned, you can create a hyperlink in the FrontPage Page view from either text or an image, and the target can be a file either within the active Front-Page web or outside of it. There are several ways to create a link, but here's the most common method:

1. In Page view, select the text or image you want to serve as a hyperlink.

2. Choose Insert ➤ Hyperlink (Ctrl+K) from the menu, or choose the Hyper-link command from the shortcut menu when you right-click the selected text or image. Alternatively, simply click the Hyperlink button on the tool-bar to open the Create Hyperlink dialog box, shown in Figure 6.2. In this dialog box, you'll specify the link's target.

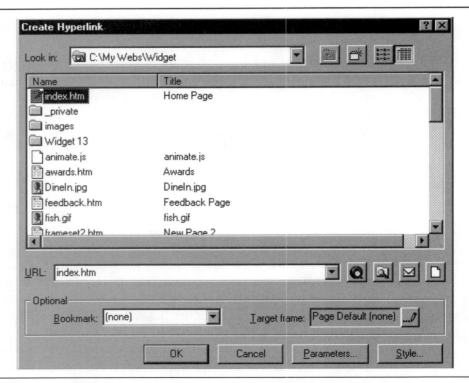

FIGURE 6.2: In the Create Hyperlink dialog box, you specify the target of the hyperlink.

3. Select a target from the current web, World Wide Web, or drives connected to your computer.

    Current FrontPage Web   Use the Look In drop-down list to select files in the active FrontPage web; FrontPage creates an internal link with a relative URL.

     World Wide Web   Type in a URL or click the Web Browser button to locate a web page on the World Wide Web. The external link uses an absolute URL.

     On Your Computer   Click the Windows Explorer button to browse and locate a file on your computer or local area network as the target of the hyperlink.

     E-mail   Click the Make a Hyperlink that Sends E-mail button and type an e-mail address in the dialog box that opens. When visitors click this hyperlink, they are presented with an e-mail form from their own e-mail program to send e-mail to the address you enter.

     New Page   Click the Create a Page and Link to the New Page button to create a new page. When you save the new page, it serves as the target for the link.

4. When you are finished defining the hyperlink, click the OK button.

When you create a text hyperlink, the selected text is underlined and displayed, by default, in blue. When you move your mouse over the text or image hyperlink, the link's target is displayed in the status bar. You can edit the hyperlink text just as you would any other text in the page.

Linking to a Page in the Current FrontPage Web

 You can link to any file in the web that's currently open in FrontPage by selecting the file in the Create Hyperlink dialog box (shown in Figure 6.2). If the file you want to use is in a folder, double-click to open the folder. Click the Up One Level button to return to the current web folder.

SKILL
6

Linking to a Bookmark

Just as in Microsoft Word, a FrontPage bookmark is a specific, named location within a page that can serve as the target for a link. You'll learn about creating bookmarks and links to bookmarks a little later in this Skill.

Specifying a Target Frame

A *frame set* is a single page that displays other pages within *frames*, or windows, in that page. It allows your browser to display multiple pages, instead of having to close a page to open another one. If the current page (the one containing the hyperlink you are defining) is part of a frame set, you can specify which frame the target file opens into when the hyperlink is clicked. For example, even though the hyperlink is in a frame on the left side of the page, you might want the target displayed in a frame to the right. You'll find out how to do this and more with frames in Skill 13, *Getting Fancier with Frames*.

Linking to a Page on the Web

To create a link to a page on the World Wide Web, enter a URL in the URL text box or click the Use Your Web Browser to Select a Page or File button in the Create Hyperlink dialog box. This opens your default Web browser, along with a message telling you to locate the URL you want. After going to the correct URL, switch back to FrontPage. The URL from the browser appears in the URL field in the Create Hyperlink dialog box.

Linking to a File on Your Computer

To create a hyperlink to a file on your computer (or your local area network) that is not part of the current web, click the Make a Hyperlink to a File on Your Computer button. This opens a standard Select File dialog box, in which you can select the file you want. Click OK to close the dialog box and create the link.

Linking to E-mail

A standard Web feature is a "return address"—a link that allows visitors to send e-mail requesting information or giving feedback. Clicking the Make a Hyperlink that Sends an E-mail button opens a dialog box where you can enter an e-mail address. Click OK to enter the e-mail address in the URL text box. Notice that

FrontPage inserts a "mailto" tag in front of the address, so that the resulting HTML looks something like this:

```
Send mail to <a
    href="mailto:webmaster@widget.com">webmaster@widget.com</a> with
    questions or comments about this Web site.
```

When visitors click an e-mail link, an e-mail form opens from their e-mail program, already addressed to the target address from the link. They can add a subject, type their message, and send it through the Internet e-mail system in the usual way.

Linking to a New Page

You can create a link to a page *and* the new page at the same time if you choose the Create a Page and Link to the New Page button in the Create Hyperlink dialog box. This is a convenient way to create a web—you can work in one page and create all its links and targets at the same time.

Clicking the Create a Page and Link to the New Page button opens the New dialog box as though you had chosen the File ➤ New ➤ Page command. Select the type of page you want to create and click OK. FrontPage creates a new page and opens the page for editing. If you're not ready to work on the page yet, choose Window from the main menu bar and switch back to the page you want to work on from the list of open pages.

If you don't even want to think about creating content for the new page now, you can click the Just Add Web Task check box before clicking OK. This creates the new page and immediately opens the Save As dialog box. Enter a name for the new page and click OK. FrontPage creates the page, saves it, adds a task for the page to the Tasks view, and closes the new page. The hyperlink to that page, however, is already in place.

Creating Links by Dragging and Copying

After you've created a few links and understand how they work, you might want to check out some other ways to create links:

- Drag a file from the FrontPage Folder List into an open page in the Page view to create a link to that file. If the file is a web page, its title appears as the link text in the page as though you had typed the title at the line where you released the mouse button. If a page is titleless, the file's name appears as the link text. (Remember that you can edit the text.)

SKILL
6

- For absolute references, simply type the URL of the target file (it must begin with a protocol, such as HTTP). When you press the space bar or press Enter after typing the URL, FrontPage automatically defines that text as a link to the URL you specified. If you want to link to an open page in a browser, copy the URL of the page from the browser's address field, paste it into your page in Page view, and press the spacebar to signal the end of the link text.

- Drag a hyperlink from a page in your browser into a page in FrontPage to create an identical link. Both your browser and FrontPage must be visible on the screen at the same time, of course, and don't just click the link or you know what will happen! You can instead right-click the link and choose Copy Shortcut, and then in FrontPage choose Edit ➤ Paste.

Revising, Deleting, and Following Hyperlinks

With FrontPage, you can change either component of a link—the text or image that a user clicks to invoke the hyperlink (the source) or the hyperlink's target. You can also disconnect the hyperlink while leaving the text or image you click to get there intact. At the click of a button (actually, several clicks), you can navigate through the hyperlink's target pages while in FrontPage.

Revising a Hyperlink

To change the text of a hyperlink, simply edit it as you would any other text. As long as the text you revise is still underlined, you'll know it's still a link. You can also change the image for an image hyperlink. Just right-click the image and choose Picture Properties from the shortcut menu. In the General tab of the Picture Properties dialog box, specify the new image in the Picture Source field, shown here:

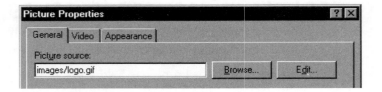

Alternatively, click the Browse button to select an image from your FrontPage web or another location. The new image in the page then serves as the image hyperlink.

To modify the hyperlink definition, select the image (click it) or position the insertion point anywhere within the link text (you need not select any of the text), and use any of the methods for creating a hyperlink; for example, choose Insert ➤ Hyperlink (Ctrl+K) or click the Hyperlink button on the toolbar. You can also right-click the link and choose Hyperlink Properties from the shortcut menu. This action displays the Edit Hyperlink dialog box, which is essentially the same as the Create Hyperlink dialog box shown earlier in this Skill. You'll see the current link definition in the URL field. You can specify a different target file, page, bookmark, e-mail address, or target frame for the link, and click OK when you're finished.

Deleting a Hyperlink

When you delete a hyperlink from a page, you are not affecting the link's target; you're only removing the reference to it. There are several ways to delete a link:

- Delete the image or all of the text for the link, and the link to the target file is deleted as well. Keep this in mind when you're editing hyperlink text, and be careful not to accidentally delete all the text. (If you do, remember Undo.)

- To delete a hyperlink but leave the link source on the page, select the link image or position the insertion point anywhere within the link text. Then choose Insert ➤ Hyperlink or click the Hyperlink button on the toolbar. In the Edit Hyperlink dialog box, delete the contents of the URL field (the name of the target), and then click OK to close the dialog box.

- If you're creating a new link in the Create Hyperlink dialog box, just click Cancel and the hyperlink will not be created.

Following Hyperlinks in FrontPage

FrontPage lets you navigate through the links in a page in much the same way you do in a browser. If a hyperlink in the current page in Page view has a web page as its target, you can open that page by holding down the Ctrl key (the pointer changes to a pointing hand) and clicking the link, or right-clicking and choosing Follow Hyperlink from the shortcut menu.

SKILL 6

When you follow a link to another page, especially a page on another server, there's always a chance the server at that site is running very slowly—or not at all. To cancel an open operation, press Esc or click the Stop button, just as you do in your browser.

Working with Bookmarks

Earlier in this Skill, you read about including a bookmark as the target for a hyperlink so when the target page is opened in a browser, the browser displays the bookmark location within the page. A bookmark lets you take a visitor to a specific section of text, rather than requiring them to locate it by scrolling through the page.

Defining a Bookmark

Creating a bookmark names a location so you can refer to it by name. Bookmarks are also referred to as *destinations* or *named targets* in HTML jargon. You can use bookmarks to link to a location on the same page as the hyperlink or to a specified location in another page.

Here's how to create a bookmark:

1. While editing a web page in Page view, move the insertion point to the line where you want to create the bookmark.

2. Although you can create a bookmark without selecting any text, it's usually a good idea to select some text that the bookmark is related to. That way, if you add more text to the paragraph, the bookmark is still attached to the text you selected.

3. Choose Insert ➢ Bookmark, which displays the Bookmark dialog box (shown next).

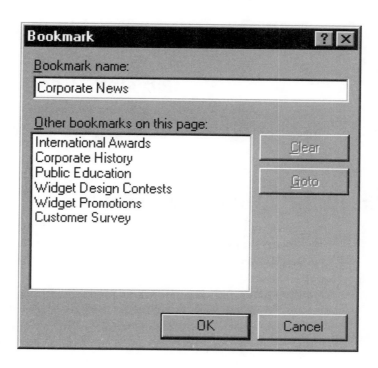

4. If you selected text before opening the dialog box, FrontPage automatically places it in the Bookmark Name field as a suggested name for the bookmark. Revise it if you wish, then click OK to create the bookmark.

 NOTE NOTE NOTE NOTE NOTE NOTE NOTE NOTE NOTE NOTE NOTE NOTE NOTE NOTE NOTE

Within a FrontPage web, each bookmark must have a unique name—using *Bookmark 1, Bookmark 2*, etc. is not a good idea. Bookmark names should clearly but briefly describe the bookmark's location so you or another author can easily select it from the list of bookmarks when you're creating a hyperlink.

The HTML tag for a bookmark is an attribute of the anchor tag <A>. If you select the text "Widgets at Home Pamphlet" and then create the bookmark name "Widgets at Home," here's how the code looks:

```
<A NAME="Widgets at Home">Widgets at Home Pamphlet</A>
```

In FrontPage, the text within the opening and closing anchor tags is underlined with a dashed line so you can tell it's a bookmark:

<u>Corporate History</u>

A browser, however, does not apply any special formatting to bookmarks; it simply uses them as reference points when they are included as the targets for hyperlinks.

Creating Hyperlinks to Bookmarks

Once you define bookmarks in your web pages, you can create hyperlinks that take users right to the spot on the page you want them to see. You can use bookmarks to link to a location on the same page as the hyperlink, or to a specified location on another page.

When you are defining a hyperlink, if the target page you select is part of the active web in FrontPage, select the page where the bookmark is defined and select the desired bookmark from the Bookmark drop-down list in the Create Hyperlink dialog box. To create a link to a bookmark in the current page (the page in which you're creating the link), just open the Create Hyperlink dialog box and choose a bookmark from the drop-down list.

In Figure 6.3, the International Awards bookmark in the awards.htm page is selected. In HTML, a reference to a bookmark name is preceded by a pound sign (#), so the complete reference for this link is:

```
awards.htm#InternationalAwards
```

If the hyperlink in Figure 6.3 was also in the awards.htm page, the HTML code would only include the pound sign and bookmark name:

```
#International Awards
```

When a user clicks this link in a browser, the page awards.htm opens, and the browser displays the International Awards bookmark location at the top of the screen—even if International Awards is in the middle of the page.

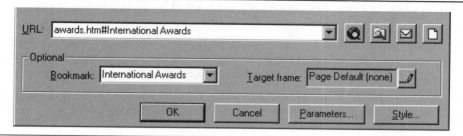

FIGURE 6.3: FrontPage automatically inserts a pound sign (#) in front of the URL to designate a hyperlink to a bookmark.

Revising, Deleting, and Going to Bookmarks

When you're editing a web page in FrontPage, you can jump to any bookmark in the page by selecting it in the Bookmark dialog box (Insert ➤ Bookmark) and clicking the Goto button. The dialog box remains open, and because the insertion point is now on a bookmark, the Clear button is enabled. Click this button to remove the bookmark from the page. Only the bookmark name is removed; text in the page isn't affected.

To revise the name of a bookmark, click anywhere within the text defined as the bookmark and choose Insert ➤ Bookmark, or right-click the text and choose Bookmark Properties from the shortcut menu. In the Bookmark dialog box, you see the name of that bookmark in the Bookmark Name field. Edit the name as needed and click OK.

FrontPage does not automatically update bookmark references in your web as it does with filenames. So, when you revise a bookmark name or delete a bookmark, FrontPage doesn't change the bookmark name or delete the reference to the bookmark in hyperlinks. You have to find and revise each link that references the bookmark. Therefore, it's best to rename bookmarks *before* you've used them as hyperlink targets—or not at all.

SKILL 6

Using and Modifying Navigation Bars

In Skill 5, you learned that you can add navigation bars to pages in FrontPage's Navigation view. To review, navigation bars are sets of hyperlink buttons located in the shared borders of each page. The links connect to pages within the current web, following the parent/child relationships laid out in Navigation view. In this section you'll learn how to take advantage of these built-in links to give visitors to your site a handy means of finding their way around your Web site.

Creating Navigation Bars

As an example, create a simple one-page web, add three other pages in Navigation view, and then we'll add some navigation buttons.

1. Choose File ≻ New ≻ Web, choose the One Page Web option, specify a location for the new web, and click OK.

2. Click the Navigation icon in the Views bar to display the Navigation view.

3. Right-click the home page and choose New Page from the shortcut menu, which will create a new page below the home page. Repeat this two more times.

4. For convenience, name the three new pages **Alan**, **Bill**, and **Charlie**. Figure 6.4 shows the resulting layout in Navigation view. All three new pages are children of the home page.

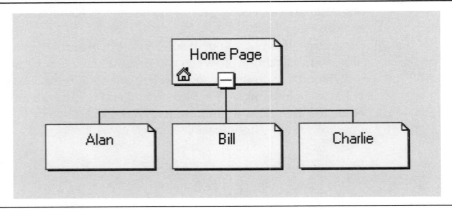

FIGURE 6.4: Three new pages created in Navigation view as children of the home page

5. To add navigation buttons to all pages in this web, first choose Format ≻ Shared Borders, which displays the dialog box of that name (shown in Figure 6.5).

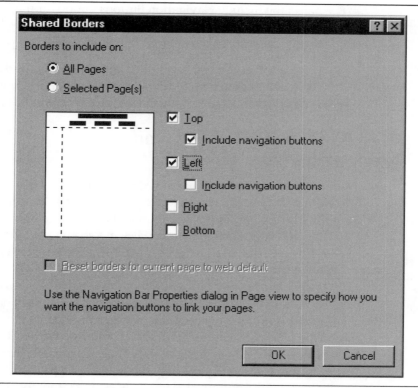

FIGURE 6.5: You create shared borders and navigation bars for your Front-Page web in the Shared Borders dialog box.

In the Shared Borders dialog box, you can choose:

- The pages in which you want shared borders to appear (all or selected pages)
- Where you want the borders to appear in each page (top, left, right, and bottom)
- Where the navigation buttons should be created (either the top or left borders—you can't put them in the bottom or right borders)

6. For this example, select the All Pages option to add borders to all pages in the web.

7. Select the Top and Left options to create borders on those sides of each page.

8. Select the Include Navigation Buttons option for the Top border only. As you make your choices, the sample page in the dialog box will show you the results, as you can see in Figure 6.5. Click OK when you're finished.

FrontPage will take a few seconds to add the borders and buttons to the pages in the web, although when it's finished the Navigation view won't look any different. When you open one of the pages, however, you'll see what's been added.

Web Pages with Borders and Navigation Bars

Figure 6.6 shows the page named Alan as it looks in Page view in our sample FrontPage web. It has a border at the top and left side, as indicated by the dotted lines. In the top border is a page banner based on the page's title, and the navigation bar with its buttons. When you click in a shared border, the dotted line becomes solid. When you click a navigation bar, the entire bar is selected.

As you can see, the four navigation buttons in Alan will allow a visitor to your site to open the home page or either of the other two pages that are children of the home page—Bill and Charlie. Because this is the page named Alan, there's just a label serving as a placeholder for that button.

All the pages have hyperlink buttons in the top border. The label on each button indicates the name of that button's target page. The target names are derived from each one's HTML page title. If you change a page's title, FrontPage automatically updates the button label in all pages that target that page.

WARNING WARNING WARNING WARNING WARNING WARNING WARNING WARNING

These borders are truly shared—any changes you make in Page view to one of the borders will be replicated in that border in all the other pages. And the changes will take place whether or not you save your page in Page view. For example, if you add text or an image to the left-hand border in one of the pages, the new material will also appear in that border in all other pages. If you delete the buttons from a page, all the other pages will lose their buttons as well.

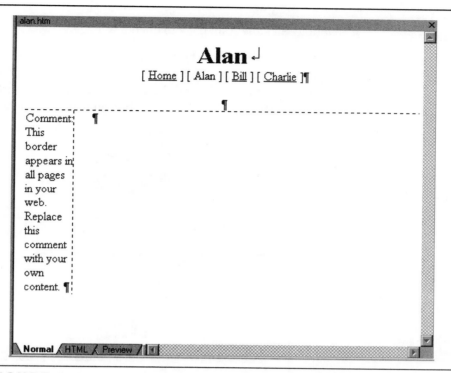

FIGURE 6.6: A page from the sample web with its shared borders at the top and left side, and navigation buttons in the top border that will take users to the other pages in the parent/child structure of this web

Revising Your Web's Structure

So far we've created a small web in which each page contains two shared borders and a navigation bar in the top border. The navigation buttons allow a visitor to access the other pages, but the links are not "hard-wired," meaning that FrontPage will update them if you change the parent/child relationships among the pages in the Navigation view. Look back at the Navigation view shown in Figure 6.4 and then at the button bar built from that layout in Figure 6.6. Let's see what happens to the buttons when you change the structure of the web in Navigation view.

1. Right-click the home page in Navigation view and choose New Page from the shortcut menu. This will create a fourth page under the home page, on the same level as the other three.

2. Name this page **David**.

3. Double-click the Alan page to open it in Page view.

Before you can even think about what needs to be done to update the buttons, FrontPage has already taken care of them. The upper part of Figure 6.7 shows the Navigation view of this web, and the lower part shows the buttons in the navigation bar in the Alan page. There's a new button that links to the new David page.

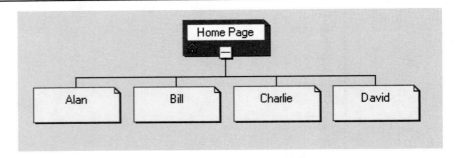

FIGURE 6.7: When you add a new page in Navigation view, FrontPage automatically updates the buttons in the navigation bars in each page.

Now rearrange the pages in the Navigation view by dragging Bill beneath Alan and David beneath Charlie, so that Bill and David are now child pages of Alan and Charlie, respectively. Figure 6.8 shows the new arrangement in the Navigation pane and the button bars in Alan and Bill. FrontPage once again revised the buttons automatically, although this time the layout of the results might not be so obvious. The reason the buttons were arranged that way will become clear in the next section.

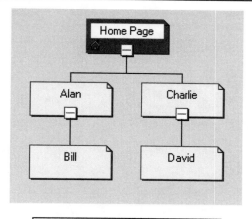

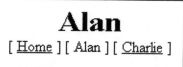

FIGURE 6.8: When you revise the parent/child relationships in Navigation view, FrontPage revises any navigation buttons.

Modifying Navigation Bars

When you created the shared bars and navigation bars for this small sample web, FrontPage set the path of the navigation buttons to a default style that served a variety of webs. The second time you rearranged the pages in the web, however (see Figure 6.8), the buttons no longer referenced every page in the web. Let's see how the targets for the buttons are determined and how you can change them.

To access the navigation bar properties, right-click the navigation bar in a page in Page view, then choose Navigation Bar Properties from the shortcut menu. This opens the Navigation Bar Properties dialog box, shown in Figure 6.9. The options shown here are the ones that FrontPage chose by default for the sample web.

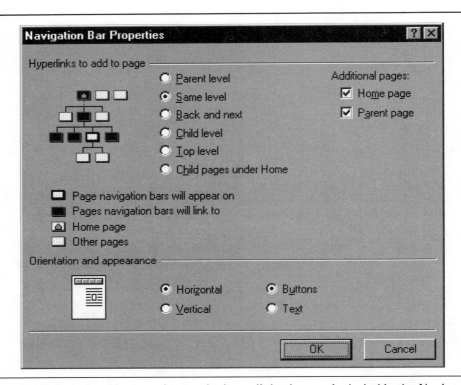

FIGURE 6.9: You can change the hyperlinks that are included in the Navigation Bar Properties dialog box.

In the Navigation Bar Properties dialog box, you can select one of six levels of pages to be the targets of the buttons in the navigation bar:

Parent Level Creates hyperlinks to the other page(s) on the same level as the parent page.

Same Level Creates hyperlinks to the other page(s) on the same level as the open page. This option was in effect for the sample web, where a button targeted each of the other pages on the same level (see Figures 6.6 and 6.7).

Back and Next Creates buttons named *Back* and *Next* that target the adjacent page(s) on the same level as the open page.

Child Level Creates hyperlinks to the page(s) below the level of the open page.

Top Level   Creates hyperlinks to the page(s) on the same level as the home page.

Child Pages under Home   Creates hyperlinks to the child pages of the home page.

In addition, you can add buttons for two other pages, both of which were selected by default in our sample web:

Home Page   Includes a hyperlink to the home page.

Parent Page   Includes a hyperlink to the parent page.
There are two orientations to choose from:

Horizontal   Aligns the navigation bar horizontally.

Vertical   Aligns the navigation bar vertically.

Finally, you can choose the appearance of the hyperlinks in the navigation bar:

Buttons   Displays the navigation bar as graphical buttons when you have chosen a theme for the page or web.

Text   Displays the navigation buttons as text, even if you have picked a theme for the pages.

As you make choices, your changes are reflected in the preview pane in the dialog box. When you are satisfied with your selections, click OK.

NOTE NOTE NOTE NOTE NOTE NOTE NOTE NOTE NOTE NOTE NOTE NOTE NOTE NOTE

You can change the text that appears in the navigation buttons that aren't named after the page they target, such as Back and Next. Choose Tools ➢ Web Settings and select the Navigation tab. There you can specify the text that will appear in the four standard buttons that are by default named Home, Up, Back, and Next.

If you choose hyperlinks for a level that doesn't exist (for example, choosing child pages when there aren't any), the hyperlinks aren't created, as you saw in Figure 6.8 for the page named Bill. It had no other pages on its level beneath Alan, so its two buttons were simply labeled Home and Up.

Modifying Shared Borders

You can change the options for the shared borders for your web by choosing Format ➢ Shared Borders. This displays the Shared Borders dialog box (shown earlier in Figure 6.5), where you can select which borders to display and decide whether to display the the navigation bars.

When you're editing a web page in Page view you can modify the borders either for that single page or the entire web. Choose Format ➤ Shared Borders, or right-click within a shared border and choose that command. You can also edit the contents of a shared border, such as by adding text, images, or formatting effects. Remember that those changes will appear in every page that has that shared border.

NOTE NOTE NOTE NOTE NOTE NOTE NOTE NOTE NOTE NOTE NOTE NOTE NOTE NOTE NOTE

You can return the borders of a single page back to the global style used for the entire web. In the Shared Borders dialog box while editing the page in Page view, select the Reset Borders for Current Page to Web Default option.

Fixing and Verifying Links

One of the most important web-management jobs is maintaining the hyperlinks in your pages. Users will quickly grow frustrated and leave your site if links take them to the wrong location or to no location at all. If you want to keep your site running smoothly, you must ensure each hyperlink references the correct target.

As part of your web's regular maintenance, you should check to see that each hyperlink target's URL is still valid and works correctly. This is especially important for external links because you have no control over the location of their targets. It's easiest if you schedule a time each week to check external links: for example, every Wednesday afternoon.

Because Web sites can have so many links, these jobs can be some of the most time-consuming aspects of managing a site—unless of course, you're using FrontPage.

Fixing Target Names Automatically

In Skill 5, you learned how to rename a file or move it to another folder in a Front-Page web. Renaming or moving a file would normally break hyperlinks that targeted that file, because the links would still target the original name or location. However, when you change a file's name or location in FrontPage, any links to that file in the current web are automatically updated to reference the new name or location. (A reminder: this *doesn't* work if you rename or move a file with Windows Explorer.)

When you rename a file that is the target of one or more links in the current web, FrontPage displays the Rename dialog box, asking you if you want to update all the hyperlinks to this file. Choose Yes and the links are revised to reference the new name, so you don't have to worry about a "dead" link. Choose No, and the file is renamed but the links still reference the old name. You might do this when you are going to create a new file with the old name to serve as the target of those hyperlinks.

When you move a file to another folder in the FrontPage web, just sit back and let FrontPage automatically update links to the file so they refer to the new location.

Verifying Links

FrontPage can also help you verify the hyperlinks in your web and find any that are broken and no longer able to access their targets. You perform this verification in the FrontPage Reports view.

The Site Summary report, which was shown in the previous chapter in Figure 5.9, displays several link-related items, including the number of:

- Links in the web

- Internal links

- External links

- Broken links

- Unverified links

To check the "health" of the hyperlinks, choose the Broken Hyperlinks report from the Reporting toolbar, or just double-click one of the link-related items in the Site Summary report. Figure 6.10 shows this report.

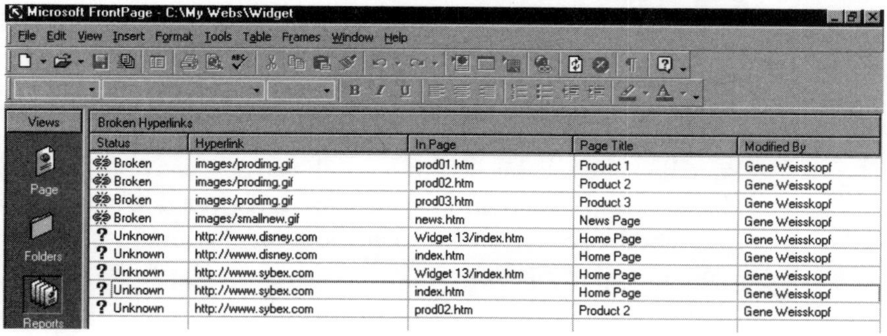

FIGURE 6.10: The Broken Hyperlinks report shows you which links are broken, unverified, or working fine.

The Status column in the Broken Hyperlinks report tells you at a glance which links are broken, a problem that you'll want to fix right away. It's easy to do so—just select a broken link in the report and click the Edit Hyperlink button on the Reporting toolbar, or right-click the item and choose that command from the shortcut menu. This opens the Edit Hyperlink dialog box, shown in Figure 6.11, which allows you to revise the link in all pages that include it, a real timesaver. You can instead choose to edit a single page that contains the link.

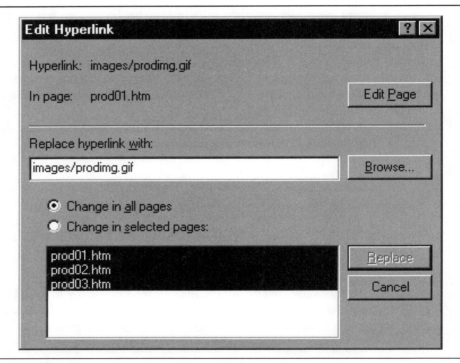

FIGURE 6.11: In the Edit Hyperlink dialog box, you can fix a broken hyperlink in all or selected pages in which it appears.

Having unverified links in your web is only a potential problem, in that FrontPage has not yet checked to see if the target files of these links are actually available at the specified URLs. Until you have verified a link, FrontPage can't tell you whether or not it is broken, so it labels the link status Unknown in the Broken Hyperlinks report.

You can start the process of verifying all hyperlinks in the current web from any view in FrontPage, as long as you have displayed the Reporting toolbar (use the View ➤ Toolbars command). If you want to verify only some links, display the Broken Links report in the Reports view. You can then select the links you want to check from those that are either broken or not yet verified. Click the Verify Hyperlinks button on the Reporting toolbar, which displays the Verify Hyperlinks dialog box, shown here, in which you can choose to verify all links or just those you selected. Click Start to start the process.

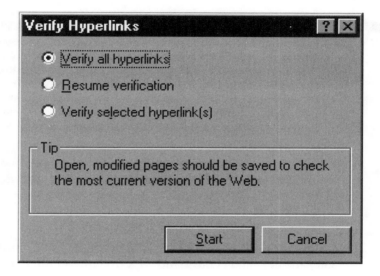

SKILL
6

NOTE NOTE NOTE NOTE NOTE NOTE NOTE NOTE NOTE NOTE NOTE NOTE NOTE NOTE NOTE

Take notice of the advice offered in the Verify Hyperlinks dialog box, which recommends that you first save any pages you've been editing in the Page view. This ensures that the hyperlinks in the most recent versions of all pages are verified.

FrontPage will verify that the targets exist for both the internal and external links in your web. This means that it may have to access the Internet to check the external links, so your usual Internet connection must be available. This process can take several minutes if there are many links in your web, especially external ones.

When the scan is complete, the Broken Hyperlinks report will show you the new status of the links. With any luck, the status of links that had previously been Unknown will now be OK, and those that had been OK won't now be broken!

The primary cause of a broken internal link is that the target file is missing as far as the link is concerned. There are two possibilities: the file isn't there, or the target specified in the link is incorrect. The quickest way to kill an internal link is to move files via Windows Explorer rather than FrontPage, which results in links that still point to the file's old location because FrontPage wasn't "aware" of the move. If the target in the hyperlink is incorrect, chances are an author typed it in rather than browsing to find it. Missing even a single character in a file's name or location results in a broken link.

WARNING WARNING WARNING WARNING WARNING WARNING WARNING WARNING

FrontPage checks only the validity of the URL for external links, not that the URL is actually the one you want! In other words, if you enter the wrong URL into a link, FrontPage might happily report that the link works just fine, even though it points to the wrong resource. That's why it's important to verify the actual result of a link, which is strictly a manual operation for someone familiar with the Web site. It's another reason to have an easy-to-find feedback link in your site, so visitors can report these types of problems.

If there are problems to resolve with broken hyperlinks and your Web site is online and in use, you need to clean up the links immediately. However, if the site is offline and under construction, you can delay the repairs until an appropriate time. Whatever your plans, you can edit the links as described earlier in this section or leave them as is for now. To create a note reminding you that a link needs fixing, select an item in the report and choose Edit ➤ Task ➤ Add Task, or right-click the item and choose Add Task from the shortcut menu. This creates a task associated with this link that reminds you that it needs your attention. The status for the link will change to Added Task.

Are You Experienced?

Now you can...

- ☑ Create internal and external hyperlinks
- ☑ Change or delete a hyperlink
- ☑ Create bookmarks
- ☑ Link to a bookmark
- ☑ Create and modify navigation bars
- ☑ Create and modify shared borders
- ☑ Verify and fix hyperlinks

SKILL
6

Using Tables to Add Structure

- ➔ **Understanding table layout**
- ➔ **Creating a table**
- ➔ **Moving between the cells in a table**
- ➔ **Selecting parts of a table**
- ➔ **Adding a caption**
- ➔ **Changing table properties**
- ➔ **Changing cell properties**
- ➔ **Changing the size of a table**

Tables are powerful and versatile tools in a Web designer's toolkit—and they're not limited to their traditional role of presenting data in rows and columns. Tables permit designers to sidestep the limitations of HTML to precisely place text, data, and images on a web page. Any attractive, graphically appealing site you run across on the Web today is probably constructed with at least a few tables lurking in the background.

The Structure of a Table

Tables provide an effective structure for a web page because they have a versatile structure of their own. In its most rudimentary form, a table is an HTML feature that helps you arrange information within rows and columns. You may have already worked with tables in a word processing program or learned about columns, rows, and cells from your spreadsheet application. Many of those skills are transferable to working with tables in FrontPage. However, you can use tables much more discreetly to provide a behind-the-scenes grid to help you position elements on your pages. Using tables in this way opens up a whole new world of possibilities for first-class web page design.

Depending on the type of information you want to present, you may want your tables to look like a traditional table (see the example in Figure 7.1), with border lines dividing its rows, columns, and cells. Other times, you may want to turn off all the borders and use the hidden border structure to present information more graphically, as shown in Figure 7.2. What you put in a table is pretty much up to you; if you can place it on a page, you can put it in a table cell.

Work Schedule for the Week of January 11, 1999							
	Mon	Tue	Wed	Thu	Fri	Sat	Sun
Celeste	X	X	X			X	X
Gerald	X	X		X	X	X	
Gordon	X			X	X	X	X
Carol			X	X	X	X	X

(As of December 7, 1998)

FIGURE 7.1: A table consists of rows, columns, and cells, as well as optional border, caption, and header cells.

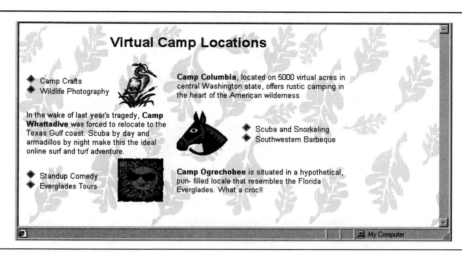

FIGURE 7.2: All the elements in this page are contained within a table.

Figure 7.1 shows a typical table with standard and special features applied to it:

- The table has six rows and eight columns; at the junction of each row and column is a cell.

- The cells in the first row have been merged into a single cell.

NOTE NOTE NOTE NOTE NOTE NOTE NOTE NOTE NOTE NOTE NOTE NOTE NOTE NOTE

By default, a column expands to include the width of its contents, and a table is, therefore, as wide as the longest entries in its cells. You can specify an exact width for a table or for any of its columns. If you don't, the table doesn't expand any wider than the window in which it is displayed; when it reaches that limit, text in cells wrap to new lines as needed.

- An optional border is displayed around the table and all its cells.

- There is a caption centered beneath the table.

- The cells with the names of the people and the days of the week are formatted as header cells, so they stand out in the table.

- The header cells have a background color.

- The days of the week and the contents of the cells beneath them are centered.

Creating a New Table

There are three ways to create a table in FrontPage:

- Dragging with the Insert Table Button
- Using the Table ➤ Insert ➤ Table command
- Drawing with the Draw table pointer

None of these is better than the others, but you'll find that you develop a preference. Even if you already know how to use one of these methods, try all three, because each might be better for creating a specific type of table.

All three methods create tables quickly and relatively painlessly. It is important, however, to think out the design of your page and how the tables impact that design before you start creating them. You should determine approximately how many columns and rows you need and in what cells to place the various page elements. This helps you create cells that enhance your design from the outset and require less tweaking in the end.

> **TIP TIP TIP TIP TIP TIP TIP TIP TIP TIP TIP TIP TIP TIP TIP TIP TIP TIP TIP TIP TIP TIP TIP TIP**
>
> **It's a good idea to save regularly while you are working with tables in case you make a significant change that negatively impacts your design. Of course, don't forget to use the Undo button to revert back to a previous step (you can reverse up to 30 actions in FrontPage).**

The following example gives you some practice creating a simple table. The table you build here will be used in several other exercises in this Skill, so even if you've had some experience with tables it's helpful to follow along.

Using the Insert Table Button

First we'll use the most direct method of creating a table; then we'll look at the other two methods.

1. Position the insertion point where you want the upper-left corner of the table to appear in the page you're editing in Page view.

2. Point to the Insert Table button on the toolbar, then press and hold down the mouse button.

3. A table template appears beneath the button, which you can use to define the dimensions of the table. Drag down and to the right to expand the number of rows and columns in the table. As you do, you'll see the size noted beneath the template.

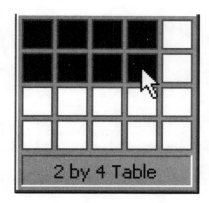

4. The table in Figure 7.1 has six rows and eight columns, so keep dragging until you have that many highlighted in the template. Then release the mouse button to create the new table.

Using the Insert Table Command

The next method for creating a table lets you define the appearance of the table as well as its dimensions.

1. Choose Edit ➢ Undo Insert to remove the table you just created.

2. With the insertion point located where you want the new table, choose Table ➢ Insert ➢ Table to open the Insert Table dialog box (see Figure 7.3).

3. Enter 6 in the Rows field and 8 in the Columns field.

4. By default, the Border Size option is set to 1 (pixel). Even if you plan to remove the border, you might want to leave it on while you're inputting the table's contents. At this point, don't change the width of the table—it spans the page by default.

5. Click OK to create the table.

SKILL 7

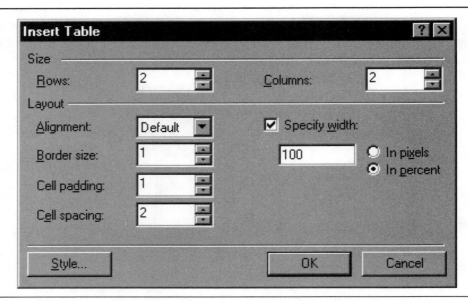

FIGURE 7.3: You can define the size and look of a table in the Insert Table dialog box.

Drawing the Table by Hand

The third method of creating tables in FrontPage involves the Draw Table feature that was first introduced by Microsoft in Word 97. Choose Table ➤ Draw Table to view the Table toolbar shown here.

The first tool, the Draw Table button, is depressed when the toolbar is activated, and the mouse pointer changes shape from an I-beam to a pencil. Use the pencil pointer to drag a rectangle, as seen in Figure 7.4, for the outside border of your table.

FIGURE 7.4: Position the pencil at the top-left corner and hold the mouse button down to drag a rectangle and create a table border.

Once the table's outside border is in place, use the pencil again to draw in column and row borders, as shown here. When you're ready to get your regular mouse pointer back, click the Draw Table button to turn the pencil tool off.

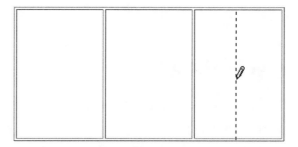

TIP TIP TIP TIP TIP TIP TIP TIP TIP TIP TIP TIP TIP TIP TIP TIP TIP TIP TIP TIP TIP TIP TIP TIP TIP

If you draw a border and it disappears, you may not be drawing a long enough line. The line needs to extend from one border to the other.

The drawing feature is very helpful when you want to add a cell or split it into smaller sections. To show or hide the Table toolbar, choose View ➢ Toolbars ➢ Table.

Viewing the HTML Code

If you want to see the code behind the tables you create, click the HTML tab at the bottom of the Page view window. The HTML coding for a table is pretty straight-forward; you really only need three tags to build a table (each has a closing tag as well). The <TABLE> tag begins the table definition, the <TR> tag defines a new row in the table, and the <TD> tag defines a single cell within the table. Here is some code that builds a small table:

```
<TABLE BORDER="1">
  <TR>
    <TD>Cell A1</TD>  <TD>Cell B1</TD>
  </TR>
  <TR>
    <TD>Cell A2</TD>  <TD>Cell B2</TD>
  </TR>
  <TR>
    <TD>Cell A3</TD>  <TD>Cell B3</TD>
  </TR>
</TABLE>
```

The resulting table has three rows and two columns. The text within the <TD> and </TD> tags is what appears in each cell. The HTML default is a table with no borders, but the FrontPage default is a border one-pixel wide, specified in the <TABLE> tag.

Working within a Table

To move between the cells in a table:

- Use the Tab key on your keyboard to move one cell to the right. If you Tab in the last cell of a table (the right-hand cell of the bottom row), a new row is automatically inserted.

- Hold down the Shift key and press Tab to move to one cell the left.

- Click within a cell with your mouse.

In the six-row and eight-column empty table you just created, enter the data from the table shown in Figure 7.1. Enter the text for the title in the first cell in the top row; later you'll merge that cell with the others in that row to allow the title to span the width of the table.

If you need to insert text before a table that occupies the first line on the page, hold Ctrl and press Home. The insertion point moves to the first cell of the table. Press Enter to insert a blank line before the table.

To move text and other elements within a table, select what you want to move and then just drag and drop it into its new location. To copy items, hold down the Ctrl key until after you release the mouse button.

You can think of each cell in a table as a mini-page. You can change a cell's background color, and just about anything you put on a page can also be placed in a cell, including images, hyperlinks, and even another table!

That's right, you can nest a table within another table, as shown in Figure 7.5. In this example, four cells in the larger, surrounding table contain a two-row by two-column table. Each of the four cells in those smaller tables contains an image.

Selecting Table Elements

To modify the look or shape of a table, you need to select one or more of its elements. To select a cell, row, column, or the entire table, move the insertion point to a cell and choose the appropriate command from the Table ➤ Select menu: Table, Column, Row, or Cell (from any cell).

You can also select various elements in the following ways:

Cell   Hold down Alt and click within the cell, as long as the pointer is displayed.

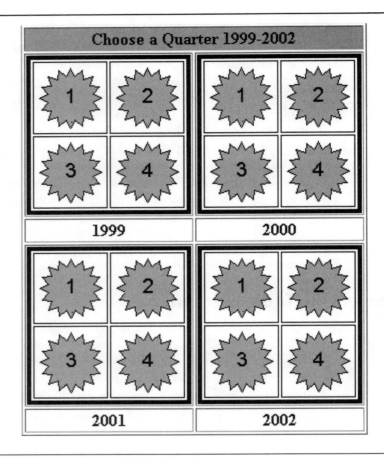

FIGURE 7.5: You can create almost any layout by nesting tables within tables.

NOTE NOTE NOTE NOTE NOTE NOTE NOTE NOTE NOTE NOTE NOTE NOTE NOTE NOTE NOTE

Don't confuse selecting a cell, which highlights the entire cell, with selecting the contents of the cell. If you select text, only the text is highlighted. When you select the entire cell, the empty space surrounding the text is also selected.

Row or Column Move the mouse pointer to the far left border of the row (or top border of the column), and the mouse pointer changes to a solid arrow pointing across the row (or down the column). Click to select the row or column.

Multiple Cells Click in the first cell and then press Shift and click in the last cell you want to select to select contiguous cells. Select one cell and then hold Ctrl and click to select non-contiguous cells. You can also drag over adjacent cells, rows, or columns to select them. To deselect individual cells, hold Ctrl and click each one.

Caption Point to the left of the caption and click.

Table Move the pointer to the left side of the table (into the area known as the selection bar) and the mouse pointer changes from an I-beam to a right-pointed arrow. Double-click on the selection bar to select the table.

When you create a table without a border, FrontPage displays dashed gridlines so you can see the limits of each cell. You can hide or display these lines by clicking the Show All button. Or, click the Preview tab to see the table without the gridlines.

Formatting a Table's Contents

You can format cell text as you would other text on a page. For example, you can make the title in the first row of our sample table a second-level heading (look back at Figure 7.1). But before you do that, you need to merge all the cells in that row into a single cell that spans the width of the table.

1. Select the first row of the table (Table ➤ Select ➤ Row).

2. Click the Merge Cells button on the Table toolbar or choose Table ➤ Merge Cells. The first row becomes a single cell; its width is determined by the total width of the cells that were merged.

3. With the insertion point still in the first row, select Heading 2 from the Style drop-down list on the Formatting toolbar.

With the data in the table, the top row merged into one cell, and the title displayed in the Heading 2 format, our sample table (shown in Figure 7.6) now looks a lot more like the one in Figure 7.1.

Skill 7

Work Schedule for the Week of January 11, 1999							
	Mon	Tue	Wed	Thu	Fri	Sat	Sun
Celeste	X	X	X			X	X
Gerald	X	X		X	X	X	
Gordon	X			X	X	X	X
Carol			X	X	X	X	X

FIGURE 7.6: The table after adding data and merging the cells in its first row.

Adding and Aligning a Caption

You can add an optional caption to a table, which appears either directly above or below the table.

1. Select any cell in the table.

2. Choose Table ➤ Insert ➤ Caption.

3. The insertion point is centered just above the table so that you can enter the caption text.

4. Type the text for the caption, such as (**As of December 7, 1998**), as in Figure 7.1.

5. When you're finished, click outside the caption.

You can also position a normal line of text just above or below the table. But unlike a caption, the text does not stay centered or move with the table.

You can apply a style or text formatting, such as bold or italic, to a caption. To delete a caption, select it and press Delete.

By default, a caption appears centered above the table, but you can instead display it below the table. To change its position, click anywhere in the caption and choose Table ➤ Properties ➤ Caption. Or right-click the caption and choose Caption Properties from the shortcut menu. In the Caption Properties dialog box, choose Bottom of Table and then click OK.

Changing the Look of a Table

Once you've created a table, you can change its appearance with the settings in the Table Properties dialog box (see Figure 7.7). Select any cell in the table and choose Table ➤ Properties ➤ Table, or right-click anywhere on the table and choose Table Properties from the shortcut menu.

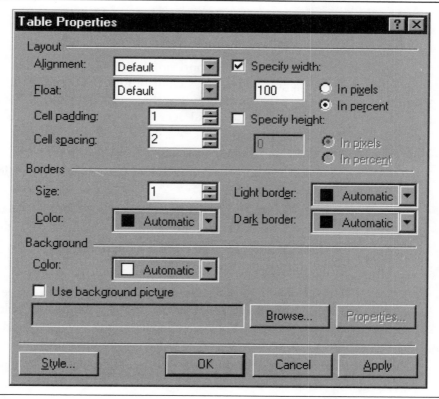

FIGURE 7.7: The Table Properties dialog box lets you adjust table format and dimensions.

Most of the options in the Table Properties dialog box affect table formatting. The Specify Width group of options affects the overall dimensions of the table and is discussed in "Changing the Size of a Table" later in this Skill. When you change one or more of the settings in the Table Properties dialog box, you can click the Apply button to apply the new settings to the table without closing the dialog box. This lets you fine-tune the settings while you watch their effects on the table.

Changing a Table's Alignment and Layout

The Layout option group includes the following choices:

Alignment   Set the horizontal alignment of the table within the width of the page. Choose Left, Center, or Right; choose Default to specify no alignment, which most browsers display as left-aligned. For the table you created earlier in this Skill, set its Alignment option to Center so it's centered in the page.

Float   Allow other page text to wrap around the table rather than appear above or below it. Choose Left or Right to float the table to the left or right of existing text.

Cell Padding   The amount of space in pixels that separates the contents of a cell from the cell's edges (picture a padded cell) ; the default is 1.

Cell Spacing   The amount of space in pixels between adjacent cells; the default is 2.

These last two options can be a little confusing until you see how they affect the cells in the table. Shown next are three copies of the same table. The one on the top has the default padding and spacing; the one in the middle has larger padding but default spacing; and the one on the bottom has default padding with larger spacing.

Sun	Mon	Tue	Wed	Thu	Fri	Sat
1	2	3	4	5	6	7

Padding -1 Spacing - 2

Sun	Mon	Tue	Wed	Thu	Fri	Sat
1	2	3	4	5	6	7

Padding - 8 Spacing - 2

Sun	Mon	Tue	Wed	Thu	Fri	Sat
1	2	3	4	5	6	7

Padding -1 Spacing - 8

Setting a Table's Background and Border Colors

The Table Properties dialog box includes two option groups that affect the table's background and borders. With the Background options, you can change the table's background to distinguish it from the surrounding page. (The settings are similar to those that affect a page's background, as discussed in "Setting Page Properties" in Skill 4.)

Color   Choose a color for the table's background; the Automatic choice specifies no color for the table's background, so the table uses the same background as the page.

Use Background Picture   Choose an image file that will fill the table's background. Select this option and either type a name or click the Browse button and select an image file or Clip Art image.

If you choose both a color and an image for a table's background, the image is displayed, not the color. However, the background color shows through a transparent color in a GIF image. If you apply background colors to individual cells (discussed in the next section), the cell background hides the table background.

TIP TIP TIP TIP TIP TIP TIP TIP TIP TIP TIP TIP TIP TIP TIP TIP TIP TIP TIP TIP TIP TIP

Use the Fill Color button on the Table toolbar to change a table's background color without opening the Table Properties dialog box. Make sure the entire table is selected first, or you'll only change the background of the selected cells.

Use the Borders options in the Table Properties dialog box to specify a size for the table's borders and to change the color of all the borders. Tables are surrounded by two borders: a light border and a dark border. Choosing different colors for the two borders gives the border a 3-D effect.

Size   Set the width of the outside table border in pixels. This does not affect the width of the inner borders separating the cells; their widths can't be changed. By default, Border Size is set to 1 pixel.

Light Border   Choose a color for one of the pair of lines that make up the table's border.

Dark Border   Choose a color for the second in the pair of border lines.

Color   Choose a color to apply to both borders when Light Border and Dark Border are set to Automatic, or for browsers that don't support Light Border and Dark Border options.

Experiment with the Borders options to see how FrontPage applies color to the border. To see how the Light and Dark Border options are interpreted, preview the page in your browser. If a browser does not support Light and Dark Border options, it applies the specified Color setting.

Changing the Look of Cells

Cells in a table have their own properties that affect alignment, background and border color, column width, and the number of columns or rows they span. We'll save the discussion of these last two items for "Changing the Size of a Table" later in this Skill.

To change the properties of a single cell, click within the cell and choose Table ➤ Properties ➤ Cell, or right-click and choose Cell Properties from the shortcut menu. You'll see the Cell Properties dialog box (shown in Figure 7.8). To change the properties of multiple cells, select them before opening the dialog box.

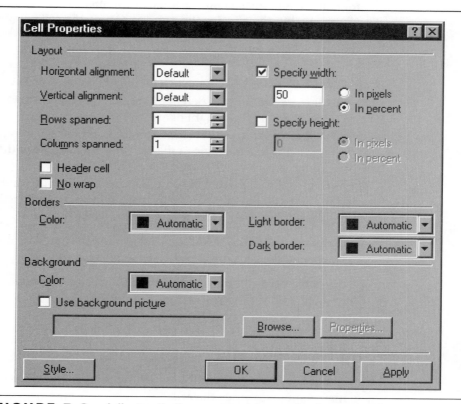

FIGURE 7.8: Adjust cell alignment and formatting in the Cell Properties dialog box.

Setting Cell Alignment and Layout

Most browsers align the contents of a cell with the left edge of the cell and center the contents vertically in the cell. You can change these alignment settings with the Horizontal Alignment and Vertical Alignment options in the Cell Properties dialog box. The horizontal choices are Default, Left, Center, Right, and Justify, and the vertical choices are Default, Top, Middle, Baseline, and Bottom.

TIP TIP TIP TIP TIP TIP TIP TIP TIP TIP TIP TIP TIP TIP TIP TIP TIP TIP TIP TIP TIP TIP TIP
You can also set the horizontal alignment in one step by clicking one of the four alignment buttons on the Standard toolbar. This changes the paragraph alignment, but the effect is the same as setting the cell's alignment. To adjust vertical alignment, click the Align Top, Center Vertically, or Align Bottom button on the Table toolbar.

By default in FrontPage, when text is longer than its cell is wide, the text wraps to a new line, expanding the height of the cell. Just like in an Excel worksheet or Word table, changing the height of one cell changes the height of the entire row. If you select the No Wrap option (see Figure 7.8), FrontPage or any typical browser doesn't wrap text to a new line in the cell, but expands the width of the column to display all the text.

Let's change the alignment of some cells in the table you built in the exercises earlier in this Skill. Follow these steps to center the contents in the cells that contain the days of the week and the cells below them:

1. Beginning with the "Mon" cell, select the cells that contain the days of the week and the cells directly below them.

2. Click the Center button on the Formatting toolbar or choose Table ➤ Properties ➤ Cell, and set the Horizontal Alignment option to Center in the Cell Properties dialog box. Then click OK.

Creating Header Cells

You can define any cells in a table as header cells to give them emphasis, which you may want to do when the cells are row or column titles. In the table you've been working on in this Skill, the days of the week and the names in the left column should be defined as header cells, as they are in Figure 7.1.

1. Select the days of the week, and then the names in the first column.

2. Choose Table ➤ Properties ➤ Cell.

3. In the Cell Properties dialog box, select the Header Cell option and then click OK.

FrontPage and most browsers display the text in header cells in boldfaced type.

Setting a Cell's Background and Border Colors

Cells have the same background and border properties as tables and pages. In the Cell Properties dialog box, you can specify an image or a color for a cell's background and the colors for the border around the cell.

When you set these options for a cell to anything but Automatic, the browser displays the colors or image you specify, overriding any backgrounds or colors used for the rest of the table. If there is no background specified for the cell or table, the page's background is used for the cell. This hierarchy of properties (Cell, then Table, then Page) is referred to as *cascading*.

Let's add some background color to some of the cells in the table we've been building:

1. If they are not already selected, select the cells that contain the days of the week and the names in the first column.

2. Choose Table ➤ Properties ➤ Cell, or right-click and choose Cell Properties.

3. Choose a color other than Automatic from the drop-down list for the Background Color (choose Silver for a light gray background).

4. Click OK to complete the job.

Changing the Size of a Table

When FrontPage creates a table, the default width is 100 percent of the width of the screen you are using to view it. It's possible to change the width of a table, to lock in a table's width, or allow it to expand and contract based on the entries in the cells or the size of the screen.

Changing Table Width

You can set the width of a table when you create it with the Insert Table dialog box or revise it with the Table Properties dialog box. First select the Specify Width option in either dialog box, then choose the measurement you want to use to define the width:

In Pixels   Enter the exact width of the table in pixels.

In Percent Enter the width as a percentage (1 to 100) of the width of the browser's window, no matter how wide that window might be. For example, entering 100 makes the table as wide as the window; entering 50 makes the table half as wide as the window.

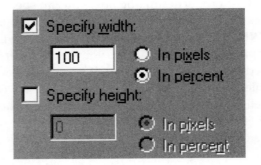

The method you choose depends on how you want your table displayed. For example, when you set the width of a table that has a lot of text or images in each cell (see Figure 7.2), you may want to maximize its visibility by setting the width as 100 percent. That way, no matter how large or small the display is, the table fills the screen. You might use this when you have a table on your home page displaying important information or hyperlinks for visitors to your site. By letting the table fit the window, all its contents will always be visible.

On the other hand, if the table is only a few columns with minimal text (see Figure 7.1), lock in the table's size in pixels so it doesn't interfere with the overall appearance of the page, even at higher resolutions.

Changing a Column's Width

There are several methods you can use to adjust the width of columns (rather than have them automatically adjust based on the width of the window). Each of these ways may be more or less useful depending on your overall goals for the table. The methods are:

- Point to any of the cell borders and, when the pointer changes to a double-headed arrow, hold the mouse button and drag the border. This can be used both to adjust cell width and cell height.

- Select the rows or columns you want to adjust and click the Distribute Rows Evenly or Distribute Column Evenly buttons on the Table toolbar.

- Specify a width in the Cell Properties dialog box. The choices are similar to those you use to set the width of a table, as discussed in the previous section. You can specify the width either in pixels or as a percentage of the table's width (*not* the window's width).

In the sample table, don't worry about drastic changes in the widths of columns that could affect the look of the table; you just want seven columns (the days of the week) to be the same width. Here's how to do it:

1. Point to the top edge of the table above the Mon column so the pointer changes to the black arrow pointing down that column; then click to select all the cells in that column.

2. Hold down the mouse button and drag to the right, straight across the top edge of the table to select all the columns until the right end of the table.

3. Click the Distribute Columns Evenly button on the Table toolbar.

Adding and Removing Cells

Once you create a table, you are still free to add or remove cells. Note that a table need not be filled with cells; each row can have a different number of cells in it. You can add either single cells or entire rows or columns.

Before you add new cells to the table, move the insertion point to a cell that's adjacent to the new ones. To add a single cell, choose Table ➤ Insert ➤ Cell; the new cell is added to the left of the insertion point. To add a row or column, select the row or column adjacent to where you want the new one and click the Insert Rows or Insert Columns button on the Table toolbar. To insert multiple rows or columns, select the corresponding number of rows or columns. Rows are inserted above the selected rows; columns are inserted to the left of the selected columns.

If you want to insert multiple rows (or columns) at the end of a table, where you can't begin by selecting multiple rows (or columns), place the insertion point in a cell in the last row (or column) and choose Table ➤ Insert ➤ Rows or Columns. In the dialog box that appears, choose Rows or Columns, the quantity to insert, and where they should be placed in relation to the active cell. For example, to add three new rows below the active cell, choose Rows, set the Number of Rows option to 3, choose Below Selection, and click OK.

**SKILL
7**

When you insert a row or column, the new one contains the same number of cells as the active one.

To delete cells from a table, select one or more cells, or entire rows or columns, and click the Delete Cells button on the Table toolbar, or choose Table ➤ Delete Cells.

Merging and Splitting Cells

You can also change the layout of a table by combining multiple cells into one and splitting one cell into multiple cells. Earlier in this Skill you merged all the cells in the top row of the table into a single, table-wide cell. Here's the general method for merging cells.

Select the cells you want to make into a single cell (they must all be adjacent and form a rectangle), and then click the Merge Cells button on the Table toolbar or choose Table ➤ Merge Cells. The borders between those cells will dissolve. The resulting single cell takes up the same amount of room in the table if the cells were empty. The amount of space may increase if there was content in the merged cells.

You can also merge cells using the Eraser on the Table toolbar. Click the Eraser button to turn it on, then drag over the border you want to erase, as shown in Figure 7.9. When you're finished, click the Eraser button again to turn it off.

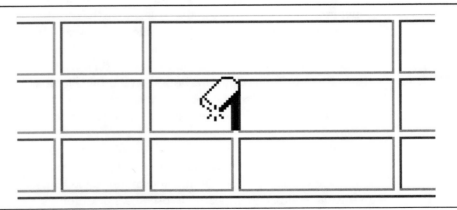

FIGURE 7.9: Drag the eraser over cells you want to merge.

To split one or more cells into multiple cells, select either a single cell or a rectangle of adjacent cells and click the Split Cells button on the Table toolbar, or choose Table ➤ Split Cells. In the Split Cells dialog box (shown here), choose whether you want to split the cells into columns or rows. A diagram in the dialog box reminds you what the effect of each is. Set the number of new rows or columns you want to create and click OK.

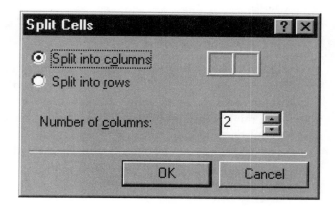

 TIP TIP TIP TIP TIP TIP TIP TIP TIP TIP TIP TIP TIP TIP TIP TIP TIP TIP TIP TIP TIP TIP TIP

For a quick and easy way to split cells, click the Draw Table tool on the Table toolbar and draw the new borders into the table.

SKILL 7

Changing Cell Span

Here's yet another way to change the cells in a table, although this method doesn't change the number of cells, it changes the size of the cells. You select the cells you want to change and choose Table ➤ Properties ➤ Cell. You'll find the two cell-spanning options in the Cell Properties dialog box (shown here).

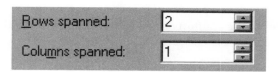

You can set one or both of the two options to have the selected cells span the specified number of rows or columns. For example, if you select a single cell and set its Rows Spanned option to 2, that cell now expands downward into the row below, effectively doubling in size. The cell that had been below it, and all the cells to the right of the cell that had been below it, are pushed to the right so that the last cell in that row now extends beyond what had been the right-hand edge of the table.

Troubleshooting Table Layout

Once you've changed cell span, the table is no longer symmetrical, as some rows and columns have a different number of cells than their neighbors. The table contains dead space—areas clearly within the boundaries of the table that contain no cells. You might also create dead space when you insert columns or rows based on a column or row that contains merged cells. For example, shown below is a table with dead space in the fourth column, created by changing the span of the first cell in column 2.

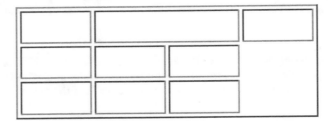

This isn't a problem once you realize the limitations of this empty area of a table. Dead space isn't a cell, so you can't select it. You can't place objects or text in it, or format it. The borders of the neighboring cells only have a single, light border rather than the double border surrounding other cells and the table.

You can't use the Draw Table tool to alter dead space. If you want to remove dead space from table, the easiest way is to move to the cell on the immediate left of the dead space and choose Table ➤ Insert ➤ Cell. Another option is simply to delete the column or row that contains the dead space.

Are You Experienced?

Now you can...

- ☑ Create a table
- ☑ Move between the cells in a table
- ☑ Select parts of a table
- ☑ Add a caption to the top or bottom of the table
- ☑ Change table properties, including layout, size, and background colors
- ☑ Change cell properties
- ☑ Merge and split cells of a table
- ☑ Troubleshoot table layout problems

SKILL
7

Displaying Images in Your Pages

- ➔ **Working with GIF and JPEG images**
- ➔ **Inserting pictures and video clips**
- ➔ **Setting picture properties**
- ➔ **Using interlaced images**
- ➔ **Creating thumbnails**
- ➔ **Making a color transparent**
- ➔ **Creating image maps**

In this Skill, you see how easy it is to add sizzle to your Web site with graphic images. You bring an image into a page in FrontPage, position it in the page and edit it. You learn several ways to improve image download time for crisp viewing and use an image to fire up several hyperlinks—a snazzy effect found on many of the best Web sites.

The World of Image Formats

Pictures in your Web sites convey information or serve as the source for hyperlinks. You can also specify a picture file as the target of a hyperlink so a browser opens and displays the picture when the user clicks its hyperlink. Pictures are also valuable as "window dressing"—livening up an otherwise humdrum, text-filled page. A bit of color can make a page more appealing and help distinguish one page from another, and logos clearly identify the Web site with a company or product.

A picture within a Web page is called an *inline image*. Because HTML is a language for presenting text, inline images are actually stored as separate files, which are then opened and displayed along with the HTML page in a browser.

NOTE NOTE NOTE NOTE NOTE NOTE NOTE NOTE NOTE NOTE NOTE NOTE NOTE NOTE

The term *image* applies to many non-text objects displayed in a Web page: line drawings, photographs, charts, geometric shapes, and textures suitable for page backgrounds. You'll see the words *picture* and *image* used interchangeably here.

Computer image files come in a wide variety of formats. A *file format* defines how information is saved in a file, not the file's content. The same is true with text, which can be saved in different formats: as a Word document, plain text (ASCII), Rich Text Format (RTF), or HTML. Two image formats have become widely-accepted standards for use on the World Wide Web: GIF and JPEG, pronounced "giff" and "jay-peg" respectively. Both file formats compress images, so the saved image is smaller than in other, noncompressed file formats. This becomes critical when the file is transferred over a network like the Internet, because smaller files take less time to transfer.

When you place an image on a page in FrontPage, you can choose GIF and JPEG pictures as well as images that were saved in other common image formats, including BMP, TIFF, TGA, RAS, EPS, PCX, PCD, and WMF (see Table 8.1). When you save the page, however, FrontPage converts the image to a

Web-appropriate format—GIF if it has 8-bit color or less, or JPEG if it has more than 8-bit color.

The GIF Format

CompuServe developed the Graphics Interchange Format (GIF) to shorten the time it takes to transfer images online. This format, which uses a `.gif` filename extension, supports up to 256 colors (or 8-bit color), often the maximum number of colors that older computers can display. Because the image is compressed for network communications, then uncompressed by the browser, GIF images arrive more quickly than, say, PCX file format.

When an image-editing program compresses and saves an image as a GIF file, it leaves nothing behind—when you open a GIF image you'll see the original picture exactly as it looked when it was saved. This is called *lossless* compression, and gives the best compression ratios when the image has many repeating patterns, such as broad fields of the same color or repetitive lines. If you want to scan your company's black and white logo into a computer file, the GIF format is probably the one to choose.

NOTE NOTE NOTE NOTE NOTE NOTE NOTE NOTE NOTE NOTE NOTE NOTE NOTE NOTE

A *compression ratio* relates the size of a file before and after compression. For example, if an image that occupies 400KB of the computer's memory is saved as a 100KB GIF file, then the compression ratio is 4:1.

The JPEG Format

The Joint Photographic Expert Group format (JPEG; the three-letter filename extension is `.jpg`) can handle many more colors than the GIF format—up to 16.7 million colors (24-bit color). Like the GIF format, JPEG compresses files, but to achieve a higher compression ratio, it uses a *lossy* compression method, which literally strips out and loses what it considers to be expendable bits of the image. When you open a JPEG file, the image you see is of a lower quality than the original image

The trick, however, is that the sophisticated JPEG compression algorithm takes out bits that you may not really notice are missing. This is especially true in richly colored images such as photographs, where a significant reduction in file size has only a slight effect on the quality of the image. When you save an image in the JPEG file format, you can specify the file size to image quality ratio. For example,

SKILL
8

you can choose a high-quality image with a larger file size, or you can choose a smaller file size with an image that's somewhat degraded. If you want to include a photograph of your company president in your Web site, the JPEG format is the one to choose.

NOTE NOTE NOTE NOTE NOTE NOTE NOTE NOTE NOTE NOTE NOTE NOTE NOTE NOTE NOTE

When saving a true-color image in the JPEG format, the image quality will be somewhat reduced, in exchange for a significant reduction in file size. Keep in mind, though, that if you were to save that image in the GIF format, you would lose significantly more quality. That's because the GIF format can store only 256 colors, so that the 16-plus million colors in the true-color image will be converted to a mere 256. To see the difference between the two formats, save a photograph to a JPEG and a GIF file and note the resulting file size and image quality of each.

Table 8.1 lists other common file formats you'll encounter when you work with images and other media on the World Wide Web.

TABLE 8.1: Common File Formats

Format Name	File Extension	Purpose, Internet Use
AIFF	.aif	digital sound, commonly used
SoundEdit	.au, .snd	digital sound, commonly used
Audio Video Interleaved	.avi	video for Windows only, so minimally used
Windows Bitmap	.bmp	images, noncompressed format used for icons, wallpaper; FrontPage can import
Encapsulated Postscript	.eps	images; FrontPage can import
Macromedia	.mmm	animation, commonly used
QuickTime Movie	.mov	audio/video scaleable compression format for Windows or Mac, the Web standard for downloadable video clips
Moving Picture Experts Group (MPEG)	.mpg	audio/video compression, seeing increasing use
PCX bitmap	.pcx	images; FrontPage can import
Portable Network Graphics	.png	Images; FrontPage can import and save
RealMedia	.ram	video; FrontPage can import
Raster	.ras	images; FrontPage can import
Targa	.tga	images; FrontPage can import

TABLE 8.1: Common File Formats *(continued)*

Format Name	File Extension	Purpose, Internet Use
Tagged Image File Format (TIFF)	.tif	images, noncompressed format often used for clipart; FrontPage can import
Wave	.wav	digital sound, commonly used for opening effects at a site
Windows Metafile	.wmf	images; FrontPage can import
Virtual Reality Modeling Language (VRML)	.wrl	3-D models, used for "virtual tour" sites

Inserting Images

To bring an image file into a page in FrontPage, first position the insertion point where you want the image to appear. Don't worry about too much precision, as you can move the image later.

Click the Insert Picture from File button on the toolbar or choose Insert ➤ Picture ➤ From File to open the Picture dialog box, shown in Figure 8.1. To add an image file from the active web, locate the image in the list of image files. You can preview JPEG and GIF files simply by selecting the file; FrontPage provides a preview in the Picture dialog box.

If the image isn't stored in the active web, click the Use Your Web Browser button to browse the Web for the image file, or click the Select a File on Your Computer button to find the image file on your local and network drives. After you have selected an image, click OK. FrontPage inserts the image into your page.

NOTE NOTE NOTE NOTE NOTE NOTE NOTE NOTE NOTE NOTE NOTE NOTE NOTE NOTE NOTE

You can also insert an image using copy and paste. Select the image in its native program, copy it to the clipboard, then switch to FrontPage and paste it on the page. If FrontPage and the other program are both displayed on the screen, you can simply drag the image into the page.

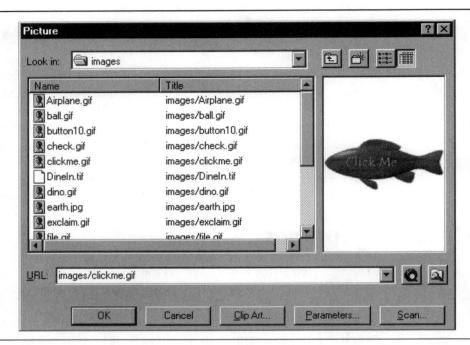

FIGURE 8.1: Specify an image to insert in the Picture dialog box.

The HTML code FrontPage creates when you insert an image in a page specifies the URL for the image, the border thickness, and the image's size:

```
<IMG BORDER="0" SRC="images/undercon.gif" WIDTH="40" HEIGHT="38">
```

Inserting Clip Art

The Microsoft Clip Art Gallery is included with FrontPage. Choose Insert ➢ Picture ➢ Clip Art from the menu or click the Clip Art button in the Picture dialog box to open the gallery, shown in Figure 8.2. The icons represent categories of images (or sounds or motion clips if you have selected one of those tabs). Click one of them to display the images in that category; click the Back button in the toolbar to return to the list of categories.

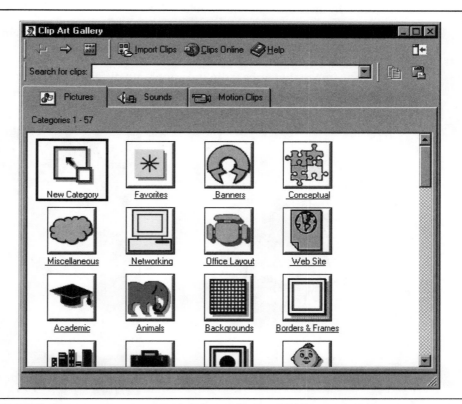

FIGURE 8.2: The Microsoft Clip Art Gallery includes a variety of pictures. Of special interest for Web developers are the bullets, backgrounds, lines, and other Web images.

Several categories have Web-related images, such as those near the bottom of the list: Web Backgrounds, Web Banners, Web Bullets and Buttons, and Web Dividers. When you've found the clip art image you want to use, click it and then click the Insert Clip button on the small toolbar of buttons that is displayed. You can either close the Clip Art Gallery or leave it open and switch back to FrontPage. Figure 8.3 shows an example of two images: a clip art picture of a lion and a larger photograph of a cat.

To insert clip art on a page:

1. Position the insertion point on the line where you want the image to appear.

2. Choose Insert ➢ Picture ➢ Clip Art or click the Insert Picture from File button and then click the Clip Art button in the dialog box.

3. In the Clip Art Gallery, select a category.

4. Select the image you want and then click the Insert Clip button to place the image on your page.

The image that appears in the page is no different from any other image. You can change its properties, size, or position, or delete it from the page.

FIGURE 8.3: It's easy to place clip art or photographs on a page in FrontPage.

Using Scanned Images

FrontPage is TWAIN–compliant (an industry standard for communications between the computer and picture input devices), so you can insert images directly i
nto a page from a scanner or digital camera attached to your computer. To insert a digital image from a device, click the Scan button in the Picture dialog box. The Camera/
Scanner dialog box appears.

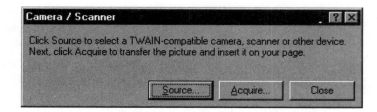

This dialog box works like a simple wizard. First, click the Source button to open a list of TWAIN-compliant devices attached to your computer.

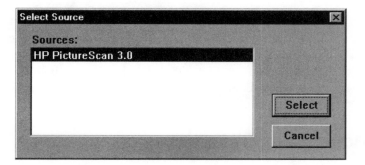

Choose the device, then click Select to return to the Camera/Scanner dialog box. Now, click the Acquire button, and FrontPage transfers control to the device you selected, which opens its own dialog boxes to walk you through the acquisition process.

NOTE NOTE NOTE NOTE NOTE NOTE NOTE NOTE NOTE NOTE NOTE NOTE NOTE NOTE NOTE

The Select Source dialog box is generated by Windows. If the device you want to use isn't on the list, use the software supplied with the device or the Add Hardware applet in the Windows Control Panel to add the scanner or camera to your system.

SKILL
8

Inserting a Video Clip

You can also include a moving image in a page, such as a video clip with an .avi or .ram extension. The process is very much the same as inserting a fixed image. Choose Insert ➤ Picture ➤ Video, then select the video clip file.

FrontPage inserts a still frame of the clip. You won't see the video running in the Page view, but you can look at the page in the Preview window in FrontPage, or use the File ➤ Preview in Browser command, to see how it looks in a browser.

Video clips take up a lot of disk space, so even a few seconds of video can be several hundred thousand bytes. For example, adding a 6MB video to a page might offer only a half-minute of moving pictures, but will add almost an hour to the time it takes a user with a 28.8 modem to download the page. The estimated time to load a page is shown in the FrontPage status bar.

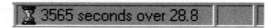

With this in mind, include a video only when its size is not a critical issue, such as when the video plays a key role in the web. Or make the video the target of a hyperlink on an otherwise unused page, and include text that tells users the estimated download time. Then, only those who are willing to wait will click the link to load the video.

Moving and Sizing Images

Before you can move or size an image, you must select it. Click the image, and a selection handle appears at each corner of the image and in the middle of each side. Not only do these indicate the image is selected, but you can use them to resize the image. When you point to any handle, the mouse pointer changes to a double arrow. Drag the handle to resize the image; if you drag a corner handle, FrontPage automatically maintains the image's *aspect ratio* (the relationship between its width and its height).

Move the selected image relative to other images and text by dragging it to a new location (drag it by the center to avoid changing its size). You can also use the Edit ➤ Cut and Paste method. Use Edit ➤ Copy and Paste, or hold Ctrl while you drag and drop, to make multiple copies of the image.

TIP TIP TIP TIP TIP TIP TIP TIP TIP TIP TIP TIP TIP TIP TIP TIP TIP TIP TIP TIP TIP TIP TIP

If you want to set the size of an image precisely, specify the size in the Picture Properties dialog box for that image, which is discussed in the "Changing Picture Properties" section later in this chapter.

Saving Embedded Images

While you can place scanned and imported images on a page, FrontPage saves all images within a web as GIF or JPEG files (videos are saved in their original format). It chooses the file format based on the number of colors in the original image. Images created with palettes of up to 256 colors are saved as GIFs; images with more colors are saved as JPEGs. The two images in Figure 8.3 are good examples. FrontPage would save the small clip art picture of a lion as a GIF; the more complex photograph of a cat is saved as a JPEG, as shown in Figure 8.4. When you insert a video clip from outside of the active web, you're given the opportunity to save the clip in the web when you save the page.

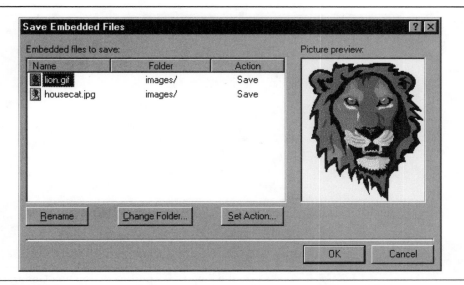

FIGURE 8.4: FrontPage saves imported images as GIFs or JPEGs.

Changing Picture Properties

When you want to fine-tune the settings for an image in a page, you use the Picture Properties dialog box. Select an image and choose Format ➤ Properties, or right-click the image and choose Picture Properties from the shortcut menu.

Setting General Properties

On the General tab of the Picture Properties dialog box, shown in Figure 8.5, you set four properties: picture source, type, alternative representations, and default hyperlink.

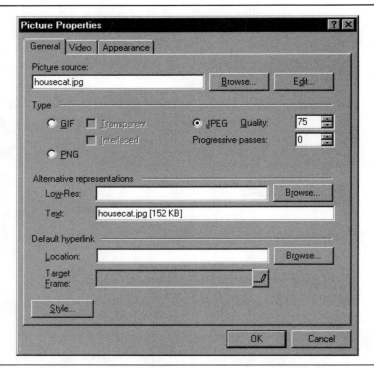

FIGURE 8.5: On the Picture Properties dialog box General tab, specify a file format and default hyperlink for the image.

Setting Picture Source Properties

The Picture Source box defines the source file for the image. If you want to replace this image with another, either enter the name and location of the new image or click the Browse button and select the file from the Picture dialog box. Selecting a different file replaces the current image in the page, so the other settings in the Picture Properties dialog box now apply to that new image. Click the Edit button to open the image in the image-editing program associated with GIF or JPEG files. In the stand-alone edition of FrontPage, the Microsoft Image Composer is associated with these file types by default. Of course, you can specify the default editor for image files on the Configure Editors tab of the Options dialog box (Tools ➤ Options).

Specifying Image Type

In the Type option group, you specify whether the image should be saved in your web as a GIF, JPEG, or PNG file. If the image file is already in one of these formats, the appropriate option is selected. If the page has not been saved and the image is in another format, choose one of the file types.

NOTE NOTE NOTE NOTE NOTE NOTE NOTE NOTE NOTE NOTE NOTE NOTE NOTE NOTE NOTE

The Portable Network Graphics format (PNG) may eventually supplant the JPEG and GIF formats on the Internet, but it is not yet widely used. Therefore, unless you have a specific reason to use PNG, you should stick with the current standards: GIF and JPEG.

Options for GIF Images   When you select the GIF option, there are two GIF-related check boxes available: Transparent and Interlaced.

A GIF image can have one transparent color (see "Making Images Transparent" later in this Skill). If you make a color in a GIF image transparent, the Transparent check box is already selected when you open the dialog box. Turn Transparent off to display the color again in the image, removing the transparent definition for that color.

When you open a GIF in a browser, the image is loaded line by line, from the top to the bottom. This happens so quickly in a small image that you hardly notice how the image appears. However, if the image is large or the network connection is slow, you see the image grow from the top down. The effect can sometimes breed impatience as users watch the slow unveiling of the image.

The Interlaced option rearranges the order of the scan lines in the image file so the image seems to appear faster. When a browser opens an interlaced GIF image, the picture occupies its space more quickly and seems to come into focus within that space, instead of appearing gradually from the top to the bottom.

Options for JPEG Images   When you save a JPEG image, you can specify the amount of compression to apply by adjusting the value in the Quality field. The default value is 75 in a range of 0 to 100. The more you compress a JPEG image,

SKILL 8

the lower the quality of the image; 100 percent is no compression, 0 percent is no quality (or at least, very little). Enter a lower number to compress the image more while further reducing the quality, or enter a higher number to improve the quality while also increasing the size of the image file. If you're saving a large JPEG image in a page, you can experiment by lowering the quality setting. See just how much the image is degraded when you later open it in FrontPage, and how much time you save from the estimated download time on the status bar.

A *progressive JPEG* is similar to an interlaced GIF; the image loads in stages, gradually increasing in quality. Use the Progressive Passes option to specify the number of stages required to completely load the image. Choosing 0 means the JPEG is not rendered progressively. This is a relatively new enhancement of the JPEG standard, so many browsers still load the entire image at once, regardless of the setting.

Specifying an Alternative for an Image

The Picture Properties dialog box lets you specify two alternatives for an image. If the image is large and takes a long time to download, you can specify a second, smaller image file in the Low-Res option (low resolution). Most browsers download and display the Low-Res image first, so the person viewing the page can see the image relatively quickly. The browser then downloads the primary image, and once it's completely downloaded, displays it instead of the low-resolution version.

NOTE NOTE NOTE NOTE NOTE NOTE NOTE NOTE NOTE NOTE NOTE NOTE NOTE NOTE NOTE

See "Creating a Thumbnail" later in this Skill for an even slicker way to handle images with long download times.

The second alternative is the Text option. Text you enter here is available to browsers to display while the image is loading, when the image is not available, or when the browser cannot handle images. For example, most browsers let users suppress downloading and displaying of images to save time online; some browsers can't handle images at all. In these cases, the browser displays the alternative text. The text you enter should describe the image so that the person viewing the page gets an idea of what was supposed to be shown.

Setting Video Properties

The Video tab of the Picture Properties dialog box has settings that affect video clip images (see Figure 8.6).

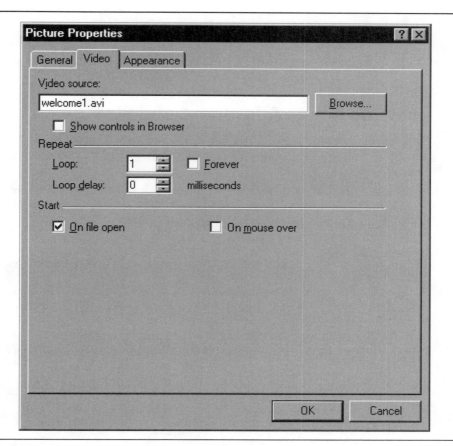

FIGURE 8.6: The Video tab in the Picture Properties dialog box

The Video Source field displays the name of the video clip file. To specify a different file, either enter a new name or click the Browse button and select a file.

If you select the Show Controls in Browser check box, the browser displays standard video controls beneath the video clip window. The video controls allow the user to start or stop the video at any time.

By default, a video clip plays only once when the page is opened in a browser. You can specify how many times the video should be played by setting the Repeat options. Set the Loop option to the number of times you want the video to play; for infinite looping, enable the Forever check box. Specify the amount of time (in milliseconds) between plays in the Loop Delay option. For example, entering 500 puts a half-second pause between playbacks.

Use the Start options to specify that the video should start when the page is opened in a browser (the On File Open check box) or when the reader moves the mouse over the video (the On Mouse Over check box).

Setting Image Alignment and Size

To align an image to the left, center, or right of the page or a table cell, treat the image as you would a paragraph. Select the image, then click one of the alignment buttons on the Formatting toolbar.

You can set other image alignment options in the Appearance tab in the Picture Properties dialog box (see Figure 8.7). You can also change the size of the image and enclose it within a border.

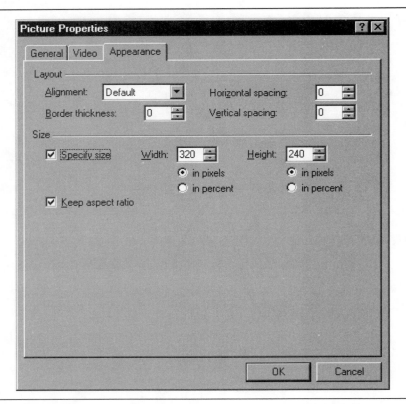

FIGURE 8.7: The Appearance tab in the Picture Properties dialog box

The Layout options include three choices for arranging an image with its surrounding text: Alignment, Horizontal Spacing, and Vertical Spacing. In the Alignment control, choose how the image should align with surrounding text:

Absbottom Aligns the image at the bottom of the current line

Absmiddle Aligns the image at the middle of the current line

Baseline Aligns the image at the bottom of the current line; this is the default in most browsers

Bottom Aligns the bottom of the image with the surrounding text

Center Aligns the center of the image with the surrounding text

Default Uses the browser's default settings

Left Aligns the image at the left margin; surrounding text is wrapped at the right side of the image

Middle Aligns the middle of the image with the surrounding text

Right Aligns the image at the right margin; surrounding text is wrapped at the left side of the image

Texttop Aligns the top of the image with the top of the tallest text in the current line

Top Aligns the top of the image with the surrounding text

In the Horizontal Spacing control, specify the number of pixels of blank space that should separate the image from any text, image, or window edge to its left or right. Use the Vertical Spacing control to specify the number of pixels between the image and any text, image, or window edge above or below it. To enclose the image in a black border, specify a thickness in the Border Thickness field. The default is zero, so no border is displayed.

Use the Size option controls to set the image's width and height. First enable the Specify Size check box. Then, enter values for image Width, Height, or both in pixels or as a percentage of page size.

If you change the width or height in pixels, you don't have to calculate the other dimension. Just make sure the Keep Aspect Ratio check box is enabled, and FrontPage maintains the aspect ratio of the image (the relationship between the height and width). As you change the size of one dimension, FrontPage automatically calculates and changes the other dimension.

SKILL 8

Working with the Picture Toolbar

If the FrontPage Picture toolbar is not already displayed, selecting an image displays it (see below). If you deselect the image by clicking elsewhere, the Picture toolbar is hidden again.

While you're working intensely with one or more images, choose View ➤ Toolbars ➤ Picture from the menu to display the Picture toolbar all the time. This prevents the page from jumping down or up whenever the toolbar is displayed or hidden.

 NOTE NOTE NOTE NOTE NOTE NOTE NOTE NOTE NOTE NOTE NOTE NOTE NOTE NOTE NOTE
You can position a toolbar anywhere on the screen by pointing to part of the toolbar's gray background and dragging the toolbar to its new location.

Making Images Transparent

When you place an image on a page that has a background color, you'll find that the fill area in the inline image may look pretty tacky. For example, the white fill area surrounding the clip art picture of the lion, on the left below, separates it from the page background. You can easily fix this problem. Select the image, click the Set Transparent Color button on the Picture toolbar, and with the mouse pointer click anywhere in the white fill area of the image. The white fill disappears and the image melds into the page's background, as shown in the lion picture on the right below.

Original image   Image with transparent color

You can make any single color in an image transparent, and it doesn't have to be the fill color (although that's the usual application). To make a different color transparent, choose the Set Transparent Color button again and click on a different color in the image. The color you originally selected becomes visible again, and the newly selected color turns transparent. You can only make GIFs transparent, so if you try to make a color transparent in any other type of image, FrontPage asks you if you want to convert it to a GIF first.

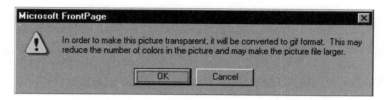

When you alter an image (for instance, by making it transparent), you're prompted to save the image again the next time you save the page.

Adding Text to an Image

One neat feature in FrontPage is the ability to add text to an image. First, select the image.

Then, click the Text button on the Picture toolbar (if the image isn't a GIF, you're prompted to convert the image), and a text box opens on the image. Enter any text you wish. You can resize the text box by selecting it, then using its handles to resize it. You can also change the font used in the box by right-clicking anywhere in the box and choosing Font from the shortcut menu.

NOTE NOTE NOTE NOTE NOTE NOTE NOTE NOTE NOTE NOTE NOTE NOTE NOTE NOTE NOTE
Adding text to an image doesn't change the image; the text is displayed on top of the image. FrontPage actually creates a separate image file for the text, which it then overlays on top of the original image.

Creating a Thumbnail

Thumbnails are alternative images that let users choose whether or not to load large image files. With a thumbnail, a smaller version of the image is loaded before the full image. If a user clicks the image, the full image is then downloaded.

FrontPage's AutoThumbnail feature creates the thumbnail image and the hyperlink to the original image, so it's very easy to create.

NOTE NOTE NOTE NOTE NOTE NOTE NOTE NOTE NOTE NOTE NOTE NOTE NOTE NOTE NOTE

You can't create a thumbnail if the picture is already smaller than the default thumbnail size; if the picture is a hyperlink or serves as an image map; or if the picture is an animation.

To create a thumbnail, select the picture in the page you're editing and click the AutoThumbnail button on the Picture toolbar. FrontPage replaces the picture with a smaller, thumbnail version that has the same filename as the original, followed by an underscore and the word *small*. For example, the thumbnail of `cyclone.jpg` is called `cyclone_small.jpg`.

FrontPage creates a hyperlink on the thumbnail that targets the full-size version. Figure 8.8 shows a section of a page with two thumbnails. Before the images were converted to thumbnails, the page took about three minutes to load with a modem speed of 28.8. The thumbnail version loads in only 3 seconds. Users can then decide whether they wish to click either thumbnail to load the full-size image.

Regional birds of winter
(335 KB)

Shore birds of summer
(418 KB)

FIGURE 8.8: These thumbnails load about 60 times faster than the page that contains full-size versions of both images.

Changing Thumbnail Options

To specify how FrontPage should create thumbnails, choose Tools ≻ Page Options and select the AutoThumbnail tab in the Page Options dialog box, shown in Figure 8.9. There are three options: Set (size), Border Thickness, and Beveled Edge. You're not setting the options for existing thumbnails or the selected thumbnail, but determining options for new thumbnails you create.

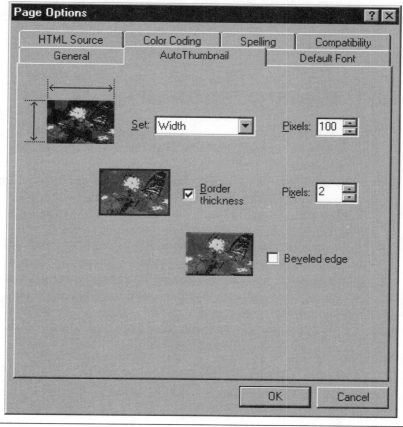

FIGURE 8.9: Set the AutoThumbnail options to change the appearance of new thumbnails you create in FrontPage.

**SKILL
8**

Use the Set option to specify the size of thumbnails you create. You only need to specify height or width; FrontPage maintains the aspect ratios of the original image when it creates the thumbnails. The Set option has four choices:

Width   Width of the thumbnail in pixels

Height   Height of the thumbnail in pixels

Shortest Side   Height or width of the shortest dimension in pixels

Longest Side   Height of width of the longest dimension in pixels

Enable the Border Thickness check box, then enter a border width in pixels to create borders around thumbnails. Enable the Beveled Edge check box to create thumbnails that have a 3-D look, like buttons.

Creating Image Maps

You've seen how you can create a hyperlink, and you know how to work with images. Now you'll see how to go one step further by creating an *image map*, which is a single image containing multiple hyperlinks. Each hyperlink is associated with a defined area of the image called a *hotspot*, which, when clicked, activates that link. In a browser, you see only the image; there is no indication it has hotspots until you move your mouse over the hotspot and the pointer changes to a hand.

You've undoubtedly encountered image maps in many, many pages on the Web. They can be informative, attractive, and intuitive, and they can also transcend language, which is an important consideration on the Internet. A typical use of an image map is literally in the form of a map, where you can click on a city, state, or area to display regional information.

Creating an image map from a geographic map works very well when you're defining hotspots for the large areas, like the Canadian provinces or the regularly shaped states in the western U.S. But the plan doesn't work so well when you try to create hotspots on smaller, irregularly shaped areas like the eastern U.S. states. Make sure you're working with an appropriate map: If all your business is in New England, you'd be better off with a regional map of the eastern United States.

You should also be aware of the following issues when you incorporate an image map in a page:

- The context of the image map must be unambiguous. Users should have no doubt that the image is a place to click to open another resource. If the image isn't completely self-explanatory, add appropriate text.

- A large image can take a long time to download on a dial-up connection (about 3,200 characters, or bytes, per second at 28,800 bps), so use large image maps with caution. Large isn't necessarily tied to the screen size of the image; the map in Figure 8.10 is a GIF image that adds only a few seconds to the page's download time. Check the time to download in the status bar before and after adding an image to determine how long it takes to load.

- Hotspots in an image map must be easy to discern, or readers will wind up on pages they had no intention of visiting. The same problem occurs if hotspots are too small or too numerous.

- You can't predict image quality for every browser—or whether the image appears at all. To ensure users can access exactly the right link, you can also include text hyperlinks as in Figure 8.10, or a link to a list of text hyperlinks.

SKILL
8

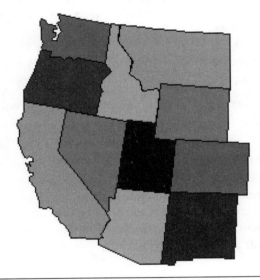

Widgets in the West
Select a state

Arizona
California
Colorado
Idaho
Montana
Nevada
New Mexico
Oregon
Utah
Washington
Wyoming

FIGURE 8.10: A geographic map can be a very practical way to implement an image map.

Defining an image map is quite simple:

1. Insert the image that serves as the image map.

2. Define a hotspot in the image for one of the hyperlinks.

3. Define the target of that hyperlink.

4. Define the other hotspots and hyperlink definitions for the rest of the image map.

We'll cover these steps in more detail in the next section, "Defining the Hotspots."

NOTE NOTE NOTE NOTE NOTE NOTE NOTE NOTE NOTE NOTE NOTE NOTE NOTE NOTE
When creating image maps in earlier versions of FrontPage, you could choose between server-side and client-side image maps. Now only client-side image maps are supported in FrontPage. These require no server interaction when a user clicks a hotspot and tend to be more reliable because the same image map will work correctly no matter which server is hosting the page. Most newer browsers support client-side image maps.

Defining the Hotspots

For this example, you can create an image map from any image in a page appropriate for the job at hand—large enough to contain the hotspots, but not so large that it takes a long time to download to a browser. The image map should also be meaningful to a user. The image we'll use here is the map that was shown in Figure 8.10. You can use any convenient image, perhaps one from the Clip Art Gallery.

Follow these steps to define the first hyperlink hotspot in this image, thereby making that image into an image map (with just one hyperlink so far). We'll start with a somewhat square state, such as Wyoming.

1. Select the image.

2. Click the Rectangular Hotspot button on the Picture toolbar so you can define a rectangular hotspot in the image.

3. Point to a corner of the state of Wyoming in the image. Notice that the pointer changes to a pencil.

4. Hold down the mouse button and drag toward the diagonally opposite corner of that state. As you drag, a rectangle expands over the image, defining the area of the hotspot.

5. When the rectangle surrounds the state, release the mouse button to open the Create Hyperlink dialog box, shown in Figure 8.11.

6. Define the target of the hyperlink just as you would for a normal hyperlink. For this example, you can either link to a file in your active web or just enter a nonexistent target. Click OK to create the link.

SKILL
8

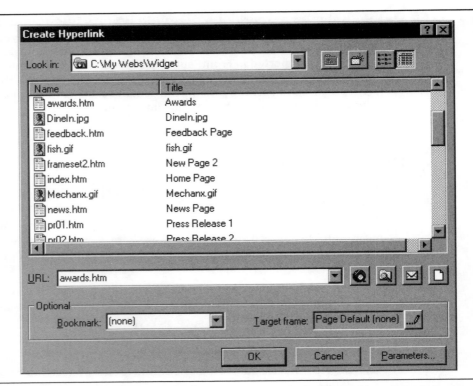

FIGURE 8.11:   Enter a target for the hotspot in the Create Hyperlink dialog box.

Let's define a second hyperlink in this image map for the state of Utah. This one is irregularly shaped, so we'll need to use the Polygonal Hotspot tool on the Picture toolbar. Select the image if it isn't still selected.

1. Click the Polygonal button on the Picture toolbar.

2. Click once (and release the mouse button) on the lower-left corner of the state of Utah in the image to begin the first line of the polygonal hotspot (this is simply a convenient beginning point).

3. Point to the lower-right corner of the state. A line extends from the first point to the mouse pointer. Click once to end this line and establish the first edge of the hotspot. Try not to overlap the rectangular hotspot you already created; otherwise there could be confusion when a user clicks in that area.

4. Continue from corner to corner, clicking each one to extend the edges of this hotspot.

5. When you reach the beginning point, double-click to end the definition of this hotspot, which will open the Create Hyperlink dialog box.

6. Define the target for this hotspot.

Now this image map has two hotspots. You can continue to create others, as needed, using the appropriate button on the Picture toolbar: Rectangular, Polygonal, or Circular. To create a circular hotspot, drag from the center of the circle outward.

Specifying a Default Hyperlink

In many image maps, there may be undefined regions that aren't covered by a hotspot. This presents a problem when a user clicks on the image, ostensibly on a hotspot, and then waits and waits for something to happen that never does.

To avoid this situation, you can define a default hyperlink for all areas of the image that aren't hotspots. This ensures that no matter where a user clicks on the image map, something happens. The default target for an image map might be a page that simply advises the user to return to the previous page and try again.

To define a default hyperlink for an image map, right-click the image and choose Picture Properties from the shortcut menu. In the General tab, enter the target for the Default Hyperlink in the Location field.

Viewing Hotspots

When you select an image map in FrontPage, each of its hotspots is outlined. When the image map is not selected, or when you are viewing it in a browser, you won't notice anything different about the image; the hotspot outlines are invisible. However, when you move your mouse pointer over a hotspot in an image map, the target of that link is displayed in the status line in FrontPage (and in most browsers, as well).

Complex graphics can obscure the hotspot outlines, making them difficult to see while you're editing the page. You can circumvent this problem by clicking the Highlight Hotspots button on the Picture toolbar. This hides the image completely while still outlining each of its hotspots, as shown in Figure 8.12, so you can get a good idea of where each lies in the image and check for areas of overlap. You can't move or resize a hotspot in this view, but you can change the target of its hyperlink definition.

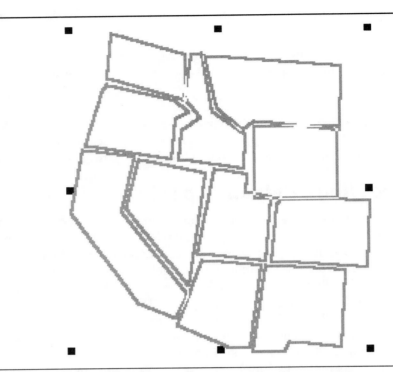

FIGURE 8.12: Highlighting hotspots allows you to check for areas of overlap.

Revising Hotspots

You change an image's hotspots in FrontPage. You can also delete a hotspot, change its size and shape, and redefine its hyperlink target. To make changes, first select the image. Then click the Select button on the Picture toolbar and click within the hotspot you want to change. You'll see selection handles appear around the hotspot's edges.

WARNING WARNING WARNING WARNING WARNING WARNING WARNING WARNING

Remember, selecting an image is much the same as selecting text. If, for example, you select an image and then type a single character, you replace the image with that character. So use caution when you are busily working on an image.

Once you've selected a hotspot, you can:

- Select the next hotspot by pressing Tab.

- Delete the selected hotspot and its hyperlink from the image by pressing Delete.

- Change the size of circles and rectangles or the shape of polygon hotspots by dragging any of their selection handles.

- Move the hotspot by dragging it (but not from a selection handle) or by selecting it and using the arrow keys on your keyboard.

- Change the target definition by right-clicking within the hotspot and choosing either the Picture Hotspot Properties or the Hyperlink command from the shortcut menu. This displays the Edit Hyperlink dialog box, which includes the same options as the Create Hyperlink dialog box you used to create the hotspot.

Are You Experienced?

Now you can...

- ☑ Insert images
- ☑ Set picture properties
- ☑ Make an interlaced image
- ☑ Create thumbnails
- ☑ Make an image transparent
- ☑ Create image maps and hotspots

SKILL
8

Getting Graphic with Image Composer

- ➔ **Using Microsoft Image Composer**
- ➔ **Creating sprites and compositions**
- ➔ **Applying effects**
- ➔ **Saving compositions and sprites**
- ➔ **Saving for the Web**
- ➔ **Creating buttons**
- ➔ **Converting images to JPEGs and GIFs**

One of the exciting Web accessories that comes with the stand-alone version of FrontPage is Microsoft Image Composer. It offers you hundreds of image-editing tools and effects that are designed for creating Web-ready images. Working with Image Composer is challenging, and there's plenty of raw material to practice with. FrontPage includes hundreds of photographic and clip art images for your composing pleasure.

Creating Web Images

Images play a big role in the life of a Web site. The images you incorporate into a page convey information, add snap and pizzazz, serve as hyperlinks, act as image maps for multiple hyperlinks, and generally just make the site a less boring place to visit. Images draw attention to surrounding text, so viewers who only intended to look at the pictures often find themselves reading nearby content. Images also accentuate text by breaking up long text entries, making them easier for users to read.

Image Composer is just what its name implies: not an image catalog or collection, but a powerful tool you can use to create fresh new images for your webs. Those images are standard graphic files that you can incorporate into *any* web, not just those you create in FrontPage. Microsoft Image Composer is no small addition to the FrontPage package. It's a powerful image-editing program that can easily stand on its own.

NOTE NOTE NOTE NOTE NOTE NOTE NOTE NOTE NOTE NOTE NOTE NOTE NOTE NOTE NOTE

Image Composer is a wonderful tool with a lot of features, but it also has a big appetite for your computer's processing power and RAM. Its official minimum hardware requirements are a 486 processor with 16MB of RAM and a video card that can display at least 256 colors, but you'll want a lot more processing power and at least twice that amount of memory to work at a decent pace.

Starting Image Composer

Start Microsoft Image Composer in any of the usual ways: choose it from the Windows Start menu or select its desktop icon. Double-click an image file in FrontPage or any other program to open that image in Image Composer.

If double-clicking an image file doesn't open the image, that means the image's file format isn't associated with Image Composer. JPEGs and GIFs are automatically associated with Image Composer, so an easy way to open the image is to convert it to a JPEG or GIF. Just save the page that contains the image, and the FrontPage saves the image in one of the two formats.

If the file type is one you use frequently, you may prefer to associate the image file type with Image Composer. That way, you can place and edit images without saving or converting them. For more information on associating file types in Frontpage, see Skill 5.

In Image Composer, you create customized works of art by combining hand-drawn work, text, scanned images, or the hundreds of sample photographs and drawings that come with Image Composer. Although many image-related programs let you combine various pieces, you'll see this process emphasized in Image Composer—both in the way the program is designed and in the way you build your images.

NOTE NOTE NOTE NOTE NOTE NOTE NOTE NOTE NOTE NOTE NOTE NOTE NOTE NOTE NOTE

Microsoft produces two other image editors: Microsoft Picture It! and Microsoft Photo Editor. Although all three programs are image editors, they're used for very different purposes. Image Composer is used to create images, the Photo Editor is used to retouch and enhance existing images, and Picture It! includes image capture utilities and image enhancement tools.

An image you create in Image Composer is called a *composition*. The basic components of every composition are *sprites*. For example, the composition in Figure 9.1 includes three sprites: a clip art image inserted from the Clip Art Gallery, an image copied from another program that serves as the image background, and text entered in Image Composer. A composition may include only a single sprite that you import and manipulate with Image Composer's tools.

FIGURE 9.1: You use Image Composer to combine sprites and create compositions.

Image Composer shares the look and feel of the programs in both Microsoft FrontPage and Microsoft Office (see Figure 9.2). Its menus, toolbars, and file-operation dialog boxes look quite familiar, so you won't have any problem finding your way around the program.

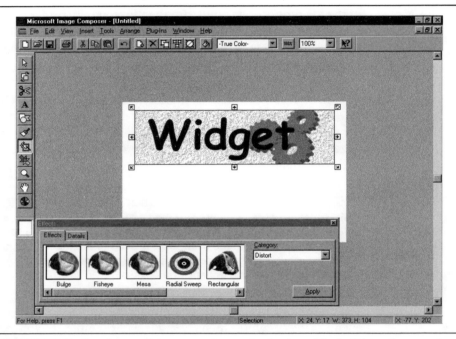

FIGURE 9.2:   Image Composer shares the look and feel of FrontPage and other Office programs.

You'll recognize the menus and toolbar at the top of the Image Composer's window, and there's a status bar at the bottom that displays pertinent information about your composition and the program. On the left side of the screen is another toolbar called the *toolbox*; each of its buttons opens a set of image-editing tools displayed in the tool palette near the bottom of the window. In Figure 9.2, the Effects tool palette is displayed. You can also open tool palettes from the Tools menu. The color that's used the next time you apply color to a sprite is displayed in the Color Swatch beneath the toolbox.

The white area beneath the toolbar and to the right of the toolbox is the composition space, where you create your composition. Think of it as a virtual page in

Image Composer that serves as the background for your image. You can change its size and color to go with the image you're creating (the default is white). Because its size is in pixels, you can specify the exact size of the images you create.

The gray area around the composition space is the workspace. Use it as a staging area where you can place sprites you need in the image or windows that display other views of your image. The size of the workspace is unlimited, so you'll never run out of room. If you scrolled the window to some far-off realm of the workspace, you can use the View ➤ Center on Composition Space (or press Home) to bring the composition space back into view.

Setting Up Your Work Area

When you save your image, the items in the workspace and composition space are saved (more on this later). Drag one of the composition guides that set the boundaries for the composition space to change its size. You can do this any time, even after you've added sprites to your composition. For more precision, open the Composition Setup dialog box (File ➤ Composition Setup):

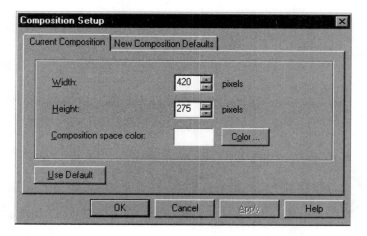

This dialog box has two tabs that are nearly identical. Both allow you to enter, in pixels, the height and width of the composition space. In the Current Composition page, you can click the Use Default button to transfer the default settings to the current composition. If you resize the composition space, you can click the Use Current button in the New Composition Defaults tab to change the default to reflect the new height and width. In both tabs, you can click the Color button to open the Color Picker and set the composition space's current or default background color.

Picking Colors for Your Web

Color is one of the most important considerations when you're creating images for display on the Web. In Image Composer, any color you use comes from a palette of colors. A palette can include millions of colors or only a few. Although your first impulse might be to plumb the depths of your artistic talent by using the largest palette possible, there are two important reasons to do exactly the opposite:

- The more colors an image contains, the larger its file becomes and the longer it takes to load.

- No matter how many colors you include in an image, the colors actually displayed in a browser are dependent on the capabilities of the browser and the computer on which it is running.

Using True Color

In the world of computers and in Image Composer, the term "true color" refers to a palette of a little more than 16 million colors. It is called 24-bit color, because that is how much computer memory is required to display one pixel in any of the 16 million colors. All of your work in Image Composer is saved with 24-bit color, so you'll never lose any colors when you save your work in Image Composer format.

To display all the colors in a true-color image, your computer's video adapter and monitor must be able to handle 24-bit color, and Windows must be set up to take advantage of these capabilities. When you display a true color image on an older computer that can't handle true color, the computer will simply approximate the true color by choosing a color from the available colors.

NOTE NOTE NOTE NOTE NOTE NOTE NOTE NOTE NOTE NOTE NOTE NOTE NOTE NOTE NOTE

To specify how many colors to display in Windows, choose Start ➣ Settings ➣ Control Panel, and double-click the Display icon (you can instead right-click the Desktop and choose Properties). You'll find a list of available color palettes on the Settings tab in the Display Properties dialog box.

You can choose a color or a color palette in Image Composer from the Composition Setup dialog box or by clicking the Color Swatch just below the toolbox to open the Color Picker dialog box. Select the True Color tab to pick a color from a palette of 16 million-plus colors (see Figure 9.3). Select a color from the palette by clicking the color, or by entering the exact RGB values in the fields for the Red,

Green, and Blue sliders. If you opened the Color Picker from the Composition Setup dialog box, you can click OK to make the color you chose the current color for the composition space.

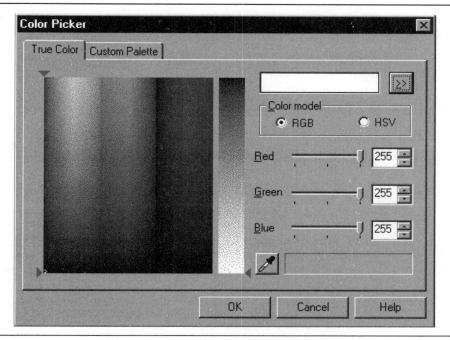

FIGURE 9.3: Use the Color Picker to choose a true color for the composition area.

Using Color Palettes

Unless you are working on an intranet and know most visitors to your site have fast connections and computers that can handle true color images, you should probably limit the images you create to 256 colors, also called *8-bit color*. There are two ways to do this:

- When you save a composition, you can convert the image into a 256-color image (more on this later). Remember that a GIF file is limited to 256 colors, so GIFs automatically use the 8-bit color palettes; only JPEGs can handle true color.

SKILL

9

- When you create an image, only choose colors from a 256-color palette. This ensures the colors you see on your screen are pretty much like the ones a browser displays.

If you choose the Custom Palette tab in the Color Picker dialog box, you can choose a 256-color palette from the Color Palette drop-down list (see Figure 9.4). Image Composer comes with several palettes; Web (Solid) and Web (Dithered) are appropriate for color images in your FrontPage webs, or choose Gray Ramp for grayscale images. If you're converting a true color image, the dithered and ramped palettes create a smoother image than the solid palettes. Once you pick a new palette, it's displayed when you click the Color Swatch.

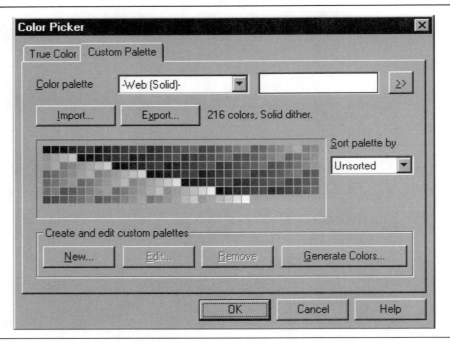

FIGURE 9.4: The Custom Palette tab in the Color Picker lets you choose a color from a 256-color palette, or select a custom palette.

Even if your computer has true color capabilities, you can view a true color composition in 8-bit color by selecting one of the custom palettes from the Color Format drop-down list on the toolbar. This allows you to see how the image looks when viewed as a 256-color image on your web.

The difference between palettes of 16 million and 256 colors isn't as large as it sounds. The human eye cannot even distinguish between several adjacent colors in the true-color palette. While richly colored photographs clearly lose quality when displayed in 256 colors, many true color images degrade only slightly. You can experiment by switching between true color and 256 colors in Image Composer to see the difference.

However, the trade-off in time is easily quantifiable. Modem transmission speeds are measured in bps (bits per second). If it takes 24 bits to describe one pixel of true color, and 8 bits to describe one pixel created from a 256-color palette, then it takes three times as long to download one true-color pixel as it does to download one 256-color pixel. Users may not notice the difference in color quality, but they always notice the difference in download time.

Working with Sprites

There are two ways to create a sprite in Image Composer: You can import an existing file or image, or create a sprite from scratch using the Image Composer tools.

Importing Sprites

The default file format for Image Composer files is MIC. The program comes with a lot of sprite files that are separated into categories. With a typical installation, they're left on the CD. (You can copy them to your hard drive during a custom installation, but they occupy about 190MB.) Image Composer has a sprite catalog with thumbnails of each of the images for easy browsing and selection.

Finding an Image in the Sprite Catalog

To see the thumbnail images of the available sprites, choose Help ➣ Sample Sprites Catalog to open the Sample Sprites Catalog help file. To browse the catalog, begin by selecting Sample Sprites ➣ Photos or Sample Sprites ➣ Web on the Contents page. Double-click any catalog category to see the thumbnails.

SKILL
9

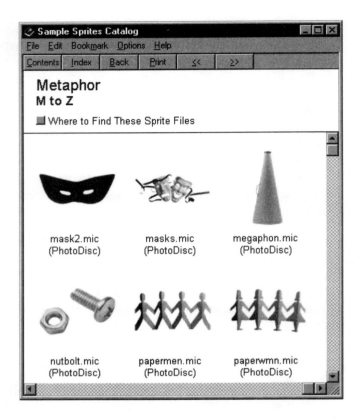

To look for a specific image (for example, an image that includes trees), move to the Index page. Enter text in the search box at the top of the page, then click the Display button.

When you've found a sprite you want to place in your composition, click the Where to Find These Sprite Files button at the top of the page. Help gives you the exact location of the file, where, as you can see in the next graphic, [Client] is the drive that contains the CD. Remember the location and file name when you insert this image into Image Composer.

Importing an Image

When you identify the name and location of the sprite or image you want to use, you can import it into Image Composer, which can handle most of the common file formats: JPEG, GIF, TIFF, Targa, and others. If you're importing a sprite from Image Composer samples, you need to insert your FrontPage CD into your CD-ROM drive.

Choose Insert ➤ From File or click the Insert Image File button on the toolbar to open the Inserts an Image File dialog box. Locate the folder where the file is located. Select the file, then click OK to insert it in the upper left corner of the workspace.

TIP TIP TIP TIP TIP TIP TIP TIP TIP TIP TIP TIP TIP TIP TIP TIP TIP TIP TIP TIP TIP TIP TIP

If you're viewing or inserting several images, you can use the Windows Explorer to find them and drag them into Image Composer.

Sizing and Moving Sprites

When a sprite is selected, it has eight handles. Seven of the handles have arrows and are used for sizing the sprite. Grab one of the handles, and drag it to resize the image. Hold the Shift key while dragging to maintain the aspect ratio of the image. The eighth handle in the upper right corner of the image is a rotation handle. Dragging the rotation handle rotates the image around its centerpoint. To size a sprite precisely (so, for example, it's the same size as the composition space), choose Tools ➤ Arrange, or click the Arrange button on the toolbox to display the Arrange tool palette, shown in Figure 9.5.

SKILL
9

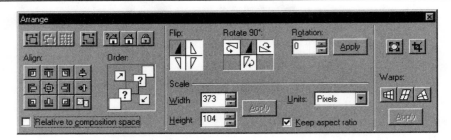

FIGURE 9.5: Use the Arrange tool palette to size and move the selected sprite.

Set the size of the sprite in pixels in the Width and Height controls. You may
need to disable the Keep Aspect Ratio check box if you're setting both the width
and the height of this sprite, thereby changing its width-to-height aspect ratio.
Click the Apply button to apply the width and height settings.

Use the Alignment tools at the left end of the palette to align the sprite in the
composition space. Enable the Relative to Composition Space check box, then use
the 12 alignment buttons to align the sprite. But first, check out the three buttons
above the Order control.

 The first button, Set Home Position, "memorizes" the sprite's current location as
its home position; the second button, Return to Home Position, returns the sprite
to its defined home position. This means you can experiment a bit, knowing that
you can precisely reposition the sprite if you don't like its new location.

 When you think the sprite is where it belongs, lock it in place with the Lock/
Unlock Position button so you can't accidentally move it. If you change your mind
and want to relocate the sprite, click the Lock/Unlock Position button again.

You don't have to use the Arrange tool palette to move a sprite; simply drag a
selected sprite to a new location. To move a sprite a small distance, use the arrow
keys on the keyboard. The default settings move the sprite one pixel in the direc-
tion you press. Hold Ctrl and use the arrow keys to move larger distances.

Creating Sprites

While Image Composer has a shapes palette and some basic drawing tools, it's
not a paint program. Many of the sprites you create are text sprites, because you
can create amazing text effects with Image Composer. To create a text sprite,
choose Tools ➤ Text, or click the Text button in the toolbox (on the left side of the
window). This opens the Text tool palette, shown in Figure 9.6.

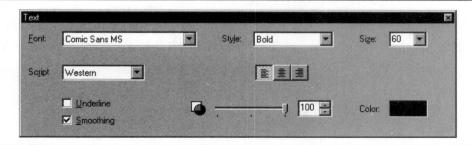

FIGURE 9.6: Use the Text tool palette to create text sprites.

Choose a font, size, and other text attributes using the controls in the palette. The slider bar is used to set opacity: how solid (opaque) or transparent the text is. 100 percent is solid. Click the Color swatch within the Text tool palette to open the Color Picker and select a color for the text.

When all the palette options are set, move the mouse pointer into the workspace, where it changes to a text tool. Hold the mouse button and drag a rectangular text box. When you release the button, the text box opens. You can instead simply click to create a default-sized text box. Type the text for your sprite, make any further adjustments in the Text tool palette, then click outside the text box to create the sprite, as shown in Figure 9.7.

FIGURE 9.7: Text sprites allow you to quickly create distinctive project or department logos.

Adding an Effect to a Sprite

Now let's put some curves into the text sprite you've just created. Make sure the sprite is selected, and click the Effects button to open the Effects tool palette.

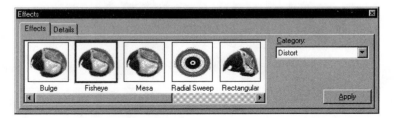

Choose a type of effect from the Category drop-down list. Browse the thumbnail samples of the post-effect macaw to see what the effect does to the selected sprite. When you've selected the effect you wish to use, click the Details tab and see if you want to change any of the optional settings for the effect. Detail options depend on the effect you select; for example, the Distort Fisheye effect has a single Spread Amount option, while Paint effects have three to five options. When you've set any details you desire, click the Apply button to apply the effect to the sprite.

NOTE NOTE NOTE NOTE NOTE NOTE NOTE NOTE NOTE NOTE NOTE NOTE NOTE NOTE NOTE
You only get one Undo operation in Image Composer. Don't adjust anything until you double-check the effect you just applied, in case you want to undo the effect.

Figure 9.8 shows the text sprite in Figure 9.7 with effects from three different categories: Fisheye (Distort), Gray Noise (Patterns), and Edge Only (Outlines). For descriptions of effects, see the "Effects Overview" in Image Composer Help.

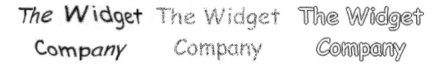

FIGURE 9.8: Apply Effects to change the appearance of a sprite.

Selecting and Arranging Sprites

There are a number of ways to select sprites:

- Click a sprite to select it.

- To move from one sprite to the next, press the Tab key.

- To select multiple sprites, select one, then hold Ctrl and select others, or use the selection tool and drag a box around the sprites you wish to select.

- To select all the sprites in the workspace, choose Edit ➤ Select All, or click the Select All button on the toolbar.

- To copy the selected sprites, click the Duplicate button on the toolbar or choose Edit ➤ Duplicate from the menu. The copy is placed on top of the existing sprite. Use the mouse to drag it to its new location.

All the sprites in Image Composer are arranged in a stack, where each sprite is assigned a position relative to the other sprites. For example, when you insert or create a new sprite, it goes to the top of the stack. When you move that sprite, it overlaps any other sprites it encounters.

You can change a sprite's order in the stack by right-clicking the sprite and choosing one of the stack-related commands. For example, if another sprite overlaps the current one, choose Bring Forward from the shortcut menu. This places the current sprite one step higher in the stack. You can repeat the command until it is high enough in the stack to overlap the other sprite or choose Bring to Front to bring the selected sprite to the very front of the stack. If you're going to be arranging a number of sprites, you might prefer to open the Arrange tool palette and use the Order control to restack the sprites.

Saving the Workspace or Composition Space

When you use the File ➤ Save command in Image Composer or click the Save button on the toolbar, you save the entire workspace, including the composition space. You can close Image Composer, open the file later, and pick up right where you left off. The file is saved as an Image Composer file, with an MIC file extension. You can't insert Image Composer files in web pages.

When you're ready to use your image in a FrontPage web (or for any other purpose), you must save the composition in an image format like GIF or

SKILL
9

JPEG. Note that when saving in an image format, you can save the entire contents of the composition space, or selected sprites (either within the workspace or composition space). Image Composer uses a Save for the Web Wizard to help you save your composition as an image. Use the Next and Back buttons to move through the wizard's steps. Once you're familiar with the process, you can instead use the File ≻ Save Selection As command to save one or more selected sprites to the format of your choice.

Choose File ≻ Save for the Web to open the wizard. In the first step, indicate whether you want to save selected sprites or the entire composition. Selected sprites don't have to be in the composition space; you can select and save sprites in the workspace. In the second step, shown in Figure 9.9, indicate whether or not the resulting image should be transparent.

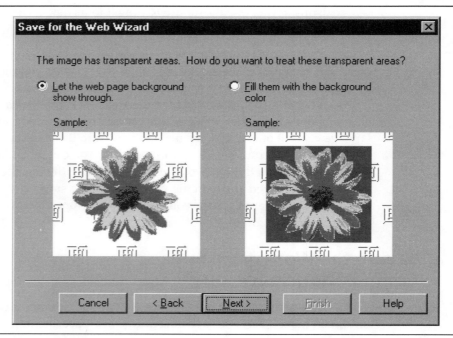

FIGURE 9.9: The Save for the Web Wizard makes it easy to create GIFs and JPEGs for use on your web pages.

In the third step, specify the background color of the page on which you intend to place the image. If you're not sure, leave the default, Tiled Background setting. In the last step, click Save to open a Save dialog box.

Select a file location, then enter a filename. You can change the file type, color format, and transparency if you want. However, the settings in the dialog box are based on the choices you just made in the wizard. If, for example, you make the image transparent, the dialog box displays only options relevant to GIFs and the transparent color is shown in the Transparent Color swatch. Click Save to save the file based on the settings you entered.

When you save to any file format other than MIC, all the sprites are saved as a single image. This is called *flattening* the composition. When you save the composition space instead of the selected sprites option in the Save for the Web wizard, sprites that hang over the composition guides are truncated, and sprites in the workspace are totally ignored.

Saving the workspace and saving sprites or compositions are unrelated operations. You can save a sprite or composition as a GIF, TIFF, JPEG, or other standard format, then save the workspace as a MIC. If you close Image Composer without saving the composition, you're prompted to save the Untitled composition, even if you've saved selected sprites from the workspace.

Adding Shapes to a Composition

Image Composer includes a small set of tools you can use to draw ovals, rectangles, arcs, and polygons. You can use shapes as borders for compositions, but you can also fill shape sprites with textures that you want to apply to other sprites (see the next section).

 Click the Shapes button or choose Tools ➤ Shapes to open the Shapes tool palette, shown in Figure 9.10. Click a shape button in the left end of the palette, set the options for Edge and Opacity, then drag in the workspace to layout the shape.

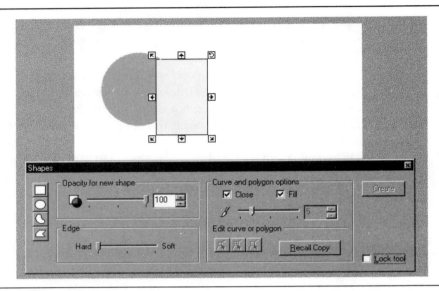

FIGURE 9.10: Use the Shapes tool palette to add regular and irregular shape sprites to your composition.

Click the Create button or select a different shape tool to create the shape. The shape is filled with the color in the color swatch. If you need to create several shapes, you can enable the Lock Tool check box to leave the selected shape tool turned on until you click to turn it off.

After you create a shape, try applying some of the effects from the Effects tool palette. To apply solid colors, click the Color Swatch and select the new color for the sprite. Select the sprite, then click the Color Fill button on the toolbar to fill the selected sprite with the color in the Color Swatch.

Transferring Textures between Sprites

One of the many fun and interesting features in Image Composer is its ability to transfer the texture from one sprite to another. In Figure 9.11, for example, the texture from the leaves sprite has been transferred to a text sprite. There are five different texture attributes you can transfer from one sprite to another:

- Color
- Opacity/transparency (0 percent is transparent; 100 percent is opaque)

- Shape

- Saturation (the fullness of the color)

- Intensity (how "pure" the color is)

FIGURE 9.11: You can transfer textures between sprites to create interesting images.

First, move the source sprite (which provides the texture) and destination sprite (the texture's recipient) so they overlap. Then, select both sprites. The sprite you overlap on the other serves as the source. If it's not clear which sprite is the source, it's easy to check: The destination sprite has hollow handles, while the handles on the source sprite are solid. If the source and destination are reversed, just press the Tab key to swap them.

Click the Texture Transfer button on the toolbox and choose a transfer technique from the thumbnails in the Texture Transfer tools palette. The easiest way to learn about texture transfers is to apply, then undo each of the transfers in turn to see how the transfer applies to real sprites. To really understand the various Map transfers, use a source or destination sprite that contains a gradient. In Figure 9.11, the Transfer Shape tool was used to transfer the leaves to the text.

SKILL
9

Table 9.1 describes each of the Texture Transfers.

TABLE 9.1: Texture Transfers

Texture Transfer	Description
Glue	Replaces the pixels in the destination sprite with opaque pixels in the source sprite, but only in the area where the two sprites overlap; "glues" the two sprites together.
Map Color	Copies the color values of the source sprite to the overlapping opaque pixels of the destination sprite, without changing the destination sprite's intensity.
Map Intensity	Copies the intensity values of the source sprite to the destination sprite without changing the destination sprite's colors.
Map Saturation	Uses the intensity of the source sprite to change the saturation of the overlapping area of the destination sprite. Saturation works exactly opposite of what you might expect: Where the source sprite is white, the destination sprite pixels becomes more intense.
Map Transparency	Uses the intensity of the source sprite to change the transparency of the destination sprite in the overlap area. Where the color is strongest in the source sprite, the pixels are made more transparent in the destination sprite.
Snip	Deletes opaque pixels from the destination sprite wherever there's an overlapping opaque pixel in the source sprite; use Snip to make a silhouette of the source pixel.
Tile	Copies the source sprite's image onto the destination sprite in a tiled manner; this texture transfer does not require the sprites to overlap, as the entire source sprite image is repeated and transferred to the entire destination sprite.
Transfer Full	Replaces only the opaque pixels of the destination sprite with the pixels, opaque and transparent, of the source sprite in the overlap area.
Transfer Shape	Replaces only the opaque pixels of the destination sprite with the opaque pixels in the source sprite in the area of overlap; use Transfer Shape to embed a portion of one sprite in another.

Optional settings for each transfer are at the right end of the Texture Transfer tools palette. After you've selected a transfer and set the options, click Apply to transfer the texture from the source sprite to the destination sprite. If you're pleased with the results, click in the workspace, then select just one of the sprites and drag it to separate them. Don't forget: Undo is an option.

Each Texture Transfer has only one source sprite, but most of the transfers can be made to multiple destination sprites in one operation.

Creating Buttons

When you consider the number of available effects and transfers you can use in Image Composer, it's easy to imagine scores of Web developers, chained to desks in dimly lit basements, painstakingly creating, warping, and snipping sprites to create the swarms of custom buttons that appear on commercial Web sites. Image Composer includes a Button Wizard to help with the process. The buttons in Figure 9.12 were created using the wizard.

FIGURE 9.12: The Button Wizard helps you create custom buttons for your web pages.

SKILL
9

To create a button, choose Insert ➤ Button to open the Button Wizard. In the first step, shown in Figure 9.13, select a button style from the list. In the second step, indicate how many buttons you'd like to create using the selected style.

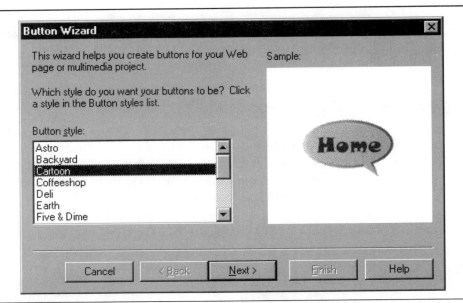

FIGURE 9.13: In the first step of the wizard, choose a button style.

In the third step, enter text for the first button. You can apply different images to each button you create. Note, however, that you can't add an MIC file to a button because MICs aren't images. When you click Next, the text for the first button is still in the text box, but the label above the text box indicates that this is the second button. Enter the text for each button, then click Next, until all buttons are entered.

In the fourth step of the Button Wizard, decide whether you want all the buttons to be the same size, or have Image Composer size each button according to its contents, as shown in Figure 9.14. (You can enter new dimensions for the buttons later, but you can't resize them by dragging.) If you choose the Same Size for All Buttons option, click the Size Preview button to find out how large the same size actually is. You can change the size using the spin box controls; you can't make the button smaller than the Minimum to Fit sizes. Click Next and then Finish to create the buttons. Image Composer dumps the buttons in a stack in the upper left corner of the screen. You can then drag them into the composition, or select and save each as a separate image.

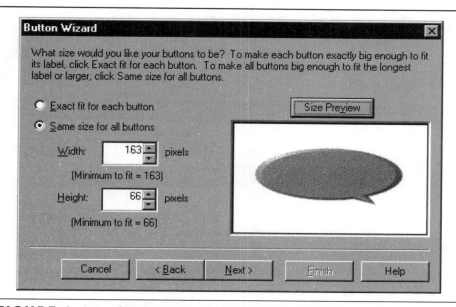

FIGURE 9.14: Choose buttons sized to fit their text, or a consistent size for all the buttons you're creating.

The Button Wizard offers limited choices: a handful of button shapes, each with a single texture. After you've created a button, however, you can edit it as you would any other sprite, such as by choosing different shapes, text attributes, and textures. To change an existing button, simply right-click it and choose Edit Button from the shortcut menu to open the Button Editor.

You can save individual buttons, or groups of buttons, but it's easiest to simply save the workspace as a MIC file. When you want to place a button in your web, copy it in Image Composer, then paste it in into FrontPage.

Using Image Composer to Convert Files

Earlier in this Skill, you learned how to use the Save for the Web Wizard with a composition or sprite. The wizard really shines, however, when you use it to convert existing images to JPEGs or GIFs for use in your web. To convert an image, open the image file directly, rather than inserting it on a page. Then, choose

File ≻ Save for the Web to launch the wizard. A progress meter appears to let you know that the wizard is building previews:

When the previews are completed, you'll find that they were worth the wait. Image Composer creates previews to show you how the file looks when saved as a GIF or JPEG with various options (see Figure 9.15). Each preview's caption includes the file format, file size, and estimated download time based on the modem speed selected in the Connection Speed drop-down list. If you change the connection speed, Image Composer recalculates the download times for each preview. After you select a preview, click the Next button to continue through the wizard and save the image file.

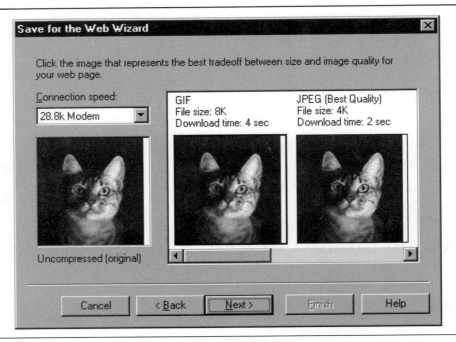

FIGURE 9.15: The Save for the Web Wizard previews allow you to choose an appropriate image format.

Of course there's a trade-off between image quality and download time, but the Save for the Web Wizard lets you see that trade-off and make high-quality decisions about the image formats you want to use in your Web site.

Are You Experienced?

Now you can...

- ☑ Import images and sprites
- ☑ Create sprites and compositions with Image Composer
- ☑ Apply effects to sprites
- ☑ Save compositions, sprites, and the workspace
- ☑ Transfer textures
- ☑ Create and edit buttons
- ☑ Convert images to JPEGs and GIFs

SKILL
9

Creating a Consistent Look for Your Web

- → **Creating a web using wizards and templates**
- → **Creating pages using templates**
- → **Applying a theme to a web or a page**
- → **Creating and linking style sheets**
- → **Copying from existing webs and web pages**

As Web sites become more sophisticated and Web design evolves into an art form all its own, Web creators face more pressure to create sites that meet acceptable standards of design. Simply throwing something together to establish a Web presence is no longer considered good business. Today, a Web site must look professional to attract repeat visitors. Although it never hurts to have a computer graphics design artist in the family, you can create a professional-looking Web site by yourself as long as you follow some simple design rules and take advantage of the built-in tools that come with FrontPage.

In this Skill, you learn how to create webs using the FrontPage wizards and templates, apply design style themes to the pages of the web, explore Cascading Style Sheets (one of the most powerful new HTML enhancements), and import pages from existing webs.

Creating a Web Using Wizards and Templates

Now that you know the fundamentals of creating a web and working with web pages, you'll find that FrontPage's templates and wizards make creating a web as easy as can be. Wizards guide you through the process of setting up the structure for the web and adding some basic content before the web is ever created. Templates are a little more modest in their approach—they still provide you with a basic structure, but require you to insert all your own content after the web is created.

You already know how to create a new one page web. The only difference is that this time, you'll choose one of the wizards or more complicated templates. In FrontPage, choose File ➢ New ➢ Web to display the New dialog box (shown in Figure 10.1).

NOTE NOTE NOTE NOTE NOTE NOTE NOTE NOTE NOTE NOTE NOTE NOTE NOTE NOTE NOTE

When you have a web open in FrontPage, the New FrontPage Web dialog box includes an Add to the Current Web option. If you select the option, all the pages associated with the new web are imported into the current web. If an incoming file has the same name as an existing file, such as `index.htm`**, you're asked to choose which one you want to keep.**

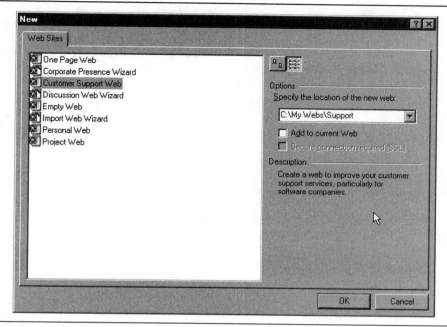

FIGURE 10.1: You can choose a wizard or a template in the New dialog box.

The choices in the New dialog box include three wizards:

> **Corporate Presence Wizard**   Helps you design a web that can be the basis for your company's debut on the Web
>
> **Discussion Web Wizard**   Helps you design a web that allows visitors to leave messages or respond to messages around an identified general topic, and organizes the messages in related threads
>
> **Import Web Wizard**   Helps you import an existing web and make it a FrontPage web, as discussed later in "Importing an Existing Web into FrontPage"

A *thread* is a group of messages that spawns from a message from someone on a particular topic. When someone else responds to that first message with another message, the thread begins. Visitors can read the first message and all of the subsequent responses, then add their own two cents (even though the responses may no longer have any relevance to the initially identified topic).

When you choose a wizard to help you create a new FrontPage web, the wizard asks you a series of questions about the content of the new Web site. For example, it may ask you about the type of pages you want in the web, the contents of the home page, and the contents of a feedback form page. It then builds the pages accordingly.

Each FrontPage web template contains a set of pages that can serve as the basis for the web you build (you'll know a new web is based on a template if its name doesn't end with "wizard"). For example, a new web based on the Project Web template, seen in Figure 10.2, can help you and other members of a team oversee a specific project.

- The Members page lets you keep track of who's involved in the project and includes a place for a picture of each member.

- The Schedule page lets you keep track of the project's schedule.

- The Status page offers you a place to create links to monthly, quarterly, and annual status reports for the project.

- The Archive page is a storehouse of links to related resources that may reside outside of the web.

- The Search page lets you search all of the pages in the web for text you specify.

- The Discussions page provides a central place to link to discussion groups in the web.

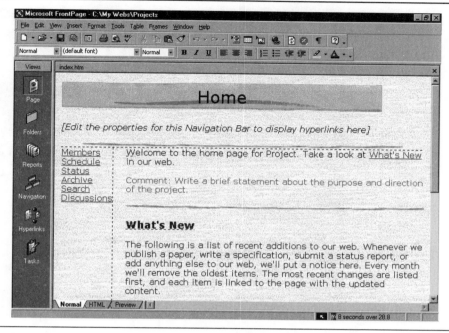

FIGURE 10.2: You can use the Project Web template as the basis for tracking work on a team project.

The Project Web contains a home page that includes an overview of the web, a What's New section, and an e-mail hyperlink for comments and questions about the web. All pages include shared borders and navigation bars.

Besides the Project Web (and the One Page Web, which you worked with in Skill 2), here's a quick rundown of the other templates:

> **Customer Support Web**   Creates a web that gives your customers a place to go for information or help with your products, particularly if those products happen to be software (see Figure 10.3)
>
> **Empty Web**   Contains all the necessary folders for a new FrontPage web, but contains no pages or other resources
>
> **Personal Web**   Creates a web you can use to provide personal information for business or personal use

SKILL
10

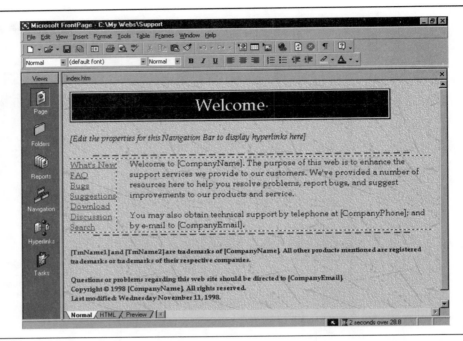

FIGURE 10.3: The Customer Support Web includes pages to provide technical assistance and support to users of a company's products.

Getting to Know Your New Web

When you create a web with a wizard or a template, it's important to explore the web in each of the views in FrontPage. The Navigation view, Hyperlinks view, and Folders view will give you an idea of the web's structure. After you are familiar with the files that make up the new web, but before you make any changes, it's a good idea to view the web in your Web browser. Then you can click all the internal hyperlinks and see if you understand how a visitor would use the web.

Sometimes the templates and wizards contain advanced elements, such as form fields (see Skill 12) and FrontPage components (see Skill 11), that may be a trifle disconcerting at first. Once you've seen these elements in operation from a browser, it's much easier to understand their purpose. Then you can decide if you want to include them before you spend time figuring out how to make them work.

Once you understand how the web works, return to FrontPage and follow the instructions in the various text and comments sections in each page to add your content. The comments are actually FrontPage components themselves, which you'll learn more about in Skill 11. In the meantime, click a comment to select it—the pointer changes to a small hand, as seen here. When you begin typing, the comment is deleted.

Comment: The picture on this page will be supplied by Tony.

When you start a new FrontPage web from a template, you can revise any of the pages, add new pages, or remove pages from the site. The template simply serves as a helpful and convenient way to get started.

You can even combine templates and wizards to add additional functionality to the web you are developing. For example, perhaps you're creating a Corporate Presence web for your company, and want to have a place for your customers to discuss topics related to your products. You can add the Discussion web to the Corporate Presence web. Just run the Corporate Presence Wizard first, and when you create the Discussion web, click the Add to Current Web check box at the bottom of the New dialog box.

Once the new pages are part of the open web, you just have to drag them into the web structure in Navigation view to create hyperlinks between the navigation bars in the appropriate pages in the webs (see Skill 5, *Managing Webs in FrontPage*).

Adding Pages Using Templates

In addition to the wizards and templates that create entire webs, you can also make use of a variety of additional templates and wizards designed to create individual pages. The majority of these templates, shown in Figure 10.4, include tables that provide a well-designed structure for the page, including suggestions for the placement of headings and graphics. All you have to do is enter your content—the design work is taken care of for you. To create a page based on a template, choose File ➤ New ➤ Page to open the New dialog box.

**SKILL
10**

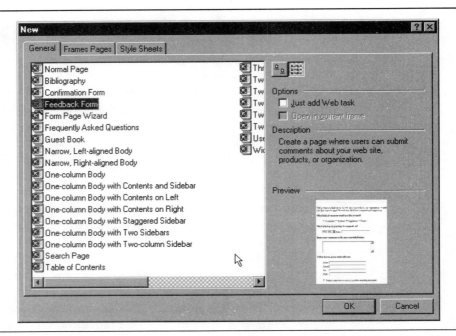

FIGURE 10.4: Creating attractive pages is a snap with the predesigned templates available in FrontPage.

NOTE NOTE NOTE NOTE NOTE NOTE NOTE NOTE NOTE NOTE NOTE NOTE NOTE NOTE NOTE

Clicking the New Page button on the toolbar creates a default new page using the Normal Page template. You must choose File ➢ New ➢ Page to create a page based on another template.

There are four different types of pages listed in Figure 10.4:

> **Structural layout**   Pages such as One-column Body and Narrow, Left-Aligned Body, that contain predesigned tables to provide a standardized structure for a page

> **Structured content**   Pages, such as Bibliography and Frequently Asked Questions, that provide structure and suggestions for presenting specific kinds of information

Forms   Forms, such as Feedback and Guest Book, that contain structural layout and FrontPage components that process input from visitors to the site (see Skill 12 for more about forms)

Frames   Structures to display multiple pages on one screen (see Skill 13 to learn about working with frames)

Select each template to see a description and a preview of the template. Placing the template into one of the categories listed above helps you decide which page best suits your purpose. When you find a template you want to use, click OK or select the Just Add Web Task check box to create the page and put it on your Task list to modify later. Adding a task is helpful when you're building the skeleton of your web and want to create multiple pages at once.

Figure 10.5 shows a newly created one-column body with a contents and sidebar page. Notice the instructions on the page showing where your headings, titles, and text go. To use the page, select the existing text and type over it. To replace a graphic, select it and insert the new graphic in its place. Once you insert your own content, the page is complete.

To create several matching pages, just add new pages using the same template.

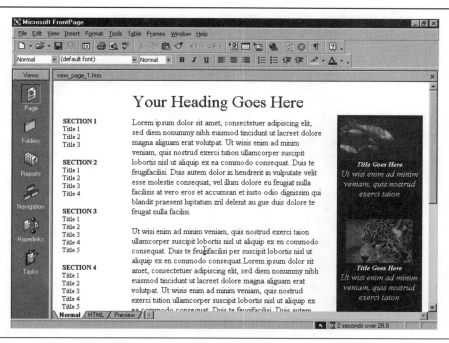

FIGURE 10.5: Insert your content into this predesigned structure to complete the page.

The page depicted in Figure 10.6, based on the Frequently Asked Questions template, not only provides you with the structural layout but suggests what the content of the page should include. This page includes a comment at the top describing how to use the page, with general instructions for creating additional questions. It's up to you, however, to figure out how to add the additional sections, create a bookmark for the new question, and create a hyperlink to the question in the Table of Contents.

> **NOTE NOTE NOTE NOTE NOTE NOTE NOTE NOTE NOTE NOTE NOTE NOTE NOTE NOTE NOTE**
>
> **The easiest way to create additional sections in the Frequently Asked Questions page is to copy one of the sections, including the bottom horizontal line, then move the insertion point to the beginning of Author Information and paste the new section. This creates the Back to Top hyperlink for you, but you still have to enter the new question and answer and create the hyperlink to the new question in the Table of Contents.**

Just as with the web templates, it's helpful to view the template pages in a browser to see how they look and function before modifying them with your own content.

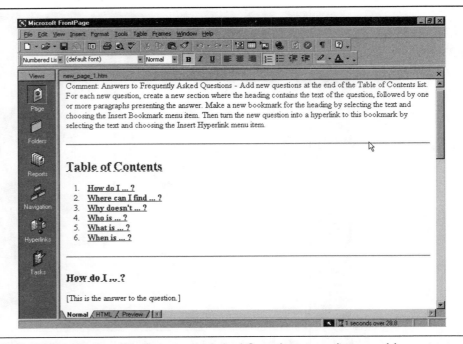

FIGURE 10.6: The Frequently Asked Questions template provides a structure for the page and guidelines for the suggested content.

Saving a Page as a Template

FrontPage doesn't limit you to the pre-existing templates that come with the software. You can save any page as a template. That template is then available in the New dialog box along with all the others.

To save a page you designed as a template, choose File ➤ Save As and choose FrontPage Template from the Save As Type drop-down list. This opens the Save As Template dialog box, shown in Figure 10.7.

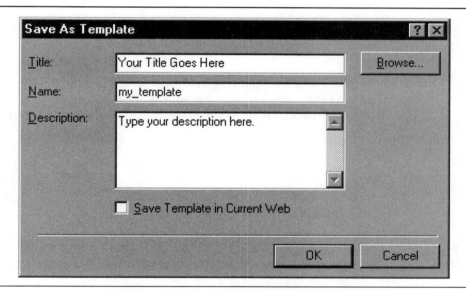

FIGURE 10.7: Use the Save As Template dialog box to save a page you create as a template.

Complete this dialog box as follows:

Title   Enter the title you want to appear in the New dialog box.

Name   Enter the name you want to use as the filename for the new page. The URL or filename for the page on which you based this template is displayed here when the dialog box opens.

Description   Enter a description of the template to appear in the Description section of the New dialog box.

Browse   Click the Browse button to save the template in a different location, or to select the name of an existing template that you want to overwrite with this new template.

**SKILL
10**

Click OK to save the new template. You may want to go to the New dialog box (File ➤ New➤ Page) to ensure your template made it and that you're satisfied with the name and description you gave it. If you want to make changes, choose File ➤ Save As again and revise the information. Click the Browse button to select the template you want to overwrite. Click OK again to save your changes.

All the files associated with each template reside in one folder (named with a `.tem` extension) within the FrontPage program folder. To remove a template from the New dialog box, you have to delete the template's folder by using the Windows Explorer, for example.

Applying Themes

In Skills 5 and 6, you learned how shared borders and navigation bars add consistency to the pages of a web. Another feature of FrontPage, *themes*, provides the ultimate in consistency. When you apply a theme to a web, FrontPage designs every page with the same background image, color scheme, buttons, navigation bars, fonts, active graphics, and other page elements. Because the theme impacts the entire web, new pages are automatically created with all the design elements of the active web.

When you create a web using a wizard, FrontPage asks you if you want to apply a theme to the web. However, you don't have to use a wizard to have a great looking web—just choose Format ➤ Theme to open the Themes dialog box, shown in Figure 10.8.

Click any of the themes to see it previewed in the preview window. You can modify each theme using the check boxes on the bottom left. These are:

Vivid Colors   Brightens the colors for some text and graphics

Active Graphics   Animates some of the page elements

Background Picture   Adds a textured background to the pages

Apply Using CSS   Bases the theme you choose on a cascading style sheet (see "Enhancing Design with Style Sheets" later in this Skill)

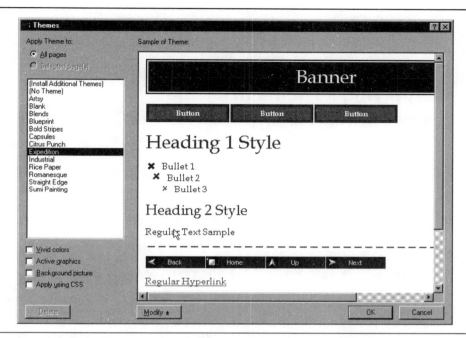

FIGURE 10.8: FrontPage includes a variety of themes that make anyone look like a professional designer.

When you turn off all these options, the background turns white. When Background Image is off and Vivid Colors is on, the background is a solid color.

To apply the theme, click the OK button. Switch to another view and open a page to see how the theme affects your web.

Changing or Removing a Theme

Once you apply a theme, you can change to another theme or remove the theme completely. To change to another theme, simply choose Format ➤ Theme and select another theme.

To remove a theme, select the No Theme option in the Themes dialog box. The preview window indicates that the current web does not use themes, and the theme is removed.

SKILL
10

When you choose the No Theme option, text returns to the style it had before the theme was applied or becomes Normal. In most cases, you need to do some manual formatting to clean up the text in your web. Of course, if that seems like too much work, you can always change your mind and reapply a theme.

Applying a Theme to a Page

There may be some pages in the web to which you don't want some or all of the theme applied. You can add, modify, and remove themes on individual pages just as easily as you can on entire webs.

While editing a page, right-click and choose Theme from the shortcut menu or choose Format ➤ Theme. This opens a dialog box with the same options that you see when choosing a theme for the entire web. If you are working in Folders view, you can choose the Selected Page(s) option to apply your choice only to the pages you had selected.

Applying Themes to Existing Webs

Although you can apply themes to existing webs, FrontPage warns you that if you apply this theme, all previous formatting is lost. Think carefully before taking this step because there is no way to undo this change. If you spent hours custom formatting a web, it can all be destroyed with one click of the mouse (yet another reason to make backup copies of *all* your important files).

Once you apply a theme to a web, your formatting choices are more limited. For example, you can no longer apply a different background unless you remove the theme from individual pages or from the entire web. If you are going to use themes, it's better to decide right from the outset than wait to apply them after you are well into designing your web.

Enhancing Design with Style Sheets

The *World Wide Web Consortium* (W3C), the group that establishes HTML standards for the World Wide Web, recently developed a new set of standards that allow Web site developers more control over the precise placement and appearance of elements on a page. FrontPage supports these standards, called Cascading Style Sheets. However, you and the visitors to your site will need one of the newer Web browsers to view the results of applying style sheets (at least as recent as Internet Explorer 3.02 or Netscape 4.0).

A *cascading style sheet* consists of style definitions or style rules that apply to specific page elements or entire pages. The reason this is valuable is that it gives you more control over how a page appears irrespective of the browser. It still isn't possible to have complete control, but style sheets give web developers many more tools than were possible before.

Let's look at a practical example. Without a style sheet, Heading 1 text appears in a large, bold version of the browser's default font. A style sheet lets you define parameters for the Heading 1 style, including font family, size, and other attributes. You can even define multiple font options to use rather than revert to the browser's default font if your first font choice isn't available on the viewer's browser.

There are three ways of applying style sheets to FrontPage web pages:

- By linking to an *external style sheet* (created in HTML and saved with a .css extension). A CSS file only contains the HTML code that defines the styles it contains. You can link one or more of the pages in your web to that one style sheet, so they all have access to the styles it contains. Then, to make a style change in the linked pages, you only have to change that one style sheet.

- By creating an *embedded style sheet* on a page, which allows you to create styles that only apply to the active page in your web.

- By applying inline styles to individual elements on a page.

You apply a style from an external or embedded style sheet by choosing it from the Style drop-down list in the Formatting toolbar, just as you select any of the standard HTML styles.

Style sheets are "cascading" because you can apply multiple styles to a page that are then interpreted by a browser in a specific order. Styles that are applied to individual elements (inline styles) take precedence over styles embedded in the page (embedded styles), and those take precedence over styles included on external style sheets.

NOTE NOTE NOTE NOTE NOTE NOTE NOTE NOTE NOTE NOTE NOTE NOTE NOTE NOTE NOTE NOTE

FrontPage themes are based on cascading style sheets. For that reason, you should not apply cascading styles to a page or a web that is already using themes. You should also avoid editing a theme's CSS file, because it may destroy the theme.

**SKILL
10**

You can specify styles for the following properties:

Alignment   Margins, padding, and text wrap

Borders   Style, color, width

Colors   Background, foreground, background image, attachment, repeat, vertical position, horizontal position

Font   Primary font, secondary font, font size

Text   Weight, style, variant, transform, decoration, indent, line height, letter spacing, alignment, vertical alignment

Creating and Linking External Style Sheets

A style sheet contains only HTML code that defines one or more styles; any other text is ignored. The only time you will view such a file is when you want to see what it contains or to modify it. Note that if you're creating a Web site as part of your company's intranet, check with your Web administrator to find out if there is a company standard style sheet you should use. Most companies have a standard design they want their Web authors to follow.

Creating an External Style Sheet

You can create an external style sheet without leaving FrontPage:

1. Create a new blank style sheet by choosing File ➤ New ➤ Page.

2. In the New dialog box, select the Style Sheets tab (see Figure 10.9) to display the style sheet templates that come with FrontPage.

3. To start with a blank style sheet file, select Normal Style Sheet and click OK. When you edit a style sheet file in FrontPage, you only see an HTML-style view of it. As you add individual styles to it, the HTML code for each will appear in the page.

4. Creating a style in a style sheet is the same as creating an embedded style for a single web page. You use the Format ➤ Style command to name the new style and set its attributes. This process is explained in the "Creating and Linking Embedded Style Sheets" section later in this Skill.

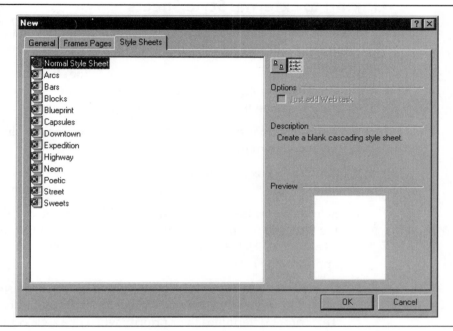

FIGURE 10.9: Choose File ➤ New ➤ Page, and you can create a new style sheet file on the Style Sheets tab in the New dialog box.

5. Continue to create new styles or modify existing ones using the Format ➤ Style command. The definition of each one will appear in the page as HTML code.

6. When you're finished, choose File ➤ Save. Verify that the file type shown in the Save As Type drop-down list is HyperText Style Sheet (*.css). Save this file to an appropriate location, such as within the current web.

The style sheet file is now available for linking to any page in your web, as described in the next section. You can edit this style sheet by opening it in Front-Page. You'll only see the HTML view, but that's all you'll need in order to see which styles are included in this sheet. You can revise the code manually or use the Format ➤ Style command to modify existing styles or to create new ones. Just be sure to use the File ➤ Save command when you're finished.

SKILL
10

Linking to External Style Sheets

Before you can use an external style sheet in FrontPage, you must create a link to it. That sheet will then be available to one or more pages in your web:

1. If there's just one page you want to link to the style sheet, open that page in FrontPage, or select it or multiple pages in Folders view (any page will do if you're linking the style sheet to all pages in the web).

2. Choose Format ➤ Style Sheet Links, which opens the Link Style Sheet dialog box shown in Figure 10.10.

3. The dialog box lists the style sheets to which links have already been created. To link to another style sheet, click the Add button.

4. Select a style sheet from the list of CSS files in the current web, or click the Select a File on Your Computer button to find a file on the Web or on a local disk. Click OK when you're finished, and the CSS file name will appear in the list of linked style sheets.

5. Continue to add more style sheets, if needed. You can use the two buttons, Move Up and Move Down, to change the order of the style sheets in the list. Their order determines their priority when one style conflicts with another (the cascading effect).

6. Once the style sheets you want are displayed in the dialog box, choose to link them either to the currently selected pages or to all pages in the web.

7. When you're finished, click OK to return to your page.

FrontPage will automatically create the necessary HTML code in the appropriate pages in your web (depending on whether you chose the Selected Pages or All Pages option). For example, the HTML for two links to style sheets named helppg.css and searchpg.css looks like this:

```
<Head>
<LINK REL="stylesheet" TYPE="text/css" HREF="helppg.css">
<LINK REL="stylesheet" TYPE="text/css" HREF="searchpg.css">
</HEAD>
```

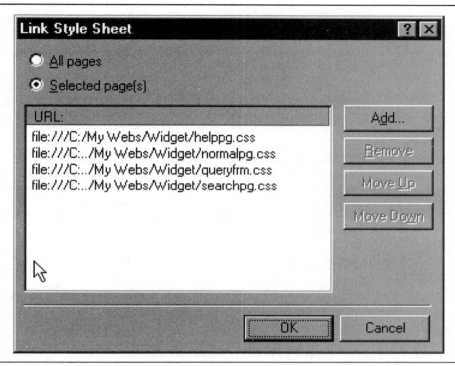

FIGURE 10.10: You can link a page or all pages in a web to an external style sheet with the Format ➤ Style Sheet Links command.

Removing a Link to an External Style Sheet

Here's how you can remove one or more links to style sheets:

1. In Folders view, first select the pages you want to unlink, unless you want to unlink a style sheet from every page in your web.

2. Choose Format ➤ Style Sheet Links.

3. Select either the All Pages or Selected Pages option.

SKILL
10

4. In the Link Style Sheet dialog box, select each of the external style sheets that you no longer want active; use the Shift-Click or Ctrl-Click techniques to select multiple names.

5. Click the Remove button, and then click OK.

This removes only the link to the style sheet; it doesn't remove the style sheet file. If you find that none of your pages is referencing an external style sheet, you can delete that CSS file in Folders view or using Windows Explorer.

NOTE NOTE NOTE NOTE NOTE NOTE NOTE NOTE NOTE NOTE NOTE NOTE NOTE NOTE NOTE

For up-to-the-minute information about the rules and structure for creating cascading styles, go to the World Wide Web Consortium's site at http://www .htmlhelp.com/reference/css/. **For help in writing HTML code and applying the standards, see** *Mastering HTML 4.0*, **by Deborah and Eric Ray, also from Sybex.**

Remember that if a page is linked to an external style sheet *and* has an embedded style sheet (discussed next), the attributes of each style will be combined. This may or may not be what you want, so consider your naming conventions before you use both types of styles.

Creating and Linking Embedded Style Sheets

FrontPage is very adept at helping you create embedded style sheets. Like the styles in a linked external style sheet, the embedded styles you create will appear in the Style drop-down list on the Formatting toolbar. You can then apply the styles as you would any others, to any element in the page.

Unlike external style sheets, however, embedded styles apply only to the active page. Although you can save a page that has embedded styles as a template and use it as the basis of other new pages, you'd be better off simply creating an external style sheet and linking it to pages as needed.

NOTE NOTE NOTE NOTE NOTE NOTE NOTE NOTE NOTE NOTE NOTE NOTE NOTE NOTE NOTE

The process of creating a style is the same whether you're creating it for an embedded style sheet or for an external one. The difference is that you save an external style sheet as a CSS file and then link Web pages to it. It doesn't matter where you are in the page when you create an embedded style, because the HTML code for the style is placed in the <HEAD> **tag on that page.**

Creating a New Embedded Style

Let's create a brand new style. We'll call it Product and assign the following formats to it:

Font:	Arial, 18 point, red, bold and italic
Paragraph:	Center alignment
Border:	Solid border

To create an embedded style sheet, first open the page for editing in Page view.

1. Choose Format ➤ Style. In the Style dialog box, shown in Figure 10.11, you can create a new style from scratch by clicking the New button. You can modify an existing style by selecting it in the drop-down list labeled List and then clicking the Modify button. You can even modify a standard HTML style, such as Heading 1, and give it the look you want.

2. Click the New button, which opens the New Style dialog box that is shown in Figure 10.12.

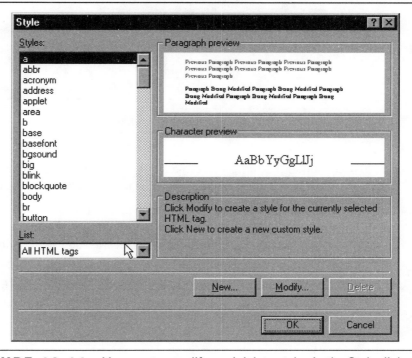

FIGURE 10.11: You create, modify, and delete styles in the Style dialog box.

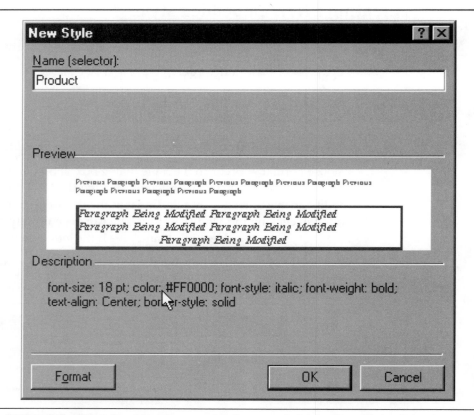

FIGURE 10.12:   You name and define a style in the New Style dialog box.

3.   Enter a descriptive name for the style in the Name field; this is the name that will appear in the Style list on the Formatting toolbar.

4.   To define the style, click the Format button and select Font. This displays the standard Font dialog box. Choose Arial for the font type, bold and italic for the font style, 18 point for the size, and red for the color. Click OK.

5.   Click the Format button again and choose Paragraph to display the standard Paragraph dialog box. This time choose Center for the alignment and click OK.

Notice the Preview pane as you make these format changes and return to the New Style dialog box. It shows you how the style you're defining will look when applied to text in a page.

6. Click the Format button once more and choose Border. In the Borders and Shading dialog box, select the Box option and choose Solid in the list of box styles. Click OK to return to the New Style dialog box.

7. That completes the style definition we wanted, so if the sample in the Preview looks about right, click OK. (Otherwise, return to any of the formatting options and fine-tune the definition.)

The embedded style is defined and ready to use. If this were not just an exercise, you would be wise to save your page at this point. Look at the HTML view of the page and you'll see the following code "embedded" in the <HEAD> section of the page:

```
<style>
<!--
.Product { font-family: Arial; font-size: 18 pt; color: #FF0000; font-
style: italic;
font-weight: bold; text-align: Center; border-style: solid }
-->
</style>
```

To apply the style, place the insertion point either on a line by itself to create a new paragraph, or within a paragraph that you want to see in this style. Then choose the style from the Style drop-down list. Note that user-defined style names are preceded by a period, so the one you just created is named ".Product" and will be found at the bottom of the list of usual HTML styles.

The new style should display the text in the paragraph in a large red italicized font, surrounded by a solid border.

Styles can save you an immense amount of work, while also ensuring that your page designs are consistent. The effects produced by the styles you apply in your documents are not "etched in stone." If you modify the definition of a style, the changes you make will immediately be reflected in any text to which you've already applied that style. If the style were in an external style sheet that you had linked to many pages in your web, the changes to the style would be reflected in all those pages.

Skill
10

Modifying an Embedded Style

To change an existing style, you basically follow the same procedure as when you created a new one. The difference is that you first choose a style from the list in the Style dialog box, and then click the Modify button. There are two lists from which you can choose:

- User-defined Styles displays all the styles that were created with the New button, and would not otherwise exist in the page.

- All HTML Tags displays the standard HTML tags that you can apply in any page, such as EM (emphasis), H1, and HR (horizontal rule).

You can modify any of the user-defined styles, but you can also modify the definitions of those standard HTML tags. The changes you make will affect *all* those tags in the current page, or in all pages linked to an external style sheet that contains the modified style. Here's a quick way to modify the effects of the Heading 1 tag:

1. Choose Format ➤ Style, and select All HTML Tags from the List option. This displays a long list of HTML tags.

2. Choose the H1 tag in the list of HTML tags, and then click the Modify button. The Modify Style dialog box which appears is the same as the New Style dialog box.

3. Make whatever changes you'd like and, when you're finished, click OK to return to your page.

NOTE NOTE NOTE NOTE NOTE NOTE NOTE NOTE NOTE NOTE NOTE NOTE NOTE NOTE NOTE
Once you have modified the definition of a standard HTML tag, the style name, such as H1 in this example, will appear in the user-defined list of styles in the Style dialog box.

The Heading 1 (H1) style still appears in its usual place in the Style drop-down list on the toolbar, but the effects it makes in the document now reflect the formatting changes you made. As with the new style you created earlier, there is an embedded style definition for the H1 tag in the <HEAD> section of the HTML code for this page. This tells a browser to override the way the browser normally displays text with the H1 tag, and use the formatting described in the style. Again, it's the "cascading" effect.

Removing a Style

You don't have to remove an embedded style from a page unless its name conflicts with another style or HTML tag. For example, if you want all the Heading 1 tags to revert to their default look in a browser, you'd want to delete the H1 style you created in the previous exercise.

To delete a style, choose Format ➤ Style. In the Style dialog box, display the user-defined list of styles (the names in the list of HTML tags cannot be deleted). Select the one you want to remove and click the Delete button.

Applying an Inline Style to Page Elements

You can apply *inline styles* to specific page elements, including the page itself, tables and cells, graphics, and horizontal lines. Inline styles supercede embedded and external style sheets so they allow even more precise formatting of individual elements. However, you can't apply an inline style globally (to other elements in the page) because the HTML code is applied only to the one element. If you want to affect all tables in a page, for example, you should create an embedded style or external style sheet.

To apply an inline style:

1. Display the Properties dialog box for the element to which you want to apply the style. For example, right-click a table or image and choose Table Properties or Picture Properties, respectively.

2. Click the Style button to open the Style dialog box. (If you don't see a Style button, it's because you can't apply inline styles to that specific element.)

3. Click the Format button and select the desired properties and values from the available options.

4. Click OK when you're finished.

NOTE NOTE NOTE NOTE NOTE NOTE NOTE NOTE NOTE NOTE NOTE NOTE NOTE NOTE NOTE

Remember that inline styles only apply to the selected element, not to all of the same elements in the page. If you apply an inline style to a table, not all tables change to that style—only the selected one changes.

SKILL
10

Using Class

When you really want to be specific, you can define a subset of a style and save it in the external or embedded style sheet as a *class*. Think of a class as a new style that you create based on a pre-existing style. For example, you define the Heading 3 style as 14 point, bold, Arial, blue. You want to apply the Heading 3 style to text, but wish to differentiate the headings that contain tips for your users. You can define a Heading 3 Tip style that is green, but that otherwise inherits all the attributes of the Heading 3 style, such as the font type and size.

To define a class for the embedded style sheet, choose Format ➤ Style and follow the same steps you use to define any style. The only difference is the way you name the new style. To define a class of the existing H3 style, you preface the new style name with H3 and a period, such as H3.Tip. In this case, you would change only the font color for this new style; it will inherit everything else from the H3 style. Here's how the HTML code would look in the <HEAD> tag for the embedded style and the new class of that style.

```
<STYLE>
<!--
h3     { font-family: Arial; font-size: 14 pt; color: #0000FF;
         font-weight: bold }
h3.tip { color: #00FF00 }
-->
</STYLE>
```

The H3.Tip style has a different color (00FF00 instead of 0000FF) from the H3 style. However, because H3.Tip is a class of H3, it inherits the font family and font weight attributes of H3, its parent class, rather than the default properties of the browser.

TIP TIP TIP TIP TIP TIP TIP TIP TIP TIP TIP TIP TIP TIP TIP TIP TIP TIP TIP TIP TIP TIP TIP

Use class names that reflect function rather than attributes. For example, the class that's applied to user tips in the page should be named "Tip" rather than something like "14-pt green."

Using Existing Files to Enhance Your Web

Whenever possible, it is wise to avoid reinventing the wheel. If you create a page or have an existing web you didn't create in FrontPage, but want to use it in your current efforts, there is no reason to start from scratch. You can import pages or entire webs into FrontPage and incorporate them in a new or existing web.

Importing an Existing Web into FrontPage

To import an existing web and make it a FrontPage web:

1. Start in FrontPage without a web open. If one is already open, choose File ➢ Close Web.

2. Choose File ➢ Import to open the New dialog box. The Import Web Wizard will already be selected.

3. Enter a location for the new web.

4. Click OK, and FrontPage will create the new web—including the necessary FrontPage folders—in the specified location for the incoming web files. It will then display the Import Web Wizard dialog box, shown in Figure 10.13.

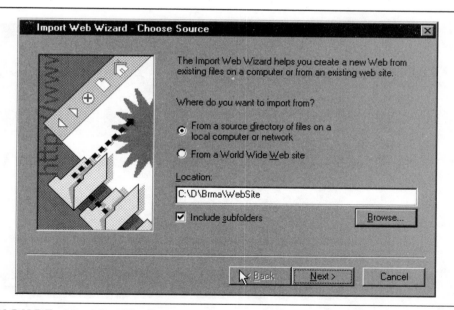

FIGURE 10.13: The first step of the Import Web Wizard asks you to identify the source of the Web site you are importing.

5. The Import Web Wizard prompts you to identify where the existing Web site resides, whether it's on a local or network computer or on the World Wide Web. Select the location and enter the address, or click the Browse button, select the folder, and click OK. If you want to import subfolders, select the Include Subfolders check box. Select Next to move on to the next page of the wizard.

6. Depending on where the site is located, the Import Web Wizard presents you with different options at this point.

   • If you're importing a web from a local computer or network (as in Figure 10.13), you see a list of all the files in the existing web (see Figure 10.14). All the filenames you see will be imported; to exclude one or more files, just select them and click the Exclude button. You can select multiple filenames in the usual way—click and Shift+click to select a group of contiguous files, or Ctrl+click to select noncontiguous files. When you are ready, click the Next button.

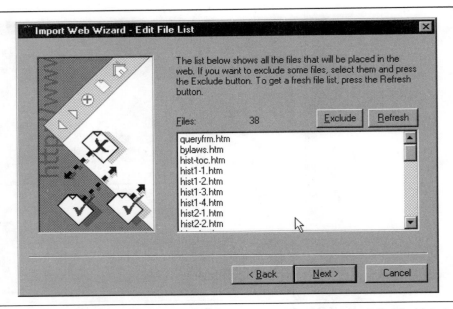

FIGURE 10.14: Choose the files you want to import in the Edit File List step of the Import Web Wizard.

- If you are importing a web from the World Wide Web, the Import Web Wizard asks you to specify how much of the web you want to import (some large sites are over a gigabyte in size!). Figure 10.15 shows that you can specify how many levels (folders within folders) of the site you want, how many kilobytes, and if you want to limit the imported files to text and image files. Click Next to move on to the last step.

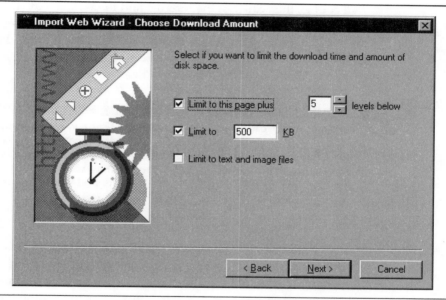

FIGURE 10.15: Indicate how much of the Web site you want to import in the Choose Download Amount step of the Import Web Wizard.

7. The last step offers you the chance to go back to a previous step or cancel the operation, if necessary. Otherwise, choose Finish.

The files from the existing Web site are imported into the new one. Now that the site is a FrontPage web, you can use all the features of FrontPage that you're already familiar with. If you import a complete site, all the relative hyperlinks should be active, but it's a good idea to click the Hyperlink Status button on the Reports toolbar to check their status. Hyperlinks that point to files outside the web but on a local drive will be broken. But you can import individual files into your FrontPage web, as you'll learn in the next section.

SKILL
10

Importing and Exporting Files

In the course of building and maintaining your FrontPage web, you'll need to bring in many different types of files, such as images for your pages, where each image is a separate file. You may also have a page that plays a tune or makes an announcement when that page is opened, which is handled by sound files in your web.

Of course, the beauty of the Internet and the Web is that you can build a Web site whose content (its pages and other files) resides anywhere on the Web; all the site's resources need not reside in the same location. Nonetheless, even if a file is accessible outside of your site, if you want to be sure that the file is always available you should save it within the confines of your own site.

TIP TIP TIP TIP TIP TIP TIP TIP TIP TIP TIP TIP TIP TIP TIP TIP TIP TIP TIP TIP TIP TIP TIP

You can import files into the active FrontPage web, and you can also export files so that copies of the files are sent to the locations you specify. While editing a page in Page view, you can open a wide variety of file types that are converted into standard HTML web pages as they are opened. These types include rich text format (RTF), text, Microsoft Word, and WordPerfect.

Importing Files

In addition to importing webs, you can use the File ➤ Import command to import any file into the active FrontPage web. Although this is the same command that was discussed earlier in this Skill in "Importing an Existing Web into FrontPage," if a web is already open, the command allows you to bring existing files into the active web.

Not only are the imported files copied into the web's location on the server, but FrontPage also examines any incoming HTML pages to keep track of any hyperlinks they contain.

FrontPage warns you if an imported file will overwrite an existing file of the same name. You can choose to exclude that file or import it and replace the existing one. Here's how you import one or more files into the active web:

1. Choose File ➤ Import, which displays the Import dialog box. This is shown in Figure 10.16, with a list of files already in it.

2. Click the Add File button, which displays a standard files dialog box. If you choose the Add Folder button, you can select a folder and all the files and subfolders within it; they are imported into a folder of the same name in your web.

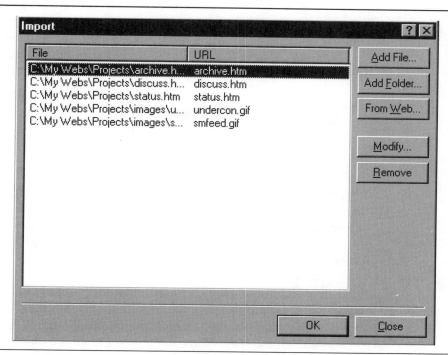

FIGURE 10.16: This dialog box lists the files you have selected to import into the active web.

3. Select a folder, then choose the files you want to import from this folder; you can select multiple files with the Shift+click or Ctrl+click method.

4. Click the Open button, which once again displays the Import dialog box.

The files you selected are listed in the dialog box, as shown in Figure 10.15. At this point, there are six different buttons from which you can choose:

OK   Imports filenames that are currently in the dialog box into the active Web.

Add File   Selects more files to add to the import list.

Add Folder   Selects a folder and all the files and subfolders in it to add to the list.

SKILL
10

Modify   Edits the URL (filename and location) of the selected file; you might need to rename an incoming file so that it does not overwrite an existing file of the same name. You can also add a folder name to the URL of an incoming file so that the file is imported into that folder in the active web.

Remove   Removes the selected filenames from the import list, but does not actually delete the files from disk.

Close   Closes the dialog box without importing the files; the list of files is still there and waiting the next time you choose File ➤ Import, until you close the current web or open another.

FrontPage tracks all the links in the HTML pages you import and incorporates them into the FrontPage web. For example, if an incoming page links to a page named summary.htm, and a page of that name already exists in the current web, then the FrontPage will show that relationship in the Hyperlinks view and in the various link-related reports.

All incoming files are placed in the active web's primary folder unless you edit the URL of an incoming file and specify a different folder, or include folders in the import list. Once the files are in the web, you can move them to other folders and let FrontPage automatically adjust links as required. For example, you may want to move all GIF and JPEG image files into the Images folder in the current web.

Exporting Files

You can select one or more files or folders in FrontPage and export them to another location outside of the FrontPage web. For example, you might want to send a page or image file to a coworker for her to incorporate into the site she is working on. There are several ways to do so.

The simplest is to use the standard copy and paste method. Right-click the selected files or folders you want to copy (usually from the Folder List or the Folders or Navigation view), choose Copy from the shortcut menu, and paste the source files and folders into the target location in Windows Explorer or another application.

If you want to export a file or folder under a new name, select it and choose File ➤ Save As, and then enter the new location and name. You can also use this method to save a file under the same name but to a new location. To change the file's type when you're saving it, select a new type in the Save As Type list in the files dialog box

To export all or some of the files and folders in a FrontPage web to another Web server, use the File ➤ Publish Web command, which is discussed in detail in Skill 14.

Opening a Page from Outside the Active Web

Usually you open HTML pages for editing from the active FrontPage web. However, you can open pages from other locations as well. Choose File ➤ Open and then either select a file from your local or network disk, specify a URL on the Internet, or click the Search the Web button to find the file on the Internet.

To open a page from disk, enter the path and filename. To open a page from the Web or your intranet, enter the address. Using this method, you can open any page from any Web site to which you have access, just as you do in your browser. Once open, you can save the page (including its images) to your local disk or web.

Of course, you must work within the constraints of upright behavior and copyright law. But this is a handy way to bring a page from a Web site into FrontPage, where you can revise it as necessary and save it to a different location.

Opening Other File Types

You can open many types of files beyond standard HTML web pages. FrontPage converts an incoming file from its native format into an equivalent-looking HTML file. You can then save it as an HTML web page in the usual way.

When you choose a file to open, FrontPage determines what type of file it is and, if it's able to, converts it as it opens it. To make it easier to find a file, and to see the types of files that FrontPage can convert, look at the Files of Type drop-down list in the Open File dialog box. When you choose one of the file types on the list, only files with the appropriate extension for that type, such as .doc or .xls, are displayed in the dialog box.

There are a wide variety of file types in the list, including several different versions of Microsoft Word, Excel, Works, and WordPerfect. The more generic Rich Text Format (RTF) and plain text (TXT) file types are also on the list.

If the incoming file contains any graphic images, FrontPage attempts to place them in the document where they belong. Since images are always separate files from the pages in which they appear, when you later save this document as an HTML page, you're asked if you also want to save the images as separate files. By saving the images, they are available the next time you open this page, either for editing in FrontPage or in a browser on your web.

SKILL
▼10

If the file you want to open is of type unknown to FrontPage, it displays a dialog box, asking you how it should convert the file—either as an HTML, RTF, or Text file. This is a last-ditch effort, and none of the choices may be appropriate. But in some cases, such as when you want to open a text file whose extension is unfamiliar to FrontPage, you can choose the appropriate file type and let FrontPage proceed.

TIP TIP TIP TIP TIP TIP TIP TIP TIP TIP TIP TIP TIP TIP TIP TIP TIP TIP TIP TIP TIP TIP TIP

If FrontPage can't open a certain file type, you may be able to save that file in the HTML format in the program that created the file. You can then open the HTML file directly from FrontPage.

Inserting a File into a Page

You can bring another file into the current page with the Insert ➤ File command. The contents of the other file appear at the insertion point's position within the page.

You'll probably find many occasions to bring another web page into the current one. For example, suppose you have an online user manual that is spread across multiple pages so that each page downloads pretty quickly. You would also like to have the entire manual in a single page so a visitor to the site can download the complete manual in one operation. You can use the Insert ➤ File command to combine each of the pages into a single page, and then save that page back to the web.

Are You Experienced?

Now you can...

- ☑ Create a consistent and well-designed web
- ☑ Create a variety of different webs using wizards and templates
- ☑ Add pages to a web using templates
- ☑ Apply a theme to a web and to an individual page
- ☑ Create and link external, embedded, and inline style sheets
- ☑ Import and export files and webs
- ☑ Copy files from webs
- ☑ Open other types of pages and pages from other sources

SKILL
10

Automating Your Web with FrontPage Components

- ➔ Creating comments, hit counters, and banner ads
- ➔ Including text, pages, and pictures automatically
- ➔ Creating a table of contents
- ➔ Including the date and time a page was last revised
- ➔ Creating hover buttons and marquees
- ➔ Including an Excel spreadsheet in a page

Once you've caught a visitor's attention with exciting, up-to-date content in your web, all you have to do is figure out how to get them to come back. This Skill introduces you to the FrontPage components and other active features that make it easy to keep your web interesting, keep your content current, and make sure visitors return to your site. FrontPage includes a number of automated features, from banner ads that appear across the top of pages to hover buttons that respond when a mouse pointer moves over them. There are even a few maintenance tricks that can automate many tasks on your web without programming or script writing.

Understanding FrontPage Components

A *FrontPage component* is a built-in object that executes either when the web page author saves the page or when the page is opened in a browser. Most FrontPage components automatically generate the appropriate HTML code for their defined tasks. Others work behind the scenes to compete specific tasks, for example, saving data that a user inputs into a form.

NOTE NOTE NOTE NOTE NOTE NOTE NOTE NOTE NOTE NOTE NOTE NOTE NOTE NOTE NOTE

In earlier versions of FrontPage, FrontPage components were referred to as WebBots or Bots. The word is derived from *robot*, which is used in Web-related circles to describe a variety of automated routines. WebBots are a subset of FrontPage components and are referenced in the HTML code when you insert a WebBot component. However, FrontPage now consistently uses the broader and more generally accepted name of *component* to refer to these objects.

You have already seen examples of several components in earlier Skills. The webs discussed in Skill 10, created from wizards and templates, freely use components such as Page Banners and Comments. You learned how themes help provide consistency by including a Page Banner component that displays the same information on each page of the web. The Comment component includes text that is not visible when the page is viewed in a browser—comments are only for the eyes of the web authors. Comments for the page are contained in HTML code within a FrontPage component that tells FrontPage to display the comment in a unique color when viewed in Page view. The more popular FrontPage components are described later in the section, "The FrontPage Components."

Inserting a FrontPage Component

You can incorporate FrontPage components into a page in several ways.

- In Page view, use the Insert ➤ Component command or select one of the components that appear on the Insert menu.

- Create a new page from a template that uses a component, including Confirmation Form, Search Page, and Table of Contents.

- Create a new web based on a wizard or template that incorporates a variety of components (including themes).

NOTE NOTE NOTE NOTE NOTE NOTE NOTE NOTE NOTE NOTE NOTE NOTE NOTE NOTE NOTE

The *Common Gateway Interface (CGI)* has been the traditional way to run automated tasks from web pages. When you perform tasks with the Front-Page components on a server configured for FrontPage (one that the FrontPage server extensions installed), you avoid having to write CGI scripts and reference their somewhat arcane parameters.

FrontPage generally treats components as separate objects in a page. For example, when you insert a Comment component (this one has its own command on the Insert menu), the result is a block of text that's displayed in the page, but is not editable there. If you try to click within the block of text, you select the entire component, as shown here.

Comment: This comment is not displayed when this page is viewed in a browser.

You know an object in a page is a FrontPage component when you simply point at it with your mouse, because the pointer changes to the FrontPage Component pointer (shown here to the left).

The FrontPage Components

You can find most of the FrontPage components with either the Insert or the Insert ➤ Component command. Here is a description of some of the more commonly used components on those menus; most are discussed later in this chapter.

Comment   Inserts a comment on a page that is invisible in Web browsers. Use this component to include notes to yourself or instructions for other Web designers who have access to the page.

Hit Counter   Displays the number of users who have visited the page that contains this component.

Include Page   Displays another web page within the current page.

Banner Ad Manager   Creates a banner ad that sequentially displays each of the pictures you specify.

Scheduled Picture   Displays an image file for a time period you set. You can also specify an optional image that's displayed before or after the specified period.

Scheduled Include Page   This is the same as the Scheduled Picture component, but you specify a page instead of an image. The result is the same as Include Page, but only within the specified time period.

Substitution   Displays the current value for the FrontPage web configuration variable you choose, such as Page URL, Author, or Description.

Table of Contents   Creates a table of contents of all the pages in your FrontPage web.

Date and Time   Displays the date or time when the page was last revised.

Confirmation Field   Displays the results of a specified field in a form, such as when a reader's input is displayed for confirmation in another page. This component is covered in the next Skill, *Letting Users Interact with Forms*.

Hover Button   Displays a button that changes in some way when you point to it (without clicking). It can change color, bevel in or out, change text, or even become a completely different button.

Marquee   Displays the text you enter as a scrolling message when viewed in a browser.

Search Form   Displays a field in which a visitor to your site can enter text to search for.

Office Spreadsheet   Displays an Excel spreadsheet that visitors to your site can use to enter data or perform calculations, even if they don't have Excel installed on their computers. You can also use the Office PivotTable and Office Chart components to insert those components into a page.

When you insert some components into a page, you see the complete result of the component immediately—for example, the Hit Counter component displays the numbers of hits on the page. Other components only leave a placeholder in the page to indicate their presence. For example, when the current date is not within the date range for the Scheduled Include Page component, all you see in Page view is the text Expired Scheduled Include Page. In a browser, however, you see nothing at all.

When the FrontPage component cannot complete its task, it produces an error message. For instance, when a page contains an Include Page component but the file to be included no longer exists, in Hyperlinks view you will see a broken hyperlink line connecting the page to the page that should be included. If you right-click the page and open its Properties dialog box, an Errors tab is available (shown here). It displays any error messages produced for that page, including those from FrontPage components.

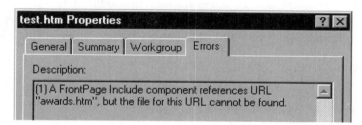

NOTE NOTE NOTE NOTE NOTE NOTE NOTE NOTE NOTE NOTE NOTE NOTE NOTE NOTE NOTE

You can insert other programmable objects into a page in FrontPage, although that discussion is beyond the scope of this book. For more information about FrontPage and programmable objects such as Java applets, ActiveX controls, and browser plug-ins, see *Mastering Microsoft FrontPage 2000*, also published by Sybex.

Inserting a FrontPage Component for Your Comments

Whether you are working on a page alone or are sharing responsibility for the development of a page with other people, there are many times when it's helpful to include a comment to document something on the page. Of course, you don't want users to see those comments. Using the FrontPage Comment component, you can place comments within your pages that are visible in Page view but invisible when viewed in a browser.

Never put confidential information in your comments. Even though comments don't appear when the page is viewed in a browser, they are still part of that page's HTML code. Visitors to your site see your comments when they view the underlying code for the page, such as with the View ➢ Source command in Internet Explorer.

To create a comment, position the insertion point where you want the comment to appear and choose Insert ➢ Comment. Enter the text of your comment in the Comment dialog box; press Enter to create a line break when the comment is displayed in the page. Click OK when you're finished, and your comment appears within the page. An example was shown earlier in this chapter.

HTML has a special tag for comments, and a browser ignores any text within that tag. FrontPage adds its own twist to the comment by displaying it in Page view in a different color (purple), along with any formatting you have applied to its displayed text.

Here is the HTML code that FrontPage uses for the comment shown earlier.

```
<!--webbot bot="PurpleText"
preview="This comment is not displayed when this page is viewed in a
browser."-->
```

The standard HTML tag for a comment is <! -- >. If you open a web page for editing in FrontPage, any comments included in this tag are not displayed in Page view's Normal view, only in HTML view. Only the comments you create with the Insert ➢ Comment command are displayed in the Normal view.

There's also a newer comment tag that you may find in other web pages, but it is not supported by all browsers. This comment tag looks like this:

```
<COMMENT>This is the text of the comment</COMMENT>
```

Counting Your Visitors

Almost always, the sole reason for publishing a Web site is to attract interest from other people. One of the nerve-racking parts of establishing a Web presence is waiting to see how many visitors find their way to your fabulous site. FrontPage takes care of counting for you with the Hit Counter component, so you can just sit back and watch the numbers grow. This is one of the components that works only when hosted by a server running the FrontPage server extensions, so you can't preview this component unless you're working with a Web server.

The first page on which you should place a hit counter is the home page for your Web site. This will show you how many visitors come to your site as a whole, because the home page is always the page that is opened first (unless a visitor specifies a specific page). You can then add counters to other pages you wish to track.

SKILL
11

To insert a hit counter, follow these steps:

1. While editing the page in Page view, position the insertion point where you want the hit counter to go on your page.

2. Choose Insert ➤ Component ➤ Hit Counter. This opens the Hit Counter Properties dialog box, shown in Figure 11.1.

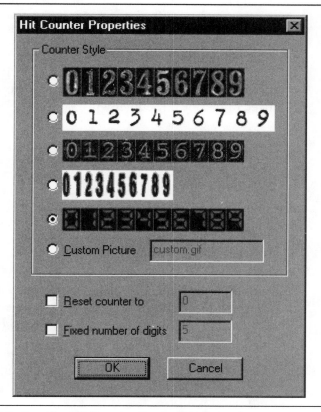

FIGURE 11.1: The Hit Counter Properties dialog box

3. Select a counter style or choose a GIF image containing the digits 0 through 9 spaced evenly across the picture (You can create your own digits in Image Composer and save them as a grouped GIF image. See Skill 9 for more about Image Composer.)

4. Select the Reset Counter To check box if you want to start the counter at a number other than 0. Enter the number in the adjacent text box. (Just like ordering new checks from the bank, it may be advantageous to start with a slightly higher number.)

NOTE NOTE NOTE NOTE NOTE NOTE NOTE NOTE NOTE NOTE NOTE NOTE NOTE NOTE

You might start the hit counter at a number greater than zero when you want the counter in a page to pick up where the counter in another page left off. For example, suppose you have a hit counter in one page that has reached 750. Now you're replacing that page with another page under a new filename. In that case, you could start the counter in the new page at 750 to continue the progression.

5. Select the Fixed Number of Digits check box if you want the counter to display zeros as placeholders. For example, if you enter 4 as the number of fixed digits, the hit counter will display 0004 when the page has been accessed four times.

6. Click OK to save the properties and insert the hit counter.

You probably want to include some message for your visitors around the hit counter like the one shown here. The example at the top is how the hit counter looks in Page view. At the bottom is the hit counter when it has been sent to a browser by a server running the FrontPage server extensions.

You are visitor # [Hit Counter] to this site.

You are visitor # 36234 to this site.

To edit the hit counter, either double-click it or right-click it and choose Front-Page Component Properties from the shortcut menu. Make any changes you want and click OK to save them.

Including Another Web Page Automatically

The Include Page component lets you easily revise many pages in your FrontPage web in only one operation. You saw an application of the Include Page component concept when you learned about shared borders in Skill 6. The actual content of each border is contained in a separate page and is linked to all the pages in the web for a consistent look. The Include Page component works in the same way. When you insert another page into an existing page, the two pages appear as if they are one. However, each page is stored separately. When the included page is revised, changes are reflected on all the pages that are linked to it.

When you click an Include Page component to select it, you can easily tell it is a FrontPage component because it will be highlighted, as shown in Figure 11.2. You can see that the image, the Widget Company title, and the horizontal line are parts of the component, and you can clearly see the telltale FrontPage component mouse pointer.

Table of Contents

International Awards

Corporate History

Public Education

FIGURE 11.2: A page in the Widget Web site takes advantage of the Include Page component.

Remember that the Include Page component offers a double benefit. It gives you a way to display the same information in any pages that reference the same included page. You also get the added benefit of being able to revise the included page and have those changes appear in all the pages that include it. In a web with many pages, this can save you hours and hours of work.

The first step in inserting an Include Page component is to create the page you want to include. Because this page is never viewed directly by users, you may want to save the page in the `_private` folder of your web. Once you create the page, here's how to place it in the active page:

1. In FrontPage, open the page in which you want to insert the Include Page component.

2. Position the insertion point where you want the included page to be displayed. In the Widget page in Figure 11.1, the component was placed at the very top of the page.

3. Choose Insert ➤ Component ➤ Include Page.

4. In the Include Page Properties dialog box, enter the URL of the page you want displayed in the current page (shown here). The page you specify must be in the active web, so it's easiest simply to click the Browse button and select the file.

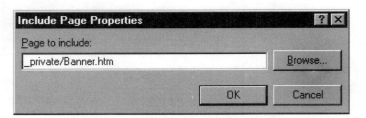

5. Finally, click OK to insert the Include Page component.

The included page is loaded into the current page and displayed as though it were actually a part of the current page. However, you can't spell-check or edit the text in the included page from the current page. To do that you have to open the included page.

Revising a FrontPage Component

You can revise a FrontPage component at any time. For example, with the Include Page component in the previous example, you can change the name of the web page it references. To revise a component, you can do any of the following:

- Double-click it.
- Select the component and choose Format ➤ Properties (or press Alt+Enter).
- Right-click it and choose the Properties command from its shortcut menu (the name of the command depends on the component, such as Comment Properties or Include Page Properties).

To edit the included page, right-click the component and choose the Open File command from the shortcut menu shown here.

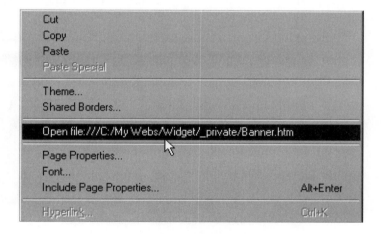

This command opens the included page for editing. Make your changes and save the page. When you switch back to the original page, choose View ➤ Refresh (F5) and the editing changes you made should be evident.

TIP TIP TIP TIP TIP TIP TIP TIP TIP TIP TIP TIP TIP TIP TIP TIP TIP TIP TIP TIP TIP TIP TIP TIP

To switch between open pages, open the Window menu and choose the page you want to switch to from the list of open pages.

If you modify the included page, you don't have to worry about updating all the pages that include this page. FrontPage handles that automatically when you save the included page.

Creating a Banner Ad in a Page

You've probably encountered countless banner ads on the Web, for better or worse. They normally appear at the top or bottom of a page and display advertising that generates revenue for the Web site that is hosting the ad. A banner ad often consists of a "moving picture show" of multiple graphic images displayed in a timed sequence. In most cases, the ad is also a hyperlink that gives a visitor more information.

FrontPage offers a component to help you create banner ads in your own web pages. Even if you don't run a commercial Web site that includes advertising, a banner ad may nonetheless serve as one means of displaying unique eye-catching information for specific pages.

To create a banner ad, place the insertion point where you want the ad to appear and choose Insert ➤ Component ➤ Banner Ad Manager; its dialog box is shown in Figure 11.3.

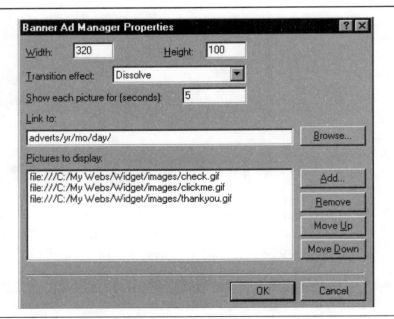

FIGURE 11.3:   The Banner Ad Manager lets you create a sequential banner ad in a page.

Creating a banner ad in FrontPage is really quite simple:

1. In the Banner Ad Manager dialog box, specify the width and height of the ad. Keep in mind that the images you choose for the ad will be displayed within the limits of this box.

2. Choose a transition effect, such as Dissolve, Box In, or Box Out.

3. Specify the number of seconds each picture should be displayed. Remember that the Web is a click-and-go place, so a shorter interval might be more useful than a longer one.

4. If you want the ad to serve as a hyperlink, enter the target in the Link To field.

5. Click the Add button to select the first picture to be displayed in the ad. As with all pictures, you can choose one from the current FrontPage web, from outside of that web, or from the Clip Art Gallery.

6. Continue to use the Add button to select more images for the ad. The ones you choose will be displayed in an endless loop, with each image being displayed for the length of time you specified.

7. When you've selected multiple images, you can change the order in which they'll be displayed by selecting one in the list and clicking the Move Up or Move Down button.

8. When you're finished, click OK to return to the page. Remember, you can always revise the parameters for the ad at a later time (see the "Revising a FrontPage Component" section earlier in this Skill).

The banner ad will appear in the page as a box of the size you specified. To see the ad in action, use the File ➤ Preview in Browser command.

Scheduling Changes in Your Web

Keeping the information in a web up-to-date is a challenge even for full-time Web site administrators. FrontPage includes two components that help you keep data current even when you're not there to take care of it. Both of these components, Scheduled Picture and Scheduled Include Page, work essentially the same as the Include Page component, except that you can set a starting and an ending date for the image or page to be included. In this way, you could have new pages in your web even when you go on vacation.

To schedule an image or a page to be included automatically, follow these steps:

1. Choose Insert ➤ Component and select either Scheduled Picture or Scheduled Include Page from the menu of components. The Scheduled Include Page Properties dialog box is shown in Figure 11.4 (the Scheduled Picture dialog box looks the same). Note that the files you select must reside within the current web.

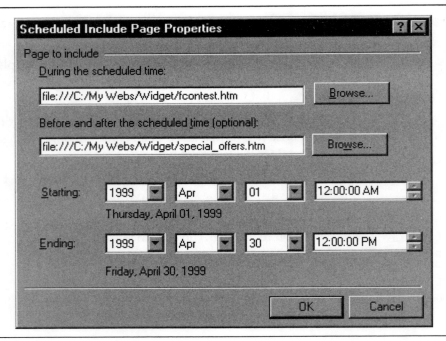

FIGURE 11.4: A Scheduled Include Page appears between the dates you specify.

2. Enter the relative URL of the page or image to include, or click the Browse button to select a file from the current web (your selection must come from the current web).

3. Select the Year, Month, Day, and Time you want to start including the image or page. Click within one of the fields and use the spin box (up and down arrows) to make the change.

4. Select the Year, Month, Day and Time to stop including the image or page.

5. Enter a relative URL to include a different page before or after the given dates. If you don't include another page, the message "Expired Scheduled Include Page/Picture" appears in its place in FrontPage, and the area is blank when viewed in a browser.

6. Click OK to schedule the page or image.

If you want to make changes in the component, right-click it and choose the Scheduled Picture or Scheduled Page Properties command from the shortcut menu. To edit an actual included page, right-click the component and choose the Open command.

TIP TIP TIP TIP TIP TIP TIP TIP TIP TIP TIP TIP TIP TIP TIP TIP TIP TIP TIP TIP TIP TIP TIP

You can insert several Scheduled Picture/Include Page components on a single page with different start and end times, but they must occupy different positions on the page.

Automating Text Entry with the Substitution Component

You can display text automatically anywhere you want in a page by taking advantage of two FrontPage features:

- While editing a page in Page view, you can insert a Substitution component that references any configuration variable and displays the text that defines that variable.

- You can create configuration variables for an entire FrontPage web that consist of a name (the variable) and a value (the definition of the variable).

This is a very powerful technique for managing information in your FrontPage webs. Its benefits are similar to using the Include Page component: It's a convenient way to display the same information in many different pages, and you can change a configuration variable's definition and have that change automatically reflected throughout your web.

Referencing a Variable in a Page

There are several built-in configuration variables in every FrontPage web. Here's how to reference one of them; the process is the same for variables you create:

1. In Page view, place the insertion point where you want to display the variable.

2. Choose Insert ➤ Component ➤ Substitution.

3. In the Substitution Properties dialog box, select one of the built-in variables from the drop-down list shown in Figure 11.5. For example, choose Author to display the name of whoever created the current page, or Modified By to display the name of the person who last worked on this page.

4. Click OK to return to the page.

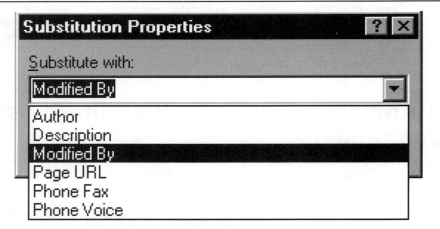

FIGURE 11.5: Using Substitution components, you can automatically insert text on a page based on web-wide values.

The Substitution component is inserted into the page, and the current value (the text) of the variable you choose is displayed.

For example, in a new page that has not yet been saved, you can create the following sentence that ends with the Page URL variable of the Substitution component:

```
This page's URL is unsaved:///new_page_1.htm.
```

That's how this variable is displayed when there is not yet a value for it. Once you save the page, thereby giving it a URL, the sentence might now look like one of the following:

```
This page's URL is http://www.widget.com/somepage.htm.
This page's URL is file:///C:/My Webs/Widget/somepage.htm.
```

The actual URL is displayed in place of the Substitution component.

NOTE NOTE NOTE NOTE NOTE NOTE NOTE NOTE NOTE NOTE NOTE NOTE NOTE NOTE NOTE
When you open a web page in Page view, any Substitution variables it contains are automatically updated. But in this case, to see the correct result for the Page URL Substitution component, you'll need to use the View ➢ Refresh command (F5).

Creating a Configuration Variable

You can create your own configuration variables in FrontPage and reference them in the pages in that web. The drop-down menu in Figure 11.5 showed two user-defined variables, Phone Fax and Phone Voice. In most cases, you create a variable only when that information needs to appear on more than one page, so you save a lot of time when you need to update the information—simply by changing that variable's definition. Here are some typical uses for variables:

Webmaster   Displays the name of whoever maintains the web; if a new person takes over the job, just enter the new name for this variable's definition.

Phone Voice   Displays a phone number to call for information.

Phone Fax   Displays a phone number for sending faxes.

Company Name   Displays the name of the company; although this won't change very often (if at all), by using a variable you're assured the name is spelled consistently throughout the web.

Company Address   Displays the company's address.

Current   Displays the most recent stock price; just update the variable's definition when you want to update the displayed price.

NOTE NOTE NOTE NOTE NOTE NOTE NOTE NOTE NOTE NOTE NOTE NOTE NOTE NOTE NOTE

Displaying the value of a configuration variable with the Substitution component is very much like displaying another page with the Include component. The text (value) of a variable, however, can be only a single line long, although it can be a long line that will wrap when displayed in the page. Even so, it's easier to update a variable than it is to update every page.

Let's create a configuration variable named Phone Voice, which displays a day and evening telephone number.

1. Open the web and choose Tools ➤ Web Settings.

2. Select the Parameters tab in the Web Settings dialog box.

3. To create a new configuration variable, choose Add.

4. In the Add Name and Value dialog box (shown in Figure 11.6), enter **Phone Voice** as the name of the variable in the Name field.

5. In the Value field, enter the text you want to appear when this variable is inserted into a page, such as **916-555-1212 (day) or 916-555-1213 (eve)**. Text wraps to the next line as needed; all the text you enter is taken as a single line when it is displayed in the page.

6. When you're finished, click OK, which returns you to the Web Settings dialog box.

7. Click Apply to incorporate the new variable into the web, or click OK to apply it and close the dialog box.

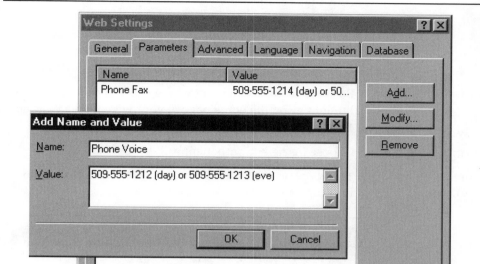

FIGURE 11.6: You can create or revise a configuration variable using the Parameters tab in the Web Settings dialog box.

Once you create a variable for a web, you can insert that variable into any page in that web using the Substitution component. You'll find the new variable name (Phone Voice in this case) on the list of variables in that component's dialog box.

Creating a Table of Contents

Just about every Web site includes some sort of table of contents, whether it's actually called that or not. The multiple pages of a Web site are just too easy to catalog within a single page of hyperlinks. Visitors to the site find such a page a great convenience, and it gives you, the Web author, a practical way to organize the important "stepping stones" in your site.

The FrontPage Table of Contents component can be used for just such a need. If you insert it into a page, it generates a complete table of contents of all the pages in your FrontPage web. Here's how to build a table of contents:

1. Position the insertion point where you want the table of contents to appear. It might be on the home page of your web or on a page appropriately titled Table of Contents.

2. Choose Insert ➤ Component ➤ Table of Contents.

3. This displays the Table of Contents Properties dialog box, where you define the scope and style of the table of contents (see Figure 11.7).

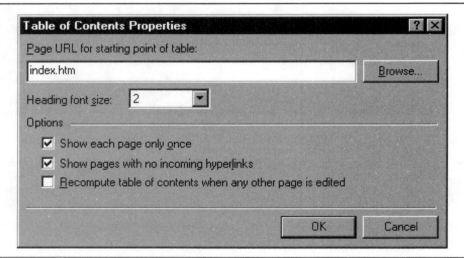

FIGURE 11.7: The Table of Contents component lets you create a list of hyperlinks to all the pages in your web.

4. First, pick the page that serves as the root of the table of contents. Normally this is the home page, because the hyperlinks it contains should lead you through the chain of hyperlinks to just about every page in the web.

5. Next choose the heading style that's used for each entry in the list. The choices are 1 through 6 (corresponding to the HTML tags <H1> through <H6>). Choose None if you want each item displayed in the default text style.

6. There may be multiple hyperlinks to many pages in the web. If you don't want to see those pages listed multiple times, choose the Show Each Page Only Once option.

7. The table of contents is built from the hyperlinks in the starting point page, but there may be pages in the web to which no other pages link. To display them as well, choose Show Pages with No Incoming Hyperlinks.

NOTE NOTE NOTE NOTE NOTE NOTE NOTE NOTE NOTE NOTE NOTE NOTE NOTE NOTE NOTE

The table of contents lists pages it finds in any other folders you may have created in this web. It will not, however, look for pages in any of the FrontPage program folders in this web, including `_private`**.**

8. The last choice, Recompute Table of Contents When Any Other Page Is Edited, is deselected by default, so the table of contents is rebuilt only when you open the page containing this FrontPage component. That should be fine in most cases, but if you're willing to put up with delays and put some strain on your server, select this option and the table of contents is updated whenever anyone makes a change to the web.

9. Finally, click OK and the Table of Contents component is inserted into the active page. Here is an example of the Table of Contents component for the Widget Web.

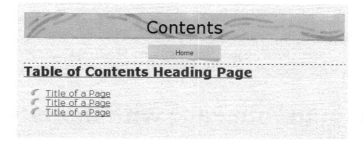

What you see in the table of contents page in Page view doesn't really look like much, but save the page and preview it in your Web browser. The result looks something like that shown in Figure 11.8 for the Widget Web. Each entry in the table of contents displays the title of a page and is a link to that page.

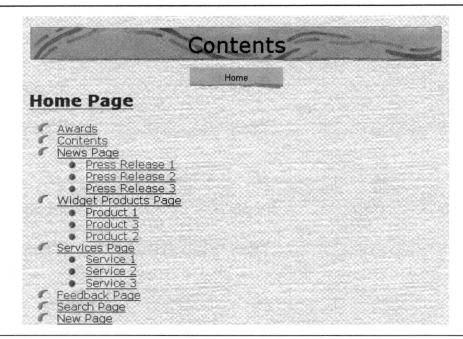

FIGURE 11.8: The Table of Contents component creates a complete table of contents for the pages in your web.

Pages that are positioned as child pages in Navigation view appear indented from their parent pages. Each page listing is a hyperlink to the actual page. Each time you save the table of contents page in Page view, the table of contents is recalculated.

Stamping Your Page with the Date and Time

The Date and Time FrontPage component is a very convenient way to display the date and/or time when the page was last revised. This information is frequently displayed on web pages to remind you and other authors of when it was last worked on, and also to let your readers know how current the information is. Would you trust pricing information displayed on a page last revised 10 months earlier?

The bottom of a page is often the place for this type of information. You might display a line that looks something like this:

```
This page was last updated on 3/11/99 at 10:15 AM.
```

This display uses two instances of the Date and Time component . Here's how you create them:

1. While editing a page in Page view, type the first part of the sentence **This page was last updated on** and end it with a space.

2. Choose Insert ➤ Date and Time (this one, like the Comment component, has its own command on the Insert menu).

3. In the Date and Time Properties dialog box (shown here), select Date This Page Was Last Edited.

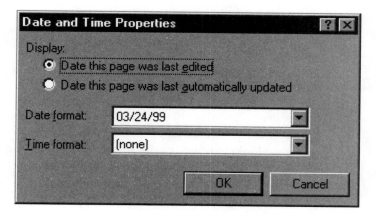

This sets the date or time when someone actually opens and then saves this page in Page view. The other option, Date This Page Was Last Automatically Updated, also updates the date or time when the page's HTML is updated by the server. For example, when you revise another page included in this page, this page's code is updated along with the Date and Time component.

4. Select an appropriate date style from the Date Format drop-down list.

5. Select (None) in the Time Format drop-down list so this component displays only the date.

6. Choose OK to return to the page, and the current date is displayed where you inserted this FrontPage component in the sentence.

7. Type the text that follows this component, starting with a space and continuing with **at** and another space.

8. Once again, choose Insert ➤ Date and Time, but this time set the Date Format option to (None), and then choose an appropriate time style from the Time Format drop-down list.

9. Choose OK to close the dialog box; the current time should be displayed in your sentence.

10. Finish the sentence with a period.

    Your completed timestamp should show the current date and time, which will update whenever you save the page. You won't see the new date and time reflected in the page until you either open it again or choose View ➤ Refresh.

Creating Hover Buttons

For whatever reason, we like to click buttons. Web users are inclined to click a button rather than click a text-based hyperlink. In Skill 9, you learned how to create great looking buttons with Image Composer. FrontPage also gives you a few more ways to have fun with buttons.

Hover buttons are buttons that change in some way when you point to them (without clicking). They can change color, bevel in or out, change text, or even become a completely different button. You can use simple rectangles as the buttons and group them together, as shown below, or use elaborate buttons you create using the Button Wizard in Image Composer. Whatever your choice, hover buttons add just a touch of sparkle.

NOTE NOTE NOTE NOTE NOTE NOTE NOTE NOTE NOTE NOTE NOTE NOTE NOTE NOTE NOTE
Hover buttons are created not from special FrontPage commands, but as standard Java applets that should be viewable in any recent version of a browser.

To create a hover button, follow these steps.

1. Position the insertion point where you want the first button to appear on your page.

NOTE NOTE NOTE NOTE NOTE NOTE NOTE NOTE NOTE NOTE NOTE NOTE NOTE NOTE NOTE
If you plan to use a custom button, save the button as a GIF file and be able to identify where the GIF is located.

2. Choose Insert ➤ Component ➤ Hover Button to open the Hover Button Properties dialog box, shown in Figure 11.9.

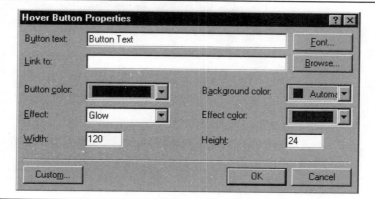

FIGURE 11.9: The Hover Button Properties dialog box

3. Enter the text you want to appear on the button. If you're using a button GIF that already has text on it, delete the text here. Click the Font button to change the font, font style, size, and color. Your choices are limited to four fonts.

4. In the Link To field, enter the URL of the target for this hyperlink button. Click the Browse button to choose a page from the active web, the World Wide Web, or your computer.

5. Choose a color for the button. If you want, you could match the button color to the background color of the page so only the text appears on the page.

6. Choose a background color for the button. Background has little effect on the button.

7. Click the Effect drop-down list and choose a transition effect for the hover button, such as Color Fill, Glow, and Reverse Glow. Experiment with different effects in Preview mode to see which you like best.

8. Choose an effect color—in other words, the color the button transitions to when a user points at it.

9. Select a width and height for the button. If you plan to use a custom button, enter the size of the button here in pixels.

10. If you want to use a custom button on your page, click the Custom button to open the Custom dialog box, shown here.

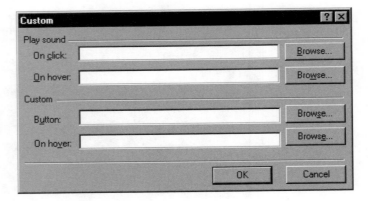

11. In the Play Sound options in the Custom dialog box, enter the URL of a sound file in the On Click field if you want a sound to play when the button is clicked, or enter the filename in the On Hover field, which will play the sound when you pass the mouse pointer over it. Browse if you need to locate the file. (You can attach a sound to each event, but that is probably overdoing it.)

12. In the Custom options, enter the location of a GIF you want to use as the button, and one you want to use on hover. If, for example, you use the first button in Figure 11.10 as the Button and the second as On Hover, the button text and color change when the user points to the button.

FIGURE 11.10: Use two identically shaped buttons with different text and colors to change one button into the other on hover.

13. Click OK to close the Custom dialog box, and again to close the Hover Button Properties dialog box.

14. Save the page and switch to Preview to see your buttons in action.

Now that you have the hang of it, if you want to edit your buttons, right-click a button and choose Hover Button Properties to reopen the hover button dialog box.

If you use the default rectangle button, you can create multiple buttons that appear connected, but you have to create them one at a time, one next to the other. Use the same effect on each button for a consistent look. You can also use the opposite effect on alternating buttons—bevel in and bevel out, glow and reverse glow—to create a more complex look.

Delivering a Message with a Marquee

Microsoft Internet Explorer first introduced the *marquee*, which is an HTML implementation of the scrolling message you might find on the marquee of a movie theater, where it displays the current schedule, or above a stock brokerage firm, where it displays a live ticker tape.

NOTE NOTE NOTE NOTE NOTE NOTE NOTE NOTE NOTE NOTE NOTE NOTE NOTE NOTE

Although the marquee is not yet a part of the HTML standard, the popularity of Internet Explorer (which can display a marquee) may eventually make the marquee an official HTML element. If a browser cannot display a scrolling marquee, it simply displays the text that would have instead scrolled across the screen.

Figure 11.11 shows an example of a marquee in a page in Page view. The marquee is added to the Widget home page, first shown in Chapter 1. Here the marquee displays a newsy and timely message that you might change every few days.

Preview the 1999 widgets on this site...

We welcome you to the home page of the world's first, and now the largest, manufacturer of widgets.

At the Widget Company, we strive to:

 Make widgets of the highest quality (the list of <u>international awards</u> proves v are succeeding).

 <u>Serve our customers</u> both in the home and in the office.

<u>Educate the public</u> on the history of widgets and their role in world history

Sponsor <u>widget design contests</u> in our schools.

<u>Promote</u> the use of widgets throughout the world.

FIGURE 11.11: A marquee can be an effective way to catch the viewer's attention and display an important message.

Of course, the only problem with the marquee in Figure 11.11 is that you can't see its most important feature—the message scrolling across the marquee from right to left, again and again. To see a marquee in action, you need to show its page in Preview mode or in a browser; shown here is a series of views of the same marquee in action.

Preview the 199

Preview the 1999 widgets on

Preview the 1999 widgets on this site...Today!

his site...Today!

Preview the

It's easy to create a marquee—it's very much like inserting a horizontal line:

1. Place the insertion point where you want the marquee to appear. As always, you can move the marquee later, if necessary.

2. Choose Insert ➤ Component ➤ Marquee, which displays the Marquee Properties dialog box (see Figure 11.12).

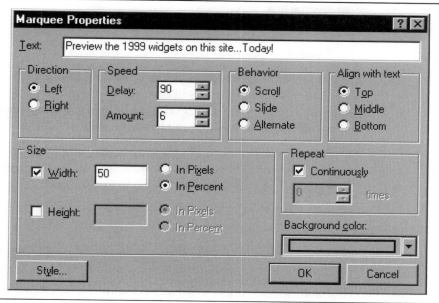

FIGURE 11.12: You can enter the text and define the size, shape, appearance, and behavior of a marquee in the Marquee Properties dialog box.

3. In the Text field, enter the text you want to display in the marquee. In this example, that's **Preview the 1999 widgets on this site...Today!** If you select text in the page before invoking the command, that text appears in this field, and the marquee replaces the text in the page.

By ignoring all the other options at this time and clicking OK, you create a functioning marquee in your page. However, you can also make a few small modifications to it:

4. To change the color of the marquee's background, select a color in the Background Color option.

5. Select the Width check box, enter **50** for the width, and select In Percent. This sizes the marquee so it is half the width of the window in which this page is displayed.

NOTE NOTE NOTE NOTE NOTE NOTE NOTE NOTE NOTE NOTE NOTE NOTE NOTE NOTE
You can also change the size of a marquee from within the page. Click it and then drag one of its selection handles, just as you can do with an image or a horizontal line.

6. That's all you need in this dialog box, so click OK.

The marquee is now half the width of the window but is aligned with the left edge of the window. Its text is in the default size and style, but it should be a little bigger for this purpose. You can change both of these aspects right in the page, treating the marquee like other objects in a page.

7. Select the marquee not by clicking (which selects the marquee component), but by pointing to the left of it and clicking. This highlights the marquee as though it were a line of text you had just selected.

8. Now click the Center button on the Formatting toolbar to center the marquee on the page.

9. Choose Heading 3 from the Style list on the Formatting toolbar so the marquee's message appears in that heading style.

10. Save the page if you want to keep your changes. Now you're ready to see the marquee in action.

11. Switch to Preview mode or choose File ➢ Preview in Browser. You'll see your message scroll across the marquee from right to left, endlessly repeating.

To modify the marquee, double-click it to open its Marquee Properties dialog box. Experiment with the Behavior options, which affect the way the message moves across the marquee. The Speed options control how fast or how slow the marquee runs. Make sure it's slow enough that your users can read it, but not so slow as to be boring.

Including an Excel Spreadsheet

An exciting new capability was introduced in FrontPage 2000 that marks its further integration into the Microsoft Office 2000 suite. You can now include "chunks" from office applications right in your FrontPage web pages. These are based on the Office Web Components and currently include spreadsheets, charts, and PivotTables. You add one or more of these in a web page with the Insert ➤ Component command.

In this exercise, you'll learn how to work with the spreadsheet component. You're likely to be impressed, because it really gives you a "live," ready-to-use Excel spreadsheet for the pages in your FrontPage webs.

First the Caveat

Before we proceed, however, it's important to point out that the Office Web Components, like the Excel spreadsheet, are *not* compatible with just any browser. In order to view and work with these components, a user must have Microsoft Internet Explorer version 4.0 or newer, as well as the Microsoft Office Web Components. Both the browser and the components are part of the Microsoft Office 2000 suite, so you'll already have them if you have installed the suite.

You can see that the Office Web Components are, at least for now, a far cry from the usual material found on the Internet, where any web page can be viewed by any browser. Nonetheless, more and more companies are utilizing in-house intranets, and the concept behind the Office Web Components will undoubtedly be welcomed in such an environment.

Another point to understand is that the file size for a spreadsheet component can grow quite large. The small example you'll build here occupies about 8,000 bytes. As you add more cells, formulas, and formatting, the file will quickly grow larger. Nonetheless, if visitors already have the Office Web Components installed on their computers, the convenience of Web-based spreadsheets might be too much to resist.

Inserting the Spreadsheet

In this exercise, we'll create a small spreadsheet that lets a visitor to your site calculate the monthly payment for a mortgage. The user enters the principal and interest, and the spreadsheet calculates the payments for both a 15-year and 30-year mortgage. You'll learn how to:

- Build the spreadsheet by entering numbers, formulas, and text.
- Modify spreadsheet properties via the Property Toolbox.
- Enhance the appearance of the spreadsheet by formatting its cells.
- Set the spreadsheet properties that determine how it will look and behave for the user.

Figure 11.13 shows the finished spreadsheet within a page in FrontPage. The text and picture above the spreadsheet were placed on the page in the usual ways. The information in the spreadsheet was entered directly within it, as you'll soon see.

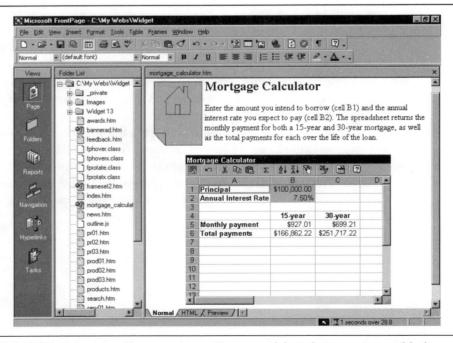

FIGURE 11.13: You can place a live spreadsheet in your pages with the Office Web Component spreadsheet.

There are several ways to include an Office Web Component in your FrontPage webs. Since we're working with FrontPage, we'll be able to use the simplest way:

1. Position the insertion point where you want the spreadsheet to appear in the page, just as you would when inserting an image or table.

2. Choose Insert ➤ Component ➤ Office Spreadsheet, and a new spreadsheet will appear in the page. It looks very much like an Excel spreadsheet, and you'll find that it behaves like one, too.

Once the spreadsheet is in the page, you are free to begin using it. You can enter data and formulas, format its cells, change the width of its columns, and so on. To make it larger or smaller, drag one of its selection handles as you would with an image.

You can also include spreadsheets in your pages that were built in Excel, Access, and Visual Basic. In fact, if you're going to get serious about making spreadsheets available in your FrontPage webs, you should consider creating them in Excel. It's just easier to work in that environment, and you'll have more tools at your fingertips.

In order to use an Excel spreadsheet as an Office Web Component, you must save it via the Excel command File ➤ Save As Web Page. This saves it as an HTML file with the appropriate code that allows it to be used in your FrontPage webs. You can then use the Insert ➤ File command in FrontPage to insert the spreadsheet into a page.

Adding Data and Formulas

We want this spreadsheet to serve as a mortgage calculator for visitors to this site. Of course, we could simply offer them a blank spreadsheet and let them do what they want with it, but that would be pretty silly. Instead, we're going to create the necessary formulas and descriptive text, so all a visitor has to enter is the amount of the loan and the interest rate. Let's build this spreadsheet:

1. Click the spreadsheet to select it, and you'll see a hashed border around it, indicating that you're now "inside" the spreadsheet, as though you were working in Excel. If you only see selection handles, click once more and that should get you inside.

2. In cell A1, enter **Principal** and press Enter. That should move the cell pointer down to A2; if not, use the arrow keys on your keyboard, or just click within the cell you want.

3. In cell A2, enter **Annual Interest Rate**.

4. The text you entered extends beyond the edge of the column. In order to see it all when we're finished we need to expand its column: simply double-click the column's right-hand edge in the column header, just to the right of the letter A that identifies this column. This will automatically size the column to match its longest entry.

5. Enter the following the indicated cells:

    - A5: **Monthly payment**
    - A6: **Total payments**
    - B4: **15-year**
    - C4: **30-year**
    - B5: **=ABS(PMT(B2/12,15*12,B1))**
    - B6: **=B5*15*12**
    - C5: **=ABS(PMT(B2/12,30*12,B1))**
    - C6: **=C5*30*12**

The two monthly payment formulas use Excel's PMT function to calculate the payment. Since this function returns a negative number for the payment, they are prefaced with the ABS function to produce the absolute value of the result (a positive number).

To see if the formulas are working correctly, enter some test data

    - B1: **$100,000**
    - B2: **7.5%**

TIP TIP TIP TIP TIP TIP TIP TIP TIP TIP TIP TIP TIP TIP TIP TIP TIP TIP TIP TIP TIP TIP TIP TIP

The spreadsheet will automatically recalculate the formulas and return the results shown in Figure 11.13. If you don't get the same results, double-check the formulas you entered and be sure they're exactly as shown above and that they reference the correct cells. If you include the dollar sign, comma, and percent sign as shown, the spreadsheet will format each of those cells so that the numbers they contain will appear as you entered them.

Formatting the Spreadsheet

We'll apply just a little formatting to spruce up this spreadsheet. To do so, we first need to open its Property Toolbox. While in the spreadsheet, click the Property Toolbox button on the spreadsheet's toolbar (not the FrontPage toolbar). Or, right-click a cell and choose that command from the shortcut menu.

The Property Toolbox serves as the menu and property dialog boxes for the spreadsheet component. You can expand or contract its options by clicking any of the option buttons: General, Format, Show/Hide, Calculations, and so on. Figure 11.14 shows the Property Toolbox with only its Format option expanded.

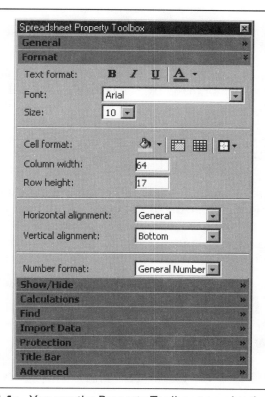

FIGURE 11.14: You use the Property Toolbox to make changes to the spreadsheets appearance, behavior, and run-time parameters.

Let's make some of the text in the spreadsheet boldfaced.

1. Select cells A1 and A2 by dragging over them with the mouse.

2. In the Property Toolbox, click the Format button to expand those options.

3. Then click the Bold button.

4. Repeat this procedure for cells A5 and A6, and B4 and C4.

5. In Figure 11.13, you can see that cells B1 and B2 are shaded, which helps the user to recognize where data is to be entered. Select those two cells and then select a color by clicking the down-arrow for the Fill Color button in the Format properties of the Property Toolbox.

6. Select cells B4 and C4 again. Center those text labels by choosing Center from the Horizontal Alignment options.

7. Expand the Title Bar options in the Property Toolbox. Enter **Mortgage Calculator** in the Title text-entry field, which changes the title that appears in the spreadsheet's title bar. You can also change the title's font and the title bar's color.

8. At some point after doing all this work, you should save this web page if you intend to keep it.

You should look at the other options in the Property Toolbox to see what the possibilities are (be sure to experiment). Then you should preview the spreadsheet to see how it would look to a visitor to your site. Remember, currently only Microsoft Internet Explorer 4.0 and later can interpret the spreadsheet component, and the Office Web Components must also be installed on each visitor's computer.

Are You Experienced?

Now you can...

☑ **Automate your web using FrontPage components**

☑ **Create page banners, banner ads, hover buttons and marquees**

☑ **Substitute images, text, and pages on a scheduled basis**

☑ **Create a table of contents of your web**

☑ **Automatically enter the time or date in a page**

☑ **Include a spreadsheet on a page**

Letting Users Interact with Forms

- ➔ **Creating forms with templates**
- ➔ **Creating forms with the Form Page Wizard**
- ➔ **Choosing a form handler**
- ➔ **Adding fields to a form**
- ➔ **Adjusting the properties of form controls**
- ➔ **Setting data validation for text boxes**
- ➔ **Using a form**

This Skill introduces you to *forms*, which allow visitors to your Web site to reverse the normal mode of Web browsing by sending information to you. If you've spent much time browsing the Web, you know that forms are being used more and more. Many of the sites you visit ask you to register in a guest book or enter personal or company information to download files. And FrontPage includes even more tools to make form creation a snap using form controls like text boxes, radio buttons, check boxes, and drop-down menus.

Creating Forms

A form lets users of your site enter information and send it to your server, moving from mere surfing into a two-way communication mode. With forms, you can find out who is visiting your site, what they liked or would like to see improved, and why they visited—user information that's impossible to acquire unless you ask.

You create a form in a web page using a variety of *form fields,* like the controls used in Windows dialog boxes, each of which lets the user enter data. Many of your users automatically understand how to use a form, because they've used the same controls to save files, select applications, and install software. Behind the form is a *form handler,* used to collect information from the form and save it in your web. Figure 12.1 shows a form in a web page containing some of the standard controls you can include in a form.

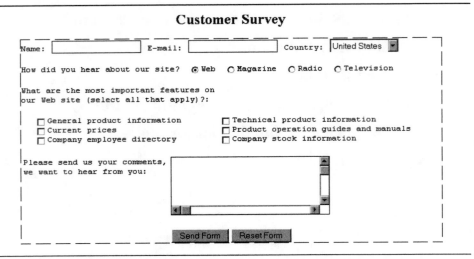

FIGURE 12.1: A form lets the user enter data and then send the data to the server.

FrontPage's form fields and their buttons on the Form toolbar are shown in Table 12.1.

NOTE NOTE NOTE NOTE NOTE NOTE NOTE NOTE NOTE NOTE NOTE NOTE NOTE NOTE NOTE

The Form toolbar is a tear-off menu—choose Insert ➤ Form and then drag the tear-off tab at the top of the menu to where you want the toolbar to appear.

SKILL
12

TABLE 12.1: Field Forms and Descriptions

Button	Form Field	Description
	New Form	Creates a new form in the page; this button is disabled when the insertion point is within a form.
	One-Line Text Box	A user enters a single line of text, such as a name, street address, or phone number (see the Name and E-mail fields in Figure 12.1).
	Scrolling Text Box	An open text box for several lines of text. The window is a fixed size, but scroll bars are displayed (see the Comments field in Figure 12.1).
	Check Box	Use check boxes to let a reader select items in the form or make more than one choice from a group of choices (see the group of six choices in Figure 12.1).
	Radio Button	Use to present mutually exclusive choices. Users can click one, and only one, radio button in a group to make a single choice from the group (see the Web, Magazine, Radio, and Television choices in Figure 12.1).
	Drop-Down Menu	Lets the user select one or more items (depending on how the field was defined) from a drop-down list (see the Country control in Figure 12.1).
	Push Button	Executes an action for the user. In the form shown in Figure 12.1, users click the Send Form button to send their entries to the form handler, or the Reset Form button to clear the form and return each control to its initial value.
	Picture	Lets you insert a picture in a form that will serve as the submit button for that form.
	Label	Links a text label to a form control so that a visitor can click either the text or the control to select the control. Must have browser that supports Dynamic HTML, such as IE4 or later.
	Form Properties	Displays the current form's Properties dialog box; this button is disabled when the insertion point is outside of a form.

Form-Building Basics

Creating a form is a three-step process: determining the data you want to collect, including controls appropriate to the data, and setting a form handler to store the data you will collect in the form.

Before you start creating the form you should decide what data you want users to be able to enter. Then, using a template, wizard, or an existing page, insert the form fields you need, like text boxes, radio buttons, and check boxes, as well as any descriptive text or images you want. Whether you use a template or not, FrontPage automatically adds the Submit Form and Clear Form push buttons to the page as soon as you place the first form field.

Finally, decide what to do with the data entered after your server receives it. For example, will it be appended to a database or added to an HTML page and displayed elsewhere on your web? Based on your decision, specify and set options for a form handler so that user data actually arrives at its destination. In most cases, when all the data in the form is sent back to the server, the information entered into each control (called the control's *value*) is paired with the name of the control. This name-value pair identifies the data elements so the server can deal with the data appropriately.

NOTE NOTE NOTE NOTE NOTE NOTE NOTE NOTE NOTE NOTE NOTE NOTE NOTE NOTE NOTE

You can place more than one form on a web page. A form is delineated in Page view by being enclosed in a dark dashed line, as you can see in Figure 12.1. Any fields you add within the dashed line are part of the form. Each form has its own properties and must have its own button to submit the data it contains to the server.

Creating a Form from a Template

You don't have to build a form "from scratch," although the process is pretty simple. Instead, when you create a new page, choose a specialized form from the page templates: Confirmation Form, Feedback Form, Guest Book, Search Page, and User Registration. (If none of the templates meet your needs, you can use the Form Page Wizard to create your form page.) You'll probably want to tweak the form that the template constructs, but it gives you a head start by placing form fields that you can copy, modify, or delete to create your finished form. To use a template, choose File ➢ New ➢ Page to open the New dialog box, shown in Figure 12.2.

Select a template to see a description and a very hard-to-see preview on the right side of the dialog box. To create the form page, select a template and click OK.

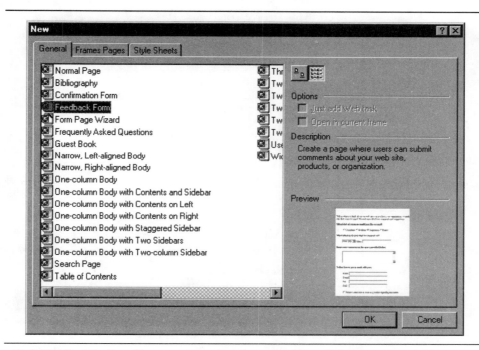

FIGURE 12.2: Choose a template from the New dialog box to quickly create a form.

Creating a Form with the Form Page Wizard

Some forms don't fall into the standard template categories, so FrontPage includes a Form Page Wizard to help you create more unique form pages. To fire up the wizard, choose File ➤ New ➤ Page and choose Form Page Wizard from the list of templates.

The first page describes the wizard; click Next to continue. The second page of the Form Page Wizard, shown next, is rather cryptic.

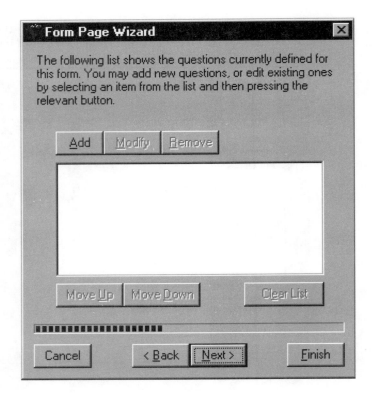

Unless you're editing an existing form, you should click the Add button to begin constructing the form's text and controls. You're prompted to choose an input type. The first items in the list create multiple fields. For example, Contact Information asks for name, address, and other similar information. Further down the list are more generic choices like Date, One of Several Options, and Paragraph. When you select an input type, a description and sample prompt appear in the dialog box. You can leave the prompt as is, but more likely you'll want to enter a new prompt that more closely matches what you want users to see above the form fields.

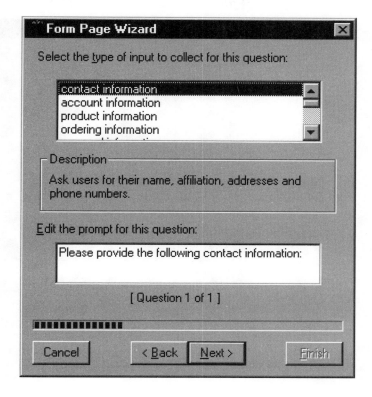

Click the Next button to see the options associated with the input type you selected. For example, when you choose Contact Information, you can choose whether you'd like users to supply just a first name, first and last, or first, last, and middle names. Do you want their fax number? Home phone? Professional survey designers tell you "the less you ask for, the more you'll get." Only ask for information you really require, so users are more likely to take the time to fill in real answers, rather than creating spurious entries for Jabba the Hutt and Winnie the Pooh.

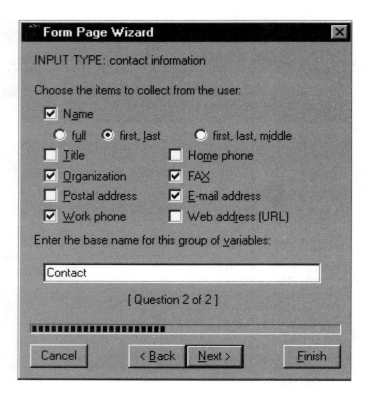

For some questions, you can choose the form field used to collect the data. If users are choosing one option from many, for example, you can present the choices in a drop-down menu or with radio buttons. If you're not sure which control type to use, think about how you've seen similar information presented online. The number of options often decides the issue: Using a drop-down list of U.S. state names is much better than using a radio button for each state.

Enter a name that's used to describe the data users enter in response to the question. This name is used internally for the form handler; users won't see it. Then click the Next button. You're returned to the list of questions, which includes the question you just entered. Select the question and click Modify if you want to alter the settings for the first question, or click Remove to delete the question. To add another question, click Add. When you have more than one question in the list, you can use the Move Up and Move Down buttons to rearrange the order of the questions. Continue adding and, if necessary, rearranging questions until you've entered all the questions required for the form.

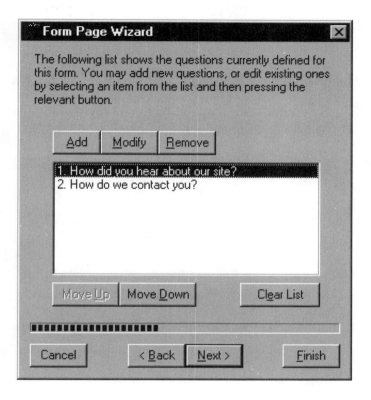

NOTE NOTE NOTE NOTE NOTE NOTE NOTE NOTE NOTE NOTE NOTE NOTE NOTE NOTE NOTE

This wizard helps you create a form page that works like any form page you create from scratch or from a template. So don't worry too much about getting the entire form completed in exactly the way you want. You'll be able to make changes later on in Page view.

With all the questions entered, click Next to move to the Presentation Options. Use the radio buttons and check boxes to indicate how you want to present the questions. If you are asking a number of questions (like an online survey or exam), users often prefer to have a table of contents, so they can jump between questions. Specify whether FrontPage should use tables to format your questions. You can always copy questions and form fields into a table later, or remove the questions from a table. Click Next to continue.

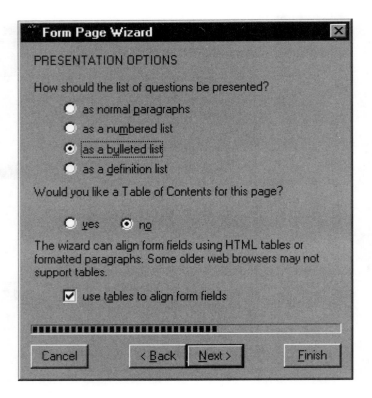

In the Output Options page of the wizard, specify the form handler you wish to use. FrontPage's form handlers are *CGI (Common Gateway Interface)* scripts, and require that the server has the FrontPage server extensions installed. You can save the results to a web page or text file, which uses the default FrontPage form handler, or indicate that you have a custom CGI script to handle this form. In the text box at the bottom of the page, enter the name (without an extension) of the web page or text file that receives the results. FrontPage creates the file if it doesn't exist.

When you've entered output options, click Next, then click the Finish button on the final page of the Form Page Wizard. The form created using the two questions in the example above is shown in Figure 12.3.

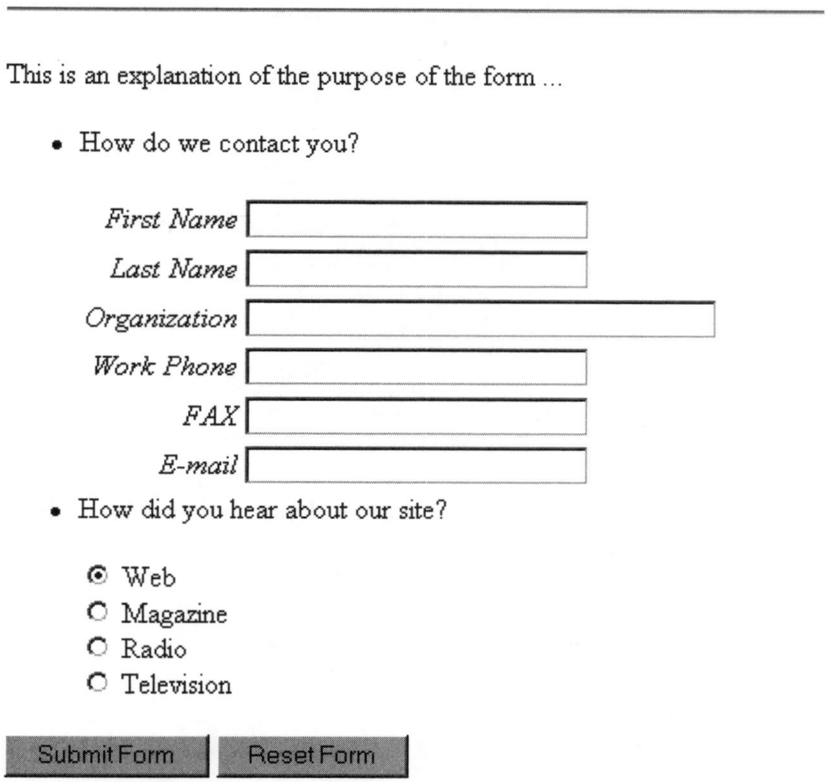

This is an explanation of the purpose of the form ...

- How do we contact you?

First Name [   ]
Last Name [   ]
Organization [   ]
Work Phone [   ]
FAX [   ]
E-mail [   ]

- How did you hear about our site?

  ⦿ Web
  ○ Magazine
  ○ Radio
  ○ Television

[Submit Form] [Reset Form]

FIGURE 12.3: The Form Page Wizard helps you create a form to collect data from your users.

Aligning Form Fields

When you create a form, you may want to align the various text elements, images, and controls it contains so that users find it easier to progress through the form. The easiest way to align objects in a form is to place them in tables. For example, the field descriptions can be in the left column of a table and the fields themselves in the right column. This method is one of the options in the Form Page Wizard and was used in Figure 12.3. There's no evidence of the table in that figure because the table has no borders. However, the table can be seen in Page view when the Show All option is enabled (as shown here).

- How do we contact you?¶

First Name:	
Last Name:	
Organization:	
Work Phone:	
FAX:	
E-mail:	

- How did you hear about our site?¶

You can also align a form's elements by applying the Formatted paragraph style to the entire form, which is how the elements of the form in Figure 12.1 were aligned. A monospaced font is used, making it easy to align objects on the screen—just press the spacebar to move objects to the right. You can place the main items in the form on separate paragraphs (press Enter) or insert a line break (press Shift+Enter) to separate groups of items. Although it's easier to space objects when you're using a monospaced font, it detracts a bit from the form's graphic appeal.

Telling the Server How to Handle the Data

When you create a form with the Form Page Wizard, you choose your form handler in the Output Options. If you create your form from scratch, you need to specify the form handler that deals with the data when it is sent to the server. Right-click anywhere within the form and choose Form Properties from the shortcut menu to open the Form Properties dialog box (shown in Figure 12.4).

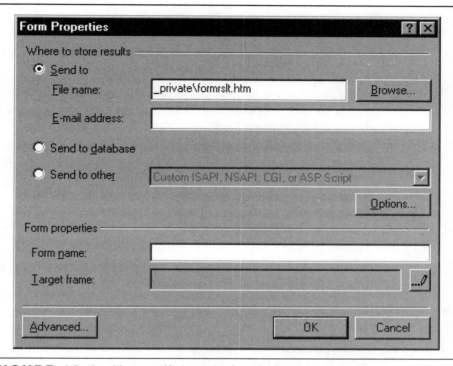

FIGURE 12.4: You specify how the form's data is sent to the server in the Form Properties dialog box.

Choosing a Form Handler

In the Form Properties dialog box, select a form-handling method:

> **Send to File Name**   If you created your form with the wizard, this text box already contains the filename you entered. Enter a new URL, or Browse to select a file.

> **Send to E-mail Address**   Enter a valid e-mail address that all user input should be sent to.

Send to Database   Enter the name of the database file to which the data should be appended. The file must already be connected with FrontPage via the Tools ➢ Web Settings command (Database tab), but this process is beyond the scope of this book. (See *Mastering Microsoft FrontPage 2000*, also from Sybex, for more information.)

Send to Other   Select this option to send user input to a custom form handler or specialized FrontPage form handler. Then, select a handler from the drop down list:

Custom ISAPI, NSAPI, CGI, or ASP Script   Sends the form results to a custom form handler created outside FrontPage.

Discussion Form Handler   Adds the data from the form to a FrontPage discussion group web.

Registration Form Handler   Allows the user to register for server-provided services.

In the Target Frame section, you can specify a frame to display form results. You'll find out more about frames in Skill 13.

Configuring the Form Handler

After you've selected a form handler, click the Options button in the Form Properties dialog box to open the dialog box for the selected form handler. When you send your results to a file or e-mail, the dialog box named Options for Saving Results of Form appears, as shown in Figure 12.5. These are the most frequently used options, so we'll review them in some depth.

This dialog box has four pages: File Results, E-mail Results, Confirmation Page (which you'll use if you're sending output to a page that appears in the user's browser to confirm the receipt of their data), and Saved Fields, which you'll always want to review.

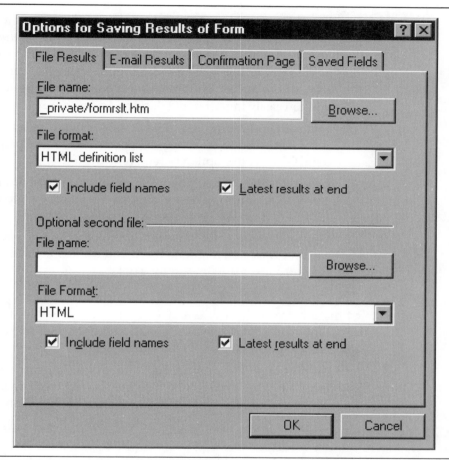

FIGURE 12.5: Use the Options for Saving Results of Form dialog box to configure the default form handler.

If you want to send user results to a file, verify or change the options on the File Results tab, shown in Figure 12.5:

> **File Name**   Enter the name of the file where the form's data is saved. If the file doesn't exist, it's created the first time data is submitted from the form. Include the relative URL of the file if it is in the active web (the _private folder might be a good place to store it).

File Format   Select one of the available file formats from the drop-down list. There are several HTML options that save the data in a web page (you need to specify a filename with an HTM or HTML extension). There are also several plain text formats; one of them, Text Database Using Comma as a Separator, creates a file where a comma is inserted between each piece of data. Most database and spreadsheet programs can read this type of file, so you can easily import it into Excel or Access, or use it as a Word merge file.

Include Field Names   By default, this option is selected so the form's data is returned to the server with each field's name paired with the field's data. Deselect this option to send only the form's data.

Latest Results at End   If you're sending the results to an HTML file, you can deselect this to write the most recent data at the top of the file. With a text file, data is always appended—added to the end.

Optional Second File   Use this group of settings to send the data to two separate files. You might do this if you wanted to have a web-ready HTML file and a text file to import for a database.

The E-mail Results tab (see Figure 12.6) includes settings for the e-mail address that should receive the results and the format that should be used in the e-mail. Use the following options in the E-mail Message Header section to specify the Subject and Reply To lines of the e-mail message:

Subject Line   Text for the Subject line of the e-mailed form results. For example, if the form is used for a membership registration, the Subject line might be Our Newest Member or Member Registration Info.

Reply-to Line   Text for the Reply To line of the e-mail message. The recipient of the e-mail clicks on this to reply to the results message. This needs to be an e-mail address or a form field with an e-mail address as a value.

Form Field Name   Enable this check box to place the results of a control (like the visitor's last name) in the Subject line or Reply To line of the e-mail. Then, type the form field name in the appropriate text box. Notice that this is enabled by default for the Reply To line. The assumption is that you'll want to include the visitor's e-mail address in the Reply To line so that the e-mail recipient can easily send mail to the visitor.

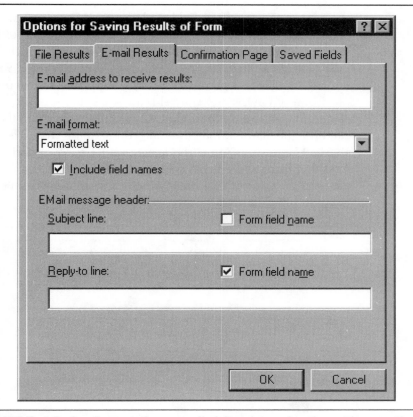

FIGURE 12.6: Format, then e-mail visitor data using the settings on the E-mail Results tab.

When a user sends in (submits) the data on a form, the FrontPage form handler returns a Confirmation page to the user. It says "Thanks" and displays the information received from the form. By default, the handler creates a plain vanilla confirmation page. You can instead specify a page in the Confirmation Page tab of the Options for Saving Results of Form dialog box.

The page you specify might be nothing more than a neatly formatted page with the message, "We received your data. Thanks!" But you can personalize the confirmation by including data from selected fields on the form that the user submitted: "Dear Sharon: Thanks for your interest in our organization..." To do this, open the confirmation page you specified in FrontPage and insert the Confirmation field component where you want to display the field. (Having the list of field names on hand makes this job easier). Save the confirmation page, and the next time it is used to confirm the receipt of data from a form, the data in the specified field replaces each Confirmation field component.

The Saved Fields tab of the Options for Saving Results of Form dialog box shows the list of fields that are captured on the form. Figure 12.7 shows the Saved Fields tab from the two-question form we created earlier. Each of the contact information fields is preceded by the group name and an underscore: for example, Contact_FirstName. The fields are saved in the order in which they're listed, so if you want to save the e-mail address first, move it to the top of the list. (You can't use the menu or toolbar while you're in this dialog box, but you can use shortcut keys: Ctrl+X or Ctrl+Delete to cut, Ctrl+V or Ctrl+Insert to paste.) Below the list of fields you created are some optional fields you can automatically capture and include with the data without having the user enter them. These include the date and time, and the type of browser.

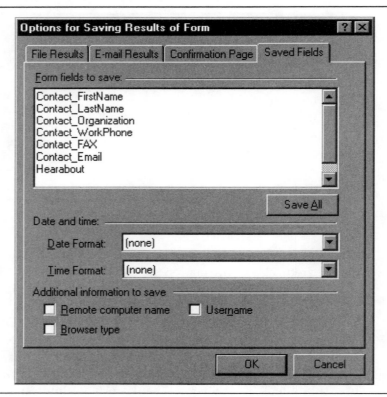

FIGURE 12.7: In the Saved Fields tab, you can specify other fields to include in the output file.

When you finish setting options, click OK to close the Options for Saving Results of Form dialog box, and again in the Form Properties dialog box to return to your form page.

Adding Fields to a Form

Some web authors prefer to create their forms from scratch. This is easy to do, because FrontPage lets you insert any of the form controls into a page. If you have not yet placed form controls on a page, when you place the first one a new form is created in the page, as evidenced by the dashed line that designates the form area. Thereafter, you can add more controls, descriptive text, and images to the form. If you want to create another form on the page, move the insertion point outside of the dashed line that defines the form.

You add a form control with the Insert ➤ Form command or by clicking a button on the Form toolbar, shown below (remember, this toolbar is a tear-off menu). Browse the toolbar, or refer to Table 12.1 for a review of the form field types.

FrontPage isn't like Visual Basic or Access; you don't drag controls and place them on the screen. Instead, you click and the field appears at the insertion point. So, before you insert a form field, you need to have a place for it. If you want the field to follow text, type the text in first. If you want to place fields in a table, it's easiest to create the table, then place the fields. For example, if you want your form to include the text string "Check here to receive our newsletter" followed by a check box, type the string, press the spacebar, then choose Insert ➤ Form ➤ Check Box, or click the Check Box button on the Form toolbar.

Microsoft publishes a large book of standards that specify how you should use product components, including controls. You don't have to read the book to develop web pages, but you should implement controls as your users expect them to be used. This allows visitors to enter information without fumbling around, and is part of what makes a site friendly. For example:

- Radio buttons should always appear in groups of two or more, because they let the reader make only one choice from several choices. If there's only one choice, use a check box.

- Only use text boxes if there are a large or unpredictable number of choices. Users would rather choose their modem from a drop-down menu than type its name. And by providing a drop-down menu, you receive consistent data.

- If the answer to a question is Yes or No, you can probably rephrase it to use a check box: "Check here to receive our newsletter" instead of "Would you like to receive our newsletter?"

- Don't ask users to enter data that you can collect automatically. Sophisticated users know that you can get the current date from their computer or your server.

- The default setting for each form field should be the setting most users are likely to choose, making one less control they have to change. Or, in a more Machiavellian worldview, the default setting should be the setting you would *like* them to choose. Some commercial sites have a notice that they offer their e-mail lists to others (for a price, of course), so they offer users the opportunity to "Check here if you don't want us to include your name in these lists." You'll notice that none of these check boxes are turned on by default.

Changing Form Field Properties

Each control in a form has a set of properties defining its name, default setting, the way it looks, the type of data it accepts (*validation*), and so on. You can adjust the properties after you enter all the fields for a form, or you can modify the properties for each as you create it. To open the properties dialog box for a control, you can do any of the following:

- Double-click the control.

- Select the control then choose Format ➣ Properties or press Alt+Enter.

- Right-click the control and choose Form Field Properties from the shortcut menu.

In the sections that follow, you learn how to change the properties for each of the form controls that you've seen in this Skill.

One-Line Text Boxes

One-line text boxes have a limited number of properties (see Figure 12.8). The first setting, Name, is found in all the controls except the radio button (which is not individually named). When you insert a control, it is given a short code-like name, such as T1 for the first one-line text box in a form; the Form Page Wizard gives controls the names you specify. As you work your way through the controls, make sure each control has a descriptive name. Don't include spaces in the names—use underscores instead.

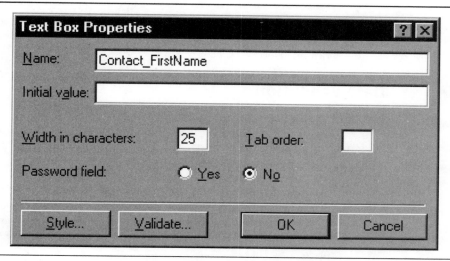

FIGURE 12.8: The Text Box Properties dialog box for a one-line text box field.

Here are the Text Box properties:

Name   Enter a name for the control to help identify the data it contains.

Initial Value   Enter the characters you want in this field when the form is opened. In some cases, a default entry can save the user some typing if the default is the typical response entered. A default entry can also serve as an example of what type of data should be entered: *Enter your name here.*

Width in Characters   Specify the width of the text box in characters (you can also select the box in the form and drag one of its selection handles to change its size). It's easier to enter data when the field is wide enough to display all or most of the text you're entering. This is not a limitation on the number of characters that can be entered but on the number of characters the user can see; you limit the number of characters through validation (see the next section).

Tab Order   Tab order specifies the order that users move through controls when they press the Tab key. Use numbers from 1–999 to set the order, with 1 being the field that the insertion point appears in when the form opens. If you don't want users to tab to a control, set its tab order value at –1. Newer browsers support tab order; others simply use the default tab order.

Password Field   If visitors will enter a password in this field, choose Yes. Whatever a user types into this field is displayed as asterisks to hide it from view. You can turn this on for any field, but users are generally not amused.

Data Validation

You can limit the type of data accepted in a one-line text box or scrolling text box by applying data validation rules to the field. You do so in the Text Box Validation dialog box (see Figure 12.9). To open the dialog box, click the Validate button in the field's Text Box Properties dialog box, or right-click the field and choose Form Field Validation.

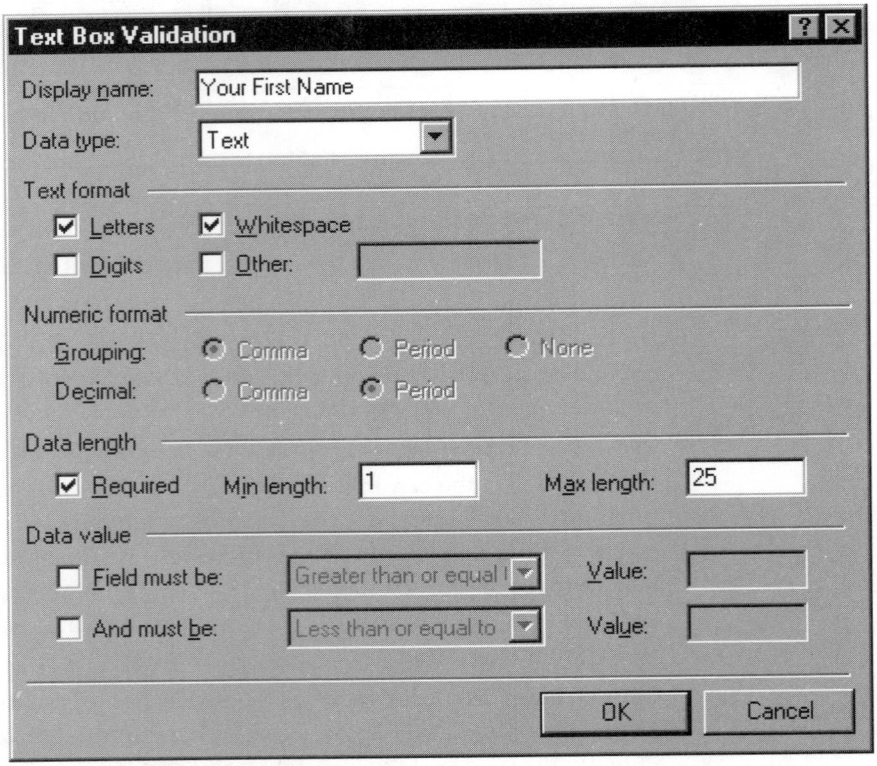

FIGURE 12.9:   You can specify the type of data accepted in a one-line or scrolling text box through data validation.

When a user submits the form's data to the server, the entry in each field is checked against any data validation that has been applied to the field. If the data in a field falls outside of the validation criteria, an error message is generated notifying the user of the problem. Whether the error message is generated on the client side or server side depends on the abilities of the browser.

If the browser supports Java, it displays validation messages before the data is ever sent to the server. Otherwise, the browser simply sends the data to the server, and the server checks the data against the validation rules. If some data is invalid, the server generates a page with the appropriate error messages and sends it back to the browser.

Display Name   When a field is mentioned in a validation message, it's identi-fied by the name you entered in the field's Text Box Properties dialog box. The name isn't usually formatted for easy reading. The Display Name is the name that appears in validation messages for the user. Instead of Contact_FirstName, you can enter Your First Name. This allows you, for example, to use exactly the same name or description that appears next to the field in the form.

Data Type   The Data Type option specifies the type of data allowed in the one-line or scrolling text box:

>   **No Constraints**   Allows any type of data in the field.
>
>   **Text**   Allows any characters to be entered into the field.
>
>   **Integer**   Requires a valid whole number, either positive, zero, or negative; ensures users don't enter alphabetic characters where a number is required.
>
>   **Number**   Allows any valid number, with or without a decimal fraction.

Once you select the Data Type, you can limit the acceptable entries for the field even further:

>   **Text Format**   When you select Text as the Data Type, you can select the type of characters allowed in the field. For example, for a field in which a member-ship number is entered, such as 123 45 6789, select the Digits and Whitespace options to allow spaces between the numbers but rule out letters.
>
>   **Numeric Format**   When you choose Integer or Number from the Data Type list, you can specify the Grouping character allowed within the entry to separate every three digits. Choose Comma, Period, or None. When you choose Number from the Data Type list, you can also specify the allowable Decimal character.

Data Length   Choose the Required option to require an entry in this field, no matter what other options have been specified. For example, you might require a first name, last name, and e-mail address from a user requesting information. Use the Min Length and Max Length fields to specify the minimum and maximum number of characters that are allowed in the field.

Data Value   Set a range of acceptable values for an entry. For example, to require a positive whole number greater than 0 but not greater than 100, choose Integer for the Data Type option, select the Required option, choose the Field Must Be option, select Greater Than, and enter 0 in the Value field. Then select the And Must Be option, choose Less Than or Equal To, and enter 100 in its Value field. If the user enters a negative number, a zero, or a number greater than 100, an appropriate error message is generated.

Changing Control Style

Click the Style button in the Text Box Properties dialog box to open the Style dialog box. Define the style for what appears in the text box in the way you define a style for text within the page, as discussed in Skill 10.

Scrolling Text Boxes

The scrolling text box is essentially the same as a one-line text box, but it allows multiple lines of text. In Figure 12.1, a scrolling text box was used to accept comments from the person filling out the form.

NOTE NOTE NOTE NOTE NOTE NOTE NOTE NOTE NOTE NOTE NOTE NOTE NOTE NOTE NOTE

Some browsers automatically wrap text when it reaches the right edge of the scrolling text box. Other browsers, however, let the text extend to the right, so the user has to press Enter to start a new line.

You can specify the width and height of a scrolling text box in its properties dialog box. As with the width of a one-line text box, these settings affect only the size of the field in the form; they do not limit the amount of text that can be entered into the field. You can apply validation rules to a scrolling text box; the choices are the same as those for a one-line text box, as discussed in "Data Validation" earlier in this chapter.

Drop-Down Menus

The Country field in the form in Figure 12.1 is a drop-down menu. The user can click the arrow in the control and select a country from the list. Drop-down menus created by the wizard or a template include some choices. When you insert a drop-down menu into a form, it is empty. You fill or modify the menu with the Drop-Down Menu Properties dialog box (shown in Figure 12.10).

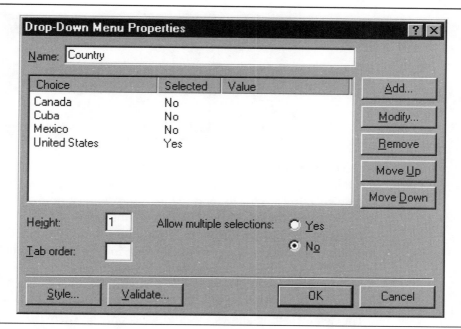

FIGURE 12.10: The Drop-Down Menu Properties dialog box for a drop-down menu form field.

To add an item to the menu, click the Add button to open the Add Choice dialog box, where you Enter what you want to appear as a choice on the menu.

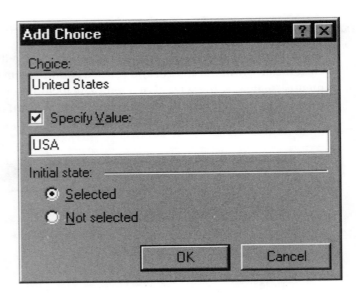

The Choice you enter is exactly what's sent to the server when a user selects this item in the menu. Optionally, you can select the Specify Value check box and enter a substitute value to send to the server. For example, you might want *United States* to appear in the list but *USA* sent to the server.

When you're adding an item to a drop-down menu, you can also specify whether the item is selected by default. For example, in Figure 12.1, United States is selected when the form opens, which is helpful if you expect most users to enter that choice. After you've created the new menu item, click OK to close the Add Choice dialog box and return to the Drop-Down Menu Properties dialog box.

The default setting allows a user to select only one item from a drop-down menu; select Yes for the Allow Multiple Selections in the properties dialog box to let a user select more than one by using Ctrl or Shift and clicking.

NOTE NOTE NOTE NOTE NOTE NOTE NOTE NOTE NOTE NOTE NOTE NOTE NOTE NOTE NOTE

It's generally more convenient for the user if you display multiple choices as a group of check boxes rather than in a pull-down menu. That way the choices are easier to read and it's also easier to see which ones are currently selected.

To rearrange the order of items in the drop-down menu, select the item in the Choice list and then click the Move Up or Move Down button to change its position in the list. A list should be in a logical order. A list with more than four or five items should be sorted. Don't worry about arranging the list around the default value; the list opens to the Selected item regardless of where it appears on the list. Click the Remove button to remove it from the list; click Modify to revise its name, value, or selected status.

You can also set validation rules for a drop-down menu in its validation dialog box, shown here.

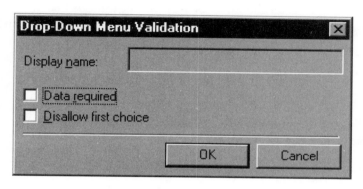

The Disallow First Choice setting lets you place an explanatory item first on the list, such as Choose a State. This item must be at the top of the list of choices; don't mark any of the other items in the list as Selected, or the item isn't displayed.

Radio Buttons

Radio buttons allow a user to make one choice from a group of choices. In Figure 12.1, four radio buttons let the user choose Web, Magazine, Radio, or Television. You define a group of radio buttons by giving each of them the same Group Name in their properties dialog box, as shown here.

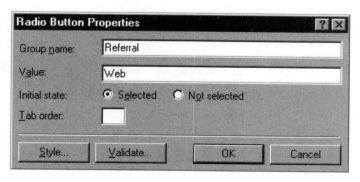

The name Referral is used for all four radio buttons in Figure 12.1. The value you assign to a radio button is sent to the server when the Submit button is selected by the user. In Figure 12.1, the radio buttons can have the same values as their respective labels. However, for longer responses you might want to use an abbreviated value thatwill take up less room in a database. This is the kind of issue that needs to be settled *before* you get to far in your form design.

You can choose to have one of the buttons in a group selected by default when the form is opened. Again, offering a default choice can be a convenience to the person who's filling out the form. If none of the buttons in a group is a default choice, you can still require the user to select a button in the validation dialog box. Select the Data Required check box and, optionally, enter a name for the group of radio buttons in the Display Name field. Applying validation to one radio button in a group applies it to all buttons in the group.

Check Boxes

The check box allows a user to select a single item by clicking the box; clicking the box again deselects it. A check mark in the box indicates it's selected. In Figure 12.1, users could check any of six check boxes to indicate the things they liked about the Web site. The properties of a check box (shown next) consist of its name, value, whether it's selected or deselected when the form is opened, and tab order.

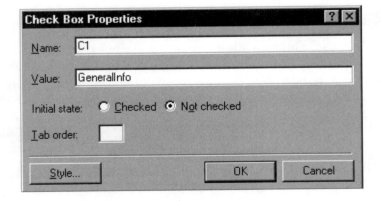

Push Buttons

There are three kinds of push button controls you can insert into a form: Submit, Reset, and Normal. Whenever you create a new form in a page, FrontPage automatically adds the Submit and Reset push buttons. These two buttons have scripts, based in part on the settings you entered in the File Results and E-mail Results tabs of the Form Properties dialog box. Normal push buttons have no attached script, but are generic buttons to which you can attach your own scripts. The Push Button Properties dialog box (shown here) lets you change the text that appears on the face of the button, the button type, and the tab order.

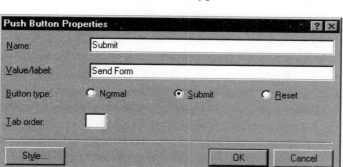

The Picture button is a substitute push button. Specifically, it's a substitute for the Submit button. Choose Insert ➤ Form ➤ Picture, or click the Picture on the Form toolbar. The standard Picture dialog box opens so you can select the image for the button.

When you click OK, the selected image is placed in the form as a button. Choosing either Form Field Properties or Picture Properties from the shortcut menu produces the same result: opening the Picture Properties dialog box (shown next). In this case the dialog box has a Form Field tab on which you name the picture form field. The other tabs in the dialog box are the same ones that appear for any image: General, Video, and Appearance.

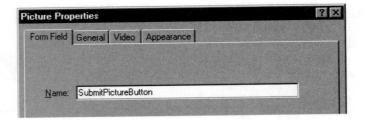

Linking Text to a Control

You can make your forms easier to navigate by giving the user a bigger target for selecting such items as check boxes and radio buttons. You will normally place descriptive text next to each control, as there was in Figure 12.1. You can link that text to the control so that clicking either the text or the control will activate (select or deselect) that control.

To link the text and the control, first select both of them, such as by dragging over them. Then choose Insert ➤ Form ➤ Label, or click the Label button on the Form toolbar. The text will now be enclosed in a dotted border, indicating that it is linked to a control. When the form is displayed in Preview mode or in a browser, clicking either the text or the control will activate the control.

Filling Out the Form in a Browser

Open a page that contains a form in your browser in the same way that you open any other page. No server interaction is involved until you press the button that submits the form's data to the server. The sample form is shown in a browser in Figure 12.11, with data entered in its various controls. At this point, a user can erase the data entered in the form by clicking the Reset Form button, which resets all the controls to their default values. If the user were ready to send the data to the server, a click of the Send Form button does the job.

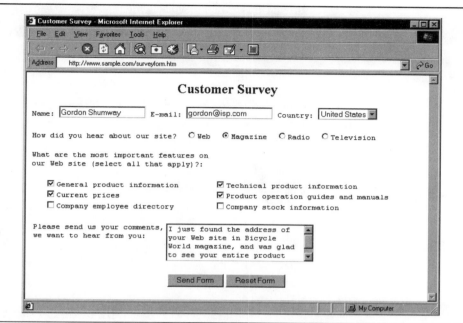

FIGURE 12.11: You open a form in a browser as you would any other page, and fill it out without any server interaction.

This form uses the default form handler, Send to File. It is this routine that sends the form's data to the server where it is saved in a file, and sends a confirmation page back to the user to verify that the data was received.

The data from this form is stored on the server in the format specified in the Options for Saving Results of Form dialog box for the form handler, shown next. For the form in Figure 12.11, the file format for the results file is Text Database Using Comma as a Separator; the file is named `feedback.txt` and stored in the web's private folder. A second copy of the data is sent to an HTML file named `feedback.htm`, also located in the web.

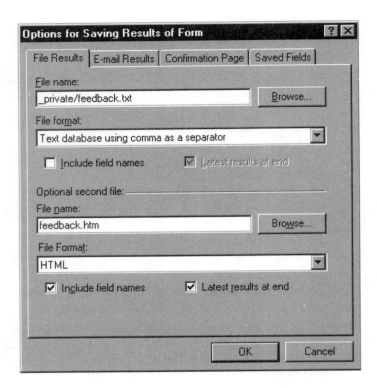

After the data from the form in Figure 12.11 is saved to the file, it contains the entry shown in Figure 12.12 (the text is actually just a single line, but Word Wrap was enabled in Notepad so all the text could be seen). There are no field names in the file, and commas are used to separate the entries from each form field. This is the type of file that most database and spreadsheet programs can easily read. For example, when you open this file in Excel, you can choose to have each control's data fall into a single column.

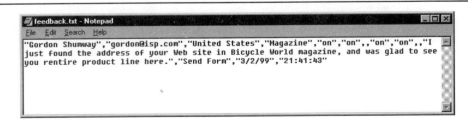

FIGURE 12.12: The data from the form is saved in a comma-delimited text file.

The HTML file, on the other hand, isn't as readily accessible to other application formats. However, it's easier to open in a browser.

The results files contain data from a single form. Each time the form is filled out and submitted, another line of data is added to each file. They continue to grow until you either delete the files or move them to another location. If you move the text file (say, at the end of the month), the next time the form is submitted, a new feedback.txt file is created.

Are You Experienced?

Now you can...

- ☑ **Create forms from scratch or by using a template or wizard**
- ☑ **Select and configure form handlers**
- ☑ **Add fields to a form**
- ☑ **Adjust the properties of form controls**
- ☑ **Set data validation for text boxes and scrolling text boxes**
- ☑ **Use a form in a browser**

Getting Fancier with Frames

- ➔ **Framing pages in a frames page**
- ➔ **Using a template to create a frames page**
- ➔ **Viewing a frames page in your browser**
- ➔ **Creating a custom frames page**
- ➔ **Adjusting the size or number of frames**
- ➔ **Modifying frame and frames page properties**

One of the ongoing controversies in Web design is in regard to the use of frames, a layout technique in which more than one page is displayed at a time. With adequate forethought, frames can be an exciting and effective design tool. Carelessly applied, they are intrusive and distracting, carving up precious screen space into difficult-to-see pieces. This Skill shows you when to use frames successfully, how to build a frames page to contain multiple pages, and how to provide users with an option to not use frames, if they prefer.

Dividing a Page into Frames

A frames page allows you to create a single web page that displays multiple pages. Each page is displayed within a separate window, or *frame*. The page containing these frames is called a *frames page* or *frames set*. When a browser opens a frames page, it also opens and displays the page assigned to each frame. Using frames, you can build all sorts of interesting and practical solutions.

Figure 13.1 shows a typical use for a frames page, which you'll build in this Skill. Perhaps without even realizing it, visitors to your frames page see several different pages in their browser:

- A frame in the top-left corner displays a banner and an image (it's surrounded by a dark border in Figure 13.1, indicating that this is the active frame, the one currently being edited).

- A frame in the top-right displays a greeting and a convenient link for taking a tour of the site.

- A frame on the left side beneath the banner's frame displays a table of contents page, which is built from the Table of Contents component discussed in Skill 11.

- A frame on the right side displays a home page when the frames page is first opened. After that, when you click a hyperlink in the table of contents frame on the left, the target of the link is displayed in this frame on the right. Therefore, what you see in this frame changes as you click different links.

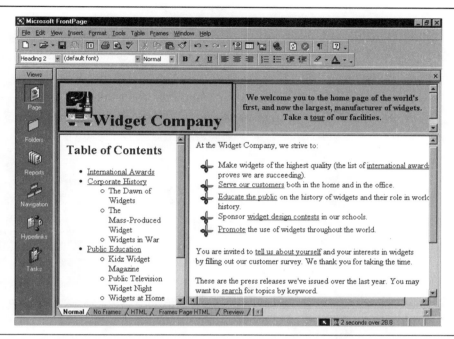

FIGURE 13.1: This frames page displays a banner and a greeting at the top, a table of contents on the left, and the target of table of contents links on the right.

When you create a frames page in FrontPage, you can create new pages to place in the frames or use existing pages from your web. You may want to create the pages that you will display in each frame first before creating the frames page.

TIP TIP TIP TIP TIP TIP TIP TIP TIP TIP TIP TIP TIP TIP TIP TIP TIP TIP TIP TIP TIP TIP TIP TIP

It's a good idea to turn off shared borders and navigation bars on any pages you are going to use as part of a frames page. They don't display properly in the frames page and take up valuable display space. The frames provide users with sufficient navigational aids, so additional buttons are unnecessary anyway.

Creating a Frames Page

When you're creating a frames page in FrontPage, you always start with a Frames template. You can choose from 10 ready-built frames page templates that provide the basic structure for your frames page. You are free to modify that structure after you create the page.

To create the frames page, make sure you're in Page view and then choose File ➤ New ➤ Page, and click the Frames Pages tab of the New dialog box, shown in Figure 13.2.

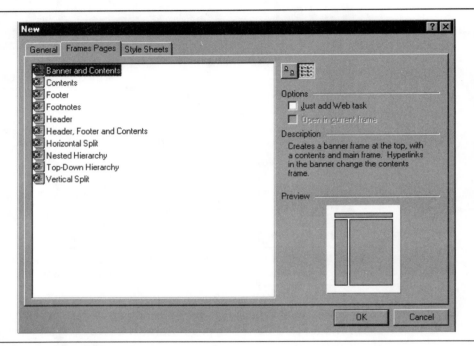

FIGURE 13.2: The Frames Pages tab of the New dialog box offers a variety of frames page templates.

Click each of the choices to see a preview of the frames page layout. Choose the layout that is closest to the structure you want for your page, and click OK to create the frames page. For this exercise, select the Banner and Contents template, which creates a three-frame page—one frame at the top spans the width of the page, and two frames below it divide the page vertically (as shown here to left).

Each frame has three buttons to help you design your page: Set Initial Page, New Page, and Help. Frames pages also have two additional views: No Frames, and Frames Page HTML, so a frames page has five View tabs. When you click the No Frames tab, you see the page that appears when a user's browser cannot display frames (as discussed later in this Skill in "Designing a No Frames Alternative"). The Frames Page HTML tab shows you the HTML for the frames page, while the HTML tab shows you the HTML for active page (as it does when you're working on a single page in Page view).

\ **Normal** / No Frames / HTML / Frames Page HTML / Preview /

The HTML for a typical FrontPage Frames page looks like this:

```
<html><head>
<title>Widget Company Web</title>
</head>
<frameset framespacing="2" rows="123,*">
  <frameset cols="*,56%">
    <frame name="banner" scrolling="no" noresize target="contents"
src="Banner.htm">
    <frame name="banner1" src="../we_welcome_you_to_the_home_page_.htm"
scrolling="no"
    noresize target="main">
  </frameset>
  <frameset cols="232,*">
    <frame name="contents" target="main" src="table_of_contents.htm">
    <frame name="main" src="index.htm">
  </frameset>
  <noframes>
  <body>
  <p>This page uses frames, but your browser doesn't support them. </p>
  </body>
  </noframes>
</frameset>
</html>
```

The content of each frame is identified between opening and closing <FRAMESET> tags. The content of the page that is displayed when the browser doesn't support tags is identified with the <NOFRAMES> tag.

NOTE NOTE NOTE NOTE NOTE NOTE NOTE NOTE NOTE NOTE NOTE NOTE NOTE NOTE NOTE

At this point, the No Frames alternative page only contains the default text "This page uses frames, but your browser doesn't support them." Later in this Skill, you'll learn how to replace this pithy text with another page.

Creating a New Page to Go into the Frame

New Page

To insert a page into a frame, you need to link the page to the corresponding section of the frames page. If you are creating the pages from scratch, make sure you're working from the Normal view tab and then click the New Page button in the frame in which you want to start working.

The insertion point moves into the frame and all of the normal page editing commands are available to you. If you prefer a larger workspace, right-click in the frame and choose Open Page in New Window from the short-cut menu. You can switch back to the frames page at any time using the Window menu. You'll see that the page you just created is displayed in its frame.

You could save and then close the new page at this point, but it's helpful to actually see the page in the context of the entire frames page—you may want to do some editing to improve its look.

Setting the Initial Page from an Existing Page

Set Initial Page...

If you already have a page you want to appear in a frame, click the Set Initial Page button. This opens the same Create Hyperlink dialog box you learned about in Skill 6. Select the page you want as the target of the hyperlink and click OK. When you open a frames page, the hyperlink in each frame is activated and the target pages, called *initial pages*, appear in the designated frames.

If the page you selected as the target for a frame is too large for that frame, in most cases horizontal and vertical scroll bars appear by default in the frame. A little later in this Skill, you'll learn how to resize the frame and eliminate unnecessary scroll bars to create a crisper, less cluttered look.

Saving a Frames Page or Its Initial Pages

Saving a frames page is no different than saving any other page, except that you need to remember that you are only saving the page's structure and the hyperlinks to each of the initial pages, not the actual content of those pages. You can still open each page separately from the frames page and make any desired editing changes, or open them alone as you would any other page for editing. The next time you open the frames page, the revised pages are included. To save the frames page, use File ➤ Save or File ➤ Save As. Figure 13.3 shows the dialog box when you save a frames page; on its right side is a diagram that indicates what aspect of the page you're actually saving to a file. For example, the diagram in

Figure 13.3 shows that the entire frames page is being saved, as opposed to the initial page for one of the frames.

To save one of the initial pages, click within its frame to make it the active frame and choose Frames ➤ Save Page or Frames ➤ Save Page As. You'll see the same dialog box, only this time the frames diagram will indicate that you're saving a single page within the frames set because only that frame in the diagram will be shaded.

When you are working on a new frames set and saving one of its initial pages for the first time, you'll see the same dialog box with the diagram indicating which frame's page you're about to save. It can be a little confusing at first if you have several new initial pages in a new frames page, so be sure to check that diagram.

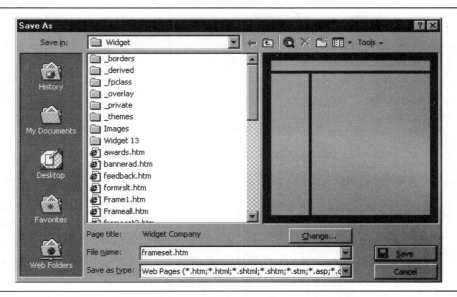

FIGURE 13.3: When you save a frames page, you are only saving the structure of the page with its corresponding hyperlinks.

TIP TIP TIP TIP TIP TIP TIP TIP TIP TIP TIP TIP TIP TIP TIP TIP TIP TIP TIP TIP TIP TIP TIP

To make a frames page the home page of your web, rename the home page in FrontPage before saving the new frames page. When you save the new page, give it the name of your previous home page, such as default.htm **or** index.htm.

Editing Pages in Frames

When you click in any of the frames while editing a frames page in Page view, a color-highlighted border appears around the frame indicating that it is active. You can edit the page in its frame or choose Open in New Window from the shortcut menu for more extensive editing.

TIP TIP TIP TIP TIP TIP TIP TIP TIP TIP TIP TIP TIP TIP TIP TIP TIP TIP TIP TIP TIP TIP TIP TIP
You can move among the frames by mouse or keyboard—click within a frame to make it active, or press F6 to make the next frame active.

Resizing a Frame

Whether you create a frame's initial page from scratch or insert an existing page, you may discover that a frame is not wide enough or tall enough to display the page effectively. This problem is easily rectified by adjusting the size of the frame. To adjust a frame's dimensions, point to the frame border. When the pointer changes to a double-headed arrow, hold down the mouse button and drag the cursor to extend the frame. When the frame is the size you want it to be, release the mouse button.

Splitting a Frame

The frames page templates are starting places for any of the frames pages you want to produce. However, you aren't limited to the frame structures that appear in the templates. You can add new frames to an existing structure or delete frames from it. For example, here's how to divide the top frame that was created by the Banner and Contents frames page template:

1. Click anywhere within the top frame to make it the active frame.

2. Choose Frames ➤ Split Frame, which displays the Split Frame dialog box (shown next).

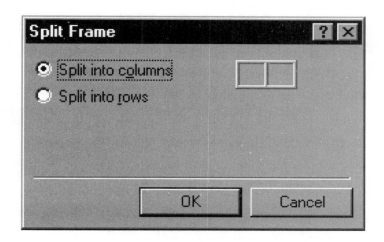

3. Select the Split into Columns option, and click OK to split the single page-wide frame into two half-page frames. The frames page now contains four frames.

Another way to split a frame is by pointing to a frame's border, holding down the Ctrl key and the mouse button, and dragging the new frame into existence.

Whichever method you use, the new frame is created with Set Initial Page, New Page, and Help buttons so you can identify or create the target page for the frame.

Creating Hyperlinks to Targeted Frames

When a user clicks a hyperlink in a page that appears in a frame, you can designate whether you want the target of that link to open in a new window, in the current window, or in a particular frame. By default, the frames template determines where a page opens. You can change the default in the Edit Hyperlink dialog box.

When you learned to create hyperlinks in Skill 6, there was one option in the Edit Hyperlink dialog box that we didn't discuss. Now is the time. Right-click a hyperlink in the page you want to redirect and choose Hyperlink Properties. The Target Frame field is located in the bottom right of the Edit Hyperlink dialog box.

Click the icon next to the Target Frame field to open the Target Frame dialog box, shown in Figure 13.4. There's a map of the active frames page on the left side of the dialog box. The right side shows a list of common targets. Notice that the default frame in Figure 13.4 is the frame named Main. Click each frame in the Current Frames Page image to see which frame is designated as Main—the name appears in the Target Setting text box.

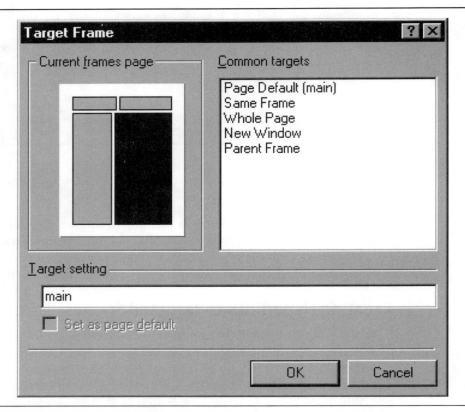

FIGURE 13.4: The Target Frame dialog box lets you designate where you want a hyperlinked page to open.

There are five options, each of which identifies a different possible location:

Page Default   This location is set by the template choice you made, and is the recommended target frame (the frame named Main in Figure 13.4).

Same Frame   The target page replaces the original page in the frame—much like a standard hyperlink.

Whole Page   The target page replaces the entire frames page in the browser window.

New Window   The target page opens in a second window of the user's browser.

Parent Frame   The target page is displayed in the frame that contains the current frameset tag. To use this option, you have to be comfortable working directly with HTML.

Any other frame in the Target Frame map is also a possible target. Click the frame in the map to display the name of that frame in the Target Setting text box.

If you want this target to be the new default target for all hyperlinks on this page (this is referring to this page only—not the entire frames page), click the Set as Page Default check box. If you don't do this, the only hyperlink affected by the changed location is the one you right-clicked on to open the dialog box. For example, for the table of contents in the left-hand frame in Figure 13.1, you would probably want to set its default target location so that all its hyperlinks opened their targets in the same location, such as the right-hand frame named Main.

NOTE NOTE NOTE NOTE NOTE NOTE NOTE NOTE NOTE NOTE NOTE NOTE NOTE NOTE NOTE

If you create a form for user input, you can send the output of the form to a frame on a frames page. Open the form's properties and click the Target Frame button to select a target frame.

Opening a Page in a Frame

When a frame does not yet have an initial page, you can click the Set Initial Page button for that frame and select a page for it. When a frame already has a page specified, you can select a different page for that frame. Open the Frame Properties dialog box, as discussed in the next section, and specify a different filename in the Initial Page field. When you click OK, that page will then be displayed in the frame.

NOTE NOTE NOTE NOTE NOTE NOTE NOTE NOTE NOTE NOTE NOTE NOTE NOTE NOTE NOTE

The File ➢ Open or File ➢ New ➢ File command opens another page that is unrelated to the frames set page. The File ➢ Close command closes the entire frames set page. There is no command for closing the initial page in a frame.

Deleting a Frame

If you would like fewer frames than the template provides (or than you created), you can delete a frame by clicking in the frame and choosing Delete Frame from the Frame menu. Although the frame and the page it displayed disappear, the page itself has not been deleted from disk.

Modifying Frame Properties

Every frames set has a set of properties, and every frame within it has its own properties. Right-click within a frame and choose Frame Properties to open the Frame Properties dialog box for that frame (see Figure 13.5). From there, you can also access the properties for the entire frames page by clicking the Frames Page button.

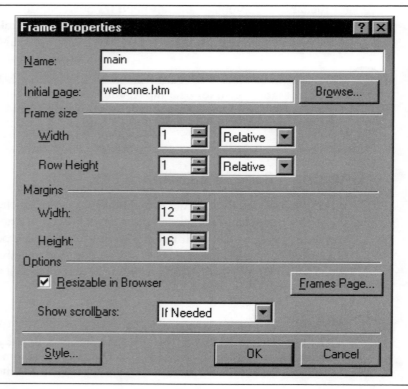

FIGURE 13.5: Use the Frame Properties dialog box to set options for an individual frame.

The major categories of frame properties are:

Name   The name given here is the default name given to the frame by the template. You should normally leave this the way it is. The names created by the templates are pretty standard, based on the purpose of the frame within the page. If you decide to change the name, however, realize that this is one instance when FrontPage does *not* automatically update any hyperlinks in other pages that target that frame name. This means that you'll have to manually edit those links to make them reference the new frame name.

Initial Page   If you want to change the page that opens in this frame, enter the new URL here or click the Browse button to select the file from the Edit Hyperlink dialog box.

Frame Size   Set Width and Row Height for the frame. By default, the sizes are set to Relative, meaning that they will adjust relative to the size of the window in which the frames set page is displayed. You can instead specify an exact size in pixels or specify a percent to make the frame variable based on the size of the browser's window.

If the frame is part of a column that contains at least one other frame, the Column Width and Height options are enabled instead of Width and Row Height. Changes to the column width affect other frames within the same column, and all other columns are adjusted accordingly.

Margins   This refers to the indentation of the contents of the frame from the frame borders.

Options   There are two options related to how the frame appears in the user's browser. If you select the Resizable in Browser check box, then users will be able to drag the borders of the frame to make it larger or smaller. Although there may be some advantages of this with certain designs, if you allow users to resize the frame display, you give up a lot of control over how your page appears to your users. Test it out first in different browsers and with different size monitors, if possible, to see how resizing affects the page before choosing this option.

The second option lets you choose whether you want scroll bars to appear. The choices are Never, Always, or If Needed. The If Needed option is probably the most reasonable in most circumstances, but there may be some frames where you want to prohibit scrolling and lock in the contents. The choice of Always rarely makes sense, but there are probably exceptions even for that.

SKILL
13

In addition to the standard property settings, there is also a Style button to take you to the cascading style sheet settings for this frame. See Skill 10 for more information about cascading style sheets.

When you finish changing the Frame Properties, click OK to save the changes.

Changing Frames Page Properties

Surprisingly, there are only two property settings that affect frames pages. These are in the standard Page Properties dialog box on an extra tab named Frames, shown in Figure 13.6. Click the Frames Page button in the Frame Properties dialog box to access these frames page properties.

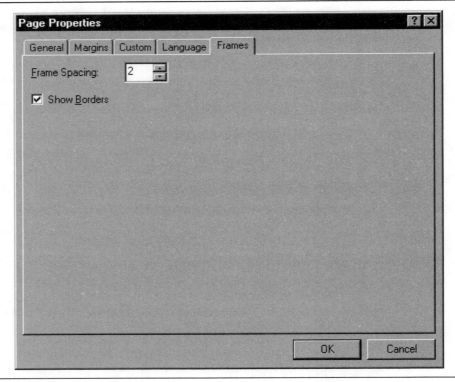

FIGURE 13.6: Set frame spacing and borders for a frames page in the Page Properties dialog box.

The first option, Frame Spacing, refers to the amount of padding that exists between frames on a page. The default setting is 2 pixels. Use the arrows to increase or decrease this setting.

The second option, Show Borders, is turned on by default, but more and more designers are discouraging the use of borders in order to give pages a cleaner look. Clearing the Show Borders check box reduces the Frame Spacing to zero. Figure 13.7 shows the same frames page displayed earlier in Figure 13.1, but this time without borders.

Whether you choose to use borders is a personal design decision. Just be cautious about the number of frames you use on a page. The frames page in Figure 13.7 is actually pretty cluttered, even when displayed in a window that is 800 × 600 pixels with just four frames and no frame borders. It would look even more crowded if it were displayed on a computer screen that was 640 × 400 pixels. If you can accomplish your objective in three, or even two frames, there is no reason to add more. A good rule is to keep borders turned on if the content of the frames is so different that you want to keep it separated—turn them off if you want the frames to be more closely tied together.

SKILL
13

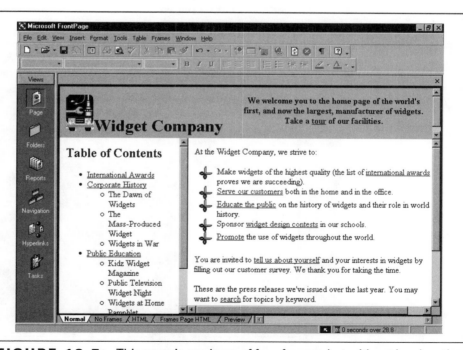

FIGURE 13.7: This page is made up of four frames, but without borders the page appears less divided.

Creating a Frame within a Frame

Just in case you thought your monitor wasn't small enough already, it's possible to set a frames page as the initial page within another frame. However, in the Normal view FrontPage can't display the frames page within a frames page. Instead you get a View Frames Page button in the intended frame, like the one shown in Figure 13.8.

Click this button to edit the frames page. If you want to see the complete frames page and its nested frames page, click the Preview tab or click the Preview in Browser button. Figure 13.9 shows a Vertical Split frames page nested within the right-hand frame of the page shown in Figure 13.1. Again, concerns about display size and appearance are paramount when you consider this option.

> **NOTE NOTE NOTE NOTE NOTE NOTE NOTE NOTE NOTE NOTE NOTE NOTE NOTE NOTE NOTE**
>
> **You may be able to avoid dealing with nested frames pages and their commensurate complexity within FrontPage if you simply split or delete the frames within a single frames page. However, you may find it less painful to go the nested route when you want to include a frames page that is already targeted by many hyperlinks in other pages.**

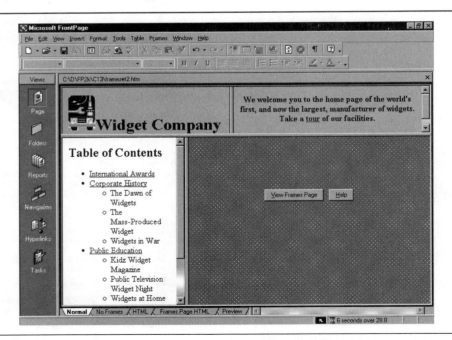

FIGURE 13.8: When you choose a frames page as the initial page of a frame, the frames page is not displayed directly.

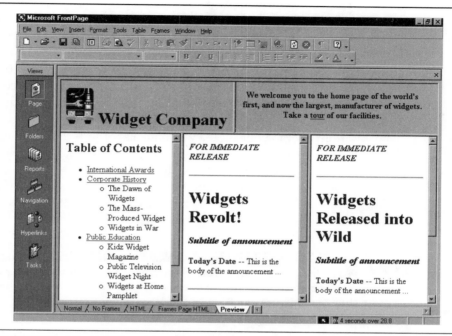

SKILL
13

FIGURE 13.9: You can preview a frames-within-a-frames page to see how it looks. This Vertical Split frames page is part of a Banner and Contents frames page.

Designing a No Frames Alternative

There may still be many people around the world who don't have access to a browser that displays frames. You can take the attitude that it's too bad for them, or you can provide them with a "frameless" way to access your site.

A frames page does not use the normal <BODY> tag to define the frames it contains, and in fact that tag need not appear in a frames page. It can be used in a frames page, however, to allow a browser that can't display frames to display a standard page when it opens the frames page. The <BODY> tag is placed within a <NOFRAMES> tag, which is ignored by a frames-enabled browser. Therefore, one browser might be able to view the frames page as a set of frames, while another browser will display only the page that is defined with the <BODY> tags.

To see the non-frames page that appears by default in a frames page template, click the No Frames tab at the bottom of the Page view. It's a simple page with the words "This page uses frames, but your browser doesn't support them." This page provides no hyperlinks to take users anywhere else in your site, so chances are that frames-challenged visitors would click the browser's Back button, which might take them back out of your site and you would never see them again.

You can avoid this by providing a way into your site without having to view frames pages. There are two accepted ways to accomplish this. The first is to create a front door to your site—a welcome mat of sorts that gives users some options, such as frames or no frames, or graphics or text only. This choice is becoming increasingly popular among Web designers.

Implementing the frames/no frames choice only requires a different target for the hyperlinks from the two buttons. The Frames button loads a frames page; the No Frames button loads your home page without frames.

NOTE NOTE NOTE NOTE NOTE NOTE NOTE NOTE NOTE NOTE NOTE NOTE NOTE NOTE NOTE

Providing users with a front door where they can choose a no frames option also accommodates those users who just don't like frames because it divides their screens too much.

Another way to accomplish this same objective is to include a page between opening and closing <NOFRAMES> tags. FrontPage already gives you this page—all you have to do is edit it so it's a bit friendlier than the default. Make sure it includes links to the rest of your web so users aren't stuck there.

Considerations in the Use of Frames

The focus of this Skill is on how to use frames as part of your web design strategy. Now that you know the basics of frames, there are a few important things to consider. We've already mentioned that frames reduce the amount of screen that's available for viewing content. Scroll bars, frame margins, and frame borders all take up critical viewing space. Until the average person accessing the Internet has a large monitor with plenty of pixels, frames make a small space uncomfortably cramped for the majority of users. For that reason, many people avoid sites that use frames, especially if the web's designers haven't provided a No Frames alternative.

Even more critical, however, is the fact that people who are visually impaired or require a speech-based interface need text-only access to be able to use screen readers and other viewing aids to retrieve information. The use of frames prevents these devices from working effectively, thereby restricting access to your site and denying some people equal access to the information on the Internet.

NOTE NOTE NOTE NOTE NOTE NOTE NOTE NOTE NOTE NOTE NOTE NOTE NOTE NOTE

Decisions about using frames on a company intranet can have larger implications. In the U.S, for example, employers are legally required to make reasonable accommodations for individuals with disabilities (similar legislation is pending in Canada). It's a good idea to discuss company policy on accessibility issues with your personnel or human resources department as part of your intranet development process.

The Internet is an incredible way to make information available to all people across all cultures and all socioeconomic levels. It can only fulfill this purpose, however, if those who are designing Web content keep all people in mind while they are developing sites.

Are You Experienced?

Now you can...

- ☑ **Insert an existing page in a frames page**
- ☑ **Use a template to create a variety of frames pages**
- ☑ **Create a custom frames page**
- ☑ **Resize frames**
- ☑ **Create a hyperlink to targeted frames**
- ☑ **Modify frame and frames page properties**
- ☑ **Include a frames page in frame**
- ☑ **Design a no-frames alternative**

Publishing Your Web Site

- ➔ Testing your Web site
- ➔ Publishing your Web site
- ➔ Renaming, moving, or deleting your Web site
- ➔ Assigning permissions to your server-hosted webs
- ➔ Running the Microsoft Personal Web Server

This chapter focuses on how to administer your webs. It begins with some tips on testing your site for reliability and usability. You then learn how to publish your web on a FrontPage server or a server that lacks the FrontPage server extensions. You also find out about user permissions and web administration using the Microsoft Personal Web Server.

Testing and Refining Your Web Site

Before you present your finished Web site to the world, you need be sure everything in it is working perfectly. There's nothing quite so anticlimactic as opening the curtains on your site and then having to close them immediately to make repairs. With that in mind, you'll now see some of the ways you can ensure the dependability of your FrontPage webs. There have been many tips and snippets of testing and maintenance advice throughout this book. Advice relating to keeping a Web site healthy applies to all sites in general, not just FrontPage webs.

In fact, when you build and maintain a web using FrontPage, many testing and maintenance chores are either eliminated or vastly simplified. For example, when you rename a file in a non-FrontPage web, the job of finding and revising all the hyperlinks that target the renamed file is a major piece of housekeeping. In FrontPage, it happens automatically.

Back Up Your FrontPage Webs

Maintaining current backups is good practice for all of your work on a computer, but it's even more important with your Web publishing. If users rely on your web for access to information, you need to quickly post a backup following a hardware or software failure. And whether you're in the process of building your Web sites or already have them up and running, you'll likely be making changes to them on a daily or weekly basis. Having a previous version of files can be a real lifesaver when you hastily click OK when asked to confirm a deletion. So be sure your FrontPage webs are included in your regular backups, or back them up separately by copying their root folder. Don't just *create* backups—*verify* your backups to ensure that they contain usable data.

Test under a Variety of Browsers

The whole purpose of the typical Web site is to deliver content to users. There are many different browsers on the market, all of which produce slightly different results when displaying the same page. Some browsers have more advanced features than others, and some are just plain outdated. When a browser is pushing a year old, its days seem numbered!

So, you should have several of the more popular browsers available for testing your FrontPage webs, and try to have both the newest and the previous version of each one. If you want to be really accommodating to visitors to your site, see how your web pages look in an older browser—one that cannot display frames, for example. If you include newer HTML features in your pages, you're leaving users with older browsers out of the picture. On the other hand, Web browsers aren't exactly expensive or difficult to obtain when you can download them for free.

SKILL 14

Many Web designers feel that it is their responsibility to include the newest, latest features in their pages, to push the envelope for the browser companies. If designers don't include new features, they reason, users won't need to download more capable browsers. If users don't demand browsers that support new features, there's no reason for software companies to include support for the latest components in their browsers. If a new technology or HTML extension is the best tool to get your message across, go for it. On the other hand, including a lot of beta components just to prove you can is an easy way to create an annoying Web site; sites that cause computers to crash in the middle of a download are incredibly unpopular.

Use Multiple Testers

It's amazing how one person can discover something that many others have missed. The more people you can corral into testing your site, the better. Each person brings a different perspective, a different interest, and a different set of talents to the job. One person tends to catch grammatical errors, while another might not notice them but finds an empty box that was supposed to display an image.

To ensure a wide range of perspectives, recruit testers with the range of skills representative of potential visitors to your site. For example, if you're creating an intranet that's used throughout the company, recruit a couple of real novices to the Web from outside of your department to help test the site. Novices who work in your department can help you pinpoint usability issues (like the placement of navigation tools), but it takes an outsider to identify places that are cloaked in departmental jargon.

Don't just sit testers in front of the computer with paper and pen. You'll learn a lot about your Web site by watching testers as they navigate through the pages. For example, three users in a row may click an image that doesn't have a link, rather than the nearby text link. By watching, you'll know that it's a good idea to either move or change the picture, or use it as a hyperlink.

Test Your Sites with and without Color

Although monochrome monitors are becoming rare, it's still a little early to assume everyone who visits your site is using a color monitor. If your site is heavy with color graphics and, especially, backgrounds, you may want to develop an alternative for those who don't have color.

If you feel there are just too few people who would benefit from this to make the extra work worthwhile, at least take the time to see how your pages look when viewed on a monochrome monitor. If they're unreadable or just plain impossible, you might consider providing a simple, pared-down alternate page.

Offer a Text-Only Page

There was a time when text-only browsers were the norm, but not any more. Nonetheless, some users may turn off the graphical image capabilities of their browsers to trim download time, cut costs, or simply make the Web tolerable when connection speeds are slow.

Other users can't choose a better browser. Blind and visually impaired visitors use Lynx or other screen reader software to interpret and read the text on your site. If all your pages use frames or many of your links are hotspots instead of textual, the site isn't accessible. To create a site that the largest percentage of visitors can load and enjoy, offer a text-only alternative page (or series of alternate pages for the site) that users open through a Text only link on the home page.

NOTE NOTE NOTE NOTE NOTE NOTE NOTE NOTE NOTE NOTE NOTE NOTE NOTE NOTE NOTE NOTE

For more information on the issues involved in designing speech-friendly sites for users with screen readers and other accessibility issues, check the World Wide Web Consortium at http://www.w3.org.

Test Your Pages at Different Screen Resolutions

One of the more frustrating aspects of creating a web page is trying to compromise on an "average" screen size. You can design your pages compactly so they nicely fill a monitor at a resolution of 640 × 480, but they might leave a lot of blank space on the right side when viewed at 800 × 600. If you design your pages for that higher resolution, a visitor working at a lower resolution might have to scroll the screen right and left to see the entire page.

NOTE NOTE NOTE NOTE NOTE NOTE NOTE NOTE NOTE NOTE NOTE NOTE NOTE NOTE NOTE

One way to avoid resolution problems is to design your pages with a tall orientation rather than a wide one. Let the visitor scroll down through a page instead of having to scroll to the right and back again. Better yet, put some of your content on another page and add a link. The majority of users don't bother to scroll, so content that exceeds page size may never be seen by most of your visitors.

SKILL
14

No matter how you design your pages, you should certainly test them at different screen resolutions. That's why FrontPage's File ➤ Preview in Browser command lets you specify a size for the browser. The command doesn't change your screen's resolution, it simply adjusts the size of the browser's window to show the equivalent amount of screen at the given resolution. Of course, this only works if your own screen is running at a resolution that's equal to or higher than the one you choose for the preview.

Test Your Sites at Different Connection Speeds

When you test your Web site on your local computer, you don't know what it's like to access the site over a slow network connection, let alone over a dial-up connection at modem speeds. So do yourself and visitors to your site a favor, and test your site over a slower, real-world connection. You might be shocked at how slowly that seemingly small image downloads at 28,800 bits per second (typically about 3,200 bytes, or characters, per second). When you've browsed through your site or others at modem speeds, you'll start to get a feel for how fast large pages or images are transferred. If pages download slowly, make use of some of the techniques you learned in earlier Skills:

- Create links to pages with multiple images or video, and make users aware of the approximate download time.

- Use thumbnails to link to large images.

- Use progressive JPEGs rather than regular JPEGs.

- Convert JPEGs to interlaced GIFs.

Don't forget to check the download estimates in the FrontPage status bar as you're constructing your pages. And if your pages are published on a high volume server, remember to test the site at peak times as well as off hours to determine real download speeds that users experience.

Test Your Hyperlinks

As emphasized in Skill 6, you must test the hyperlinks in your site on a regular basis to ensure they still connect to their target URLs and that the targets are the files you expect them to be. The Verify Hyperlinks command on the Reporting toolbar can do the first part of this job by testing to see if a link actually has a valid target URL.

The second part is a little more difficult, however. There's really no automated way to confirm the target of an external hyperlink is still *relevant* to you and your site. When a link goes outside of your Web site and your control, you have to click the link and see what the server returns. Having multiple testers go through your site on an ongoing basis is one way to find broken links. Large corporate Web sites often have full time Web gardeners, who have the job of following each link and "rooting out" dead links and orphaned pages.

Provide an Opportunity for Feedback

Browsing a Web site is often a read-only process, where visitors to a site get a lot of information without returning any. It's important to give visitors the opportunity to let you know how things are going so they can report problems, leave comments, or ask questions.

In fact, on a busy site the visitors are actually doing a lot more testing of the site than you ever will! Therefore, you should either have a form on a page for accepting their comments or simply include an e-mail hyperlink on your home page, such as "Please e-mail any questions or comments to webcrafter@widget.com."

Visit Other Sites

Some of your best ideas about what works, and what doesn't work, come from browsing other sites. There are many sites that maintain lists of popular Web sites, which can server as starting points for you. The following site lists popular sites that were chosen by its own reviewers and then voted for by its visitors:

```
http://www.toptenlinks.com/
```

Another site worth visiting is the World Wide Web Consortium (W3) site at:

```
http://www.w3.org/
```

W3 is the organization responsible for HTML, and their site contains numerous resources on HTML usage and information on changing language standards. For example, the W3 site includes Tim Berners-Lee's Style Guide for online hypertext at:

```
http://www.w3.org/Provider/Style/Overview.html
```

Publishing a Web to a Server

After you've finished creating and testing your web, you need to give it some wider distribution, putting it on a Web server where users can access it. You can publish your web on the Internet or on a local intranet. In FrontPage lingo, *publishing* a web means copying it either to a different server or with a different name on the same server. You use the File ➤ Publish Web command to do the job.

> **&** NOTE NOTE NOTE NOTE NOTE NOTE NOTE NOTE NOTE NOTE NOTE NOTE NOTE NOTE NOTE
>
> **If you create your FrontPage web on the same server that is hosting it, then the world might be seeing your work virtually as you do it. This isn't a good idea, because users are browsing in a construction zone. You should either create your webs in a private folder or on another server, like the Microsoft Personal Web Server, which is discussed later in this Skill.**

All the Internet web pages you view in your browser are stored on a Web server. Many Internet service providers (ISPs) offer Web hosting services for customer's web pages at a minimal charge. ISPs are also called WPPs: Web Presence Providers. Before you can publish your web, speak to your Web server's administrator at the ISP/WPP and ask for:

- The protocol used at the ISP, such as FTP or HTTP Post

- The URL for the Web server, including the folder where you are to publish your files

- A connection to your ISP when you're actually publishing the web

Before you publish your web on an intranet, speak with the Web server's administrator. Ask about conventions for naming webs and folders, see if the FrontPage Server Extensions are installed on the server, and get the name of the folder your web should be published in.

Publishing your web is a convenient way to back up the entire web with all its folders and files. The resulting copy is a fully functional FrontPage web, so you can make changes and perform tests on that web while leaving the original up and running for users. Often, site maintenance begins and ends with publishing: Publish a copy to an internal server to work on, make changes or corrections, then publish the copy back to the public server.

Publishing a Web to a FrontPage Server

It's easy to publish a web to a FrontPage server—either the Microsoft Personal Web Server or another server that includes the FrontPage Server Extensions. For example, when you've finished building a Web site on a local PC, you can use FrontPage to publish the entire site to the Internet or intranet server that hosts this site. If you've pulled a copy of a web for maintenance, you can just publish the updated files. Follow the steps below to publish your web:

1. In FrontPage, open the web you want to publish.

 2. Choose File ➤ Publish Web, or click the Publish Web button on the toolbar.

3. In the Publish Web dialog box, shown in Figure 14.1, select the server, or a folder on disk, to which you want to copy the web. Enter the location and a name for the web. Remember that the web's name is also used to name the folder in which it resides, so the name must follow the naming conventions used on the server.

4. Click the Browse button if you need to select another location.

5. If you are only updating the files in an existing web, select the Publish Changed Pages Only check box (if that option isn't displayed, first click the Options button). This is the option to choose if you've been doing mainte-nance work on a copy of a web.

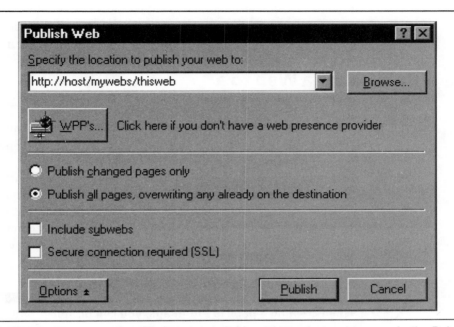

FIGURE 14.1: Specify a server or folder destination and a name in the Publish Web dialog box.

NOTE NOTE NOTE NOTE NOTE NOTE NOTE NOTE NOTE NOTE NOTE NOTE NOTE NOTE NOTE

You can exclude individual pages from any publishing process. Display the Properties dialog box for a page (right-click the page and choose Page Properties from the shortcut menu) and choose the Workgroup tab. There you'll find a check box labeled Exclude This File When Publishing the Rest of the Web. By default, it is not selected, so select it to keep this file from being published. Use the Publish Status report in Reports view to see which files are marked to be included or excluded.

6. You can select the Include Subwebs check box so that all webs within the root web are also created at the destination.

7. If the server supports secure connections using Secure Sockets Layer, select the Secure Connection Required (SSL) option.

8. When you're ready, click Publish.

If the destination web name you enter doesn't exist within the server's root web, a new folder of that name is created and the web is copied there. All the files and folders within the published web are duplicates of the current web.

Publishing a Web to a Non-FrontPage Server

You can publish a FrontPage web to a server that does not have the FrontPage Server Extensions. You can do so either with the traditional File Transfer Protocol (FTP) or with Microsoft's Web Publishing Wizard.

Of course, your published Web site won't offer all the FrontPage features that are available under a server with the FrontPage Server Extensions, as mentioned in "The FrontPage Server Extensions" in Skill 1. For example, if you included a server-assisted feature in a page, such as the Hit Counter component, that feature won't be operable when hosted by a server that does not have the FrontPage Server Extensions.

NOTE NOTE NOTE NOTE NOTE NOTE NOTE NOTE NOTE NOTE NOTE NOTE NOTE NOTE NOTE NOTE

When creating a page in FrontPage, you can disable FrontPage features that will not be supported by a non-FrontPage server. Choose Tools ➤ Page Options and select the Compatibility tab. Clear the check box labeled Enabled with Microsoft FrontPage Server Extensions, and then click OK. You'll find that several of the items on the Insert ➤ Component menu are now disabled, such as Hit Counter. These are the ones that require a FrontPage-aware server.

Publishing from FrontPage with FTP

You can publish your web via FTP to a server that doesn't include the Front-Page Server Extensions. Just about all Web servers support FTP, so that shouldn't be a problem. The process is essentially the same as copying any other files to that server.

There are many programs on the market that make it easy to upload and download files via FTP. Windows 95, 98, and NT have command-line FTP already built in, although having to resort to arcane commands is a little too reminiscent of the "old days." But you don't need to leave FrontPage, because it's already able to upload your web via FTP.

NOTE NOTE NOTE NOTE NOTE NOTE NOTE NOTE NOTE NOTE NOTE NOTE NOTE NOTE NOTE

When you use some other FTP program to copy a FrontPage web to a server that is not running the FrontPage Server Extensions, you need not include any folders whose names begin with _VTI_. These are used only by FrontPage and are not needed outside of it.

Before you publish your web to a non-FrontPage server, however, you need some specific information that you would need for FrontPage or any FTP program:

- The URL of the FTP server to which you're copying your web, such as ftp://host.com.

- Your username and password if the FTP server requires you to log in.

- The name of the folder you have access to on the server, if you are normally limited to specific folders.

- The name of the destination subfolder within your folder on the server where the web will reside.

In FrontPage, you begin by following the publishing procedure described in the previous section.

1. Open the web you wish to publish.

2. Choose File ➤ Publish Web.

3. In the Publish Web dialog box, you need to specify an FTP server as the destination for the transfer, so click the Browse button to display the Open Web dialog box.

4. Open the Look In drop-down list. Near the bottom of the list you should see the item FTP Locations, as shown next. To define a new FTP connection or modify the settings of an existing one, choose Add/Modify FTP Locations. This opens the dialog box shown in Figure 14.2.

SKILL
14

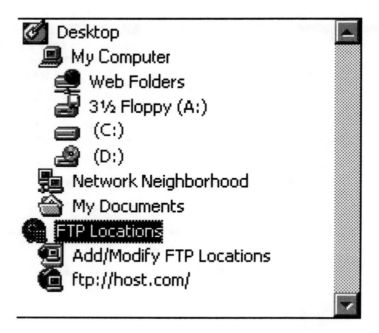

In the Add/Modify FTP Locations dialog box, you enter the basic information you normally need to log on to an FTP server. You can create multiple FTP definitions; just click the Add button when you've completed one to add it to the FTP Sites list. Then you can define another, if you want. You can also select an existing FTP connection in the list and click Modify to revise its settings, or Remove to delete it from the list. Click OK when you're finished defining the FTP connection to return to the Open Web dialog box.

Once you've defined one or more FTP connections, you can select one from the Look In drop-down list in the Open Web dialog box. Your computer will then attempt to connect to that FTP server. If it does so successfully, FrontPage can then publish your web to this FTP server by uploading the necessary files to the folder you specified in the FTP connection settings.

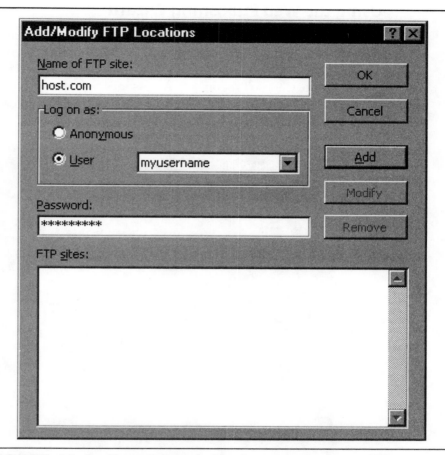

FIGURE 14.2: You define the settings for connecting to your FTP server in the Add/Modify FTP Locations dialog box.

TIP TIP TIP TIP TIP TIP TIP TIP TIP TIP TIP TIP TIP TIP TIP TIP TIP TIP TIP TIP TIP TIP TIP

On a typical FTP server, FrontPage will not be able to create a new folder for the web you are publishing. Therefore, if you want a new folder for the web, you should arrange to have it created ahead of time and specify that folder in the FrontPage FTP settings.

Using the Web Publishing Wizard

Another tool for publishing your FrontPage webs to non-FrontPage servers is the Web Publishing Wizard, which helps you through the process of connecting to the server and uploading the files. You can start this Wizard from the Windows Start menu. Choose Programs ➢ Accessories ➢ Internet Tools ➢ Web Publishing Wizard. The initial dialog box is shown in Figure 14.3, where you click the Next button to continue.

FIGURE 14.3: The opening step of the Web Publishing Wizard

The Web Publishing Wizard walks you through the process of copying your web to the server. It starts by letting you select the folder or files that you want to copy (shown in Figure 14.4).

FIGURE 14.4: The Web Publishing Wizard starts by letting you select the folder and files you want to copy to another server.

You can either type in the name of the folder or file that you want to copy, click the Browse Folders button and select a folder, or Browse Files and select a single file. If you selected a folder, you probably want to select the Include Subfolders check box to include your Images and private folders in the published web. Click the Next button to continue. In the Descriptive name text box, type a name for the Web server (see Figure 14.5).

If you use a particular protocol to publish to an Internet service provider's server (or to your intranet), click the Advanced button to select the connection method from the list. When in doubt, choose Automatically Select Connection Method before you click Next.

FIGURE 14.5: The Name the Web Server step of the Web Publishing Wizard

Specify the URL for the server you're publishing to (see Figure 14.6), including any specific folder your ISP has assigned to you. For example, if your company's intranet administrator assigns you the folder with your name on the server www.mycompany.com, you would enter http://www.mycompany.com/myname as the URL. Make sure the local folder is the folder you wish to publish.

If you haven't published to the selected server in the past, you'll need to identify how you connect with the server in the next step of the wizard. If you choose Dial-Up Networking, select the connection from the list or choose New Dial-Up Connection to open the Dial-Up Networking Make New Connection dialog box.

The Web Publishing Wizard begins to copy the folder or file you selected to the destination server if the server is on a network. If the URL you designated is an Internet Service Provider's server or otherwise requires a dial-up connection, the Microsoft Connection Wizard opens, and locates the server you indicated.

After the wizard connects with the server, a progress meter is displayed to keep you posted on the progress. After it successfully publishes your web, the Web Publishing Wizard closes.

FIGURE 14.6: Enter the URL for your Web server

Renaming, Moving, or Deleting a Web Site

You can perform several management tasks on the active web in FrontPage. You should *only* perform these procedures from within FrontPage so it can complete the entire job and update its own indexes of your web.

Renaming a Web Site

When you create a web, the name you give it is also used to name the actual folder on the disk where the web resides. You can rename your web at any time within FrontPage. In the process, FrontPage will automatically update the name in all file references, such as links to images or the targets within hyperlinks.

Select Tools ➤ Web Settings, and choose the General tab in the Web Settings dialog box, shown in Figure 14.7. In the Web Name field, enter the new name for the web. Remember, the name must be compatible with the file-naming conventions of the server or operating system under which you're working.

You can change the web's name at any time, but because a web's name is part of its URL, you should avoid changing the name once the web is in service. Users who have added your site to their Favorites or Bookmarks won't be able to find your page if you change the URL.

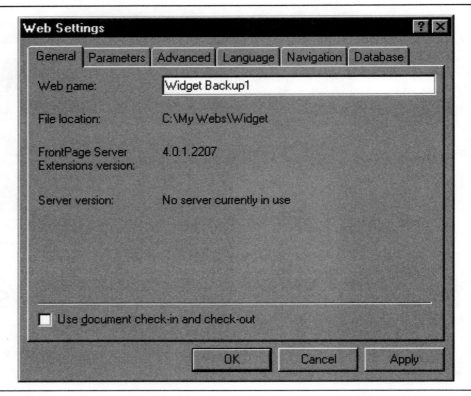

FIGURE 14.7: Change a web's name or title in the FrontPage Web Settings dialog box.

Moving a Web Site

There is no specific command in FrontPage for moving a web to another location, but you can do so in two steps. First, copy the web to the new location with the File ➤ Publish Web command. Then delete the original web, as discussed next.

Deleting a Web Site

Here's how to delete a FrontPage web from its server or from your local disk:

1. Open that web in FrontPage.

2. Display its files either in the Folder List or in Folders view.

3. Select the top-most folder in this web, the one that has the same name as the web.

4. Choose Edit ➤ Delete or press the Delete key. A dialog box is displayed that offers two choices for deleting the web. You can choose to remove only the FrontPage-related files from the web, while leaving everything else, or delete the entire web so that nothing remains. If you choose the second option, the web, with all its folders and files, is erased—completely and irrevocably.

WARNING WARNING WARNING WARNING WARNING WARNING WARNING WARNING

Use caution, and be sure you really want to delete a web before you proceed.

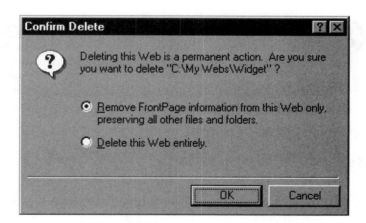

Keeping Your Web Secure

After your webs are published, there is always at least one person, an *administrator*, who has full access rights to FrontPage's root web (the server folder that contains all other FrontPage webs). The administrator can create or delete FrontPage webs, create or delete files within a web, and assign access rights (permission) for those webs to others, either as browsers, authors, or other administrators. Unless your server has been set up to restrict access to a FrontPage web, anyone can browse through the files in all FrontPage webs by default, although they are not allowed to make changes to those files.

When you install FrontPage on a computer running a Web server, you are asked for the name of a person who serves as administrator. If the name you give is not already a registered user on your server, you're also prompted for a password. The name of the person you provide is then an administrator of the FrontPage root web and, by definition, all FrontPage webs within it. This administrator can then restrict or assign access rights to others as needed.

The security restrictions and access rights for your FrontPage webs are dependent on the host server. The rest of this Skill assumes your server has the FrontPage Server Extensions installed. Your rights to access your web once it's published are dependent on the host server's administrator. Some administrators give you full permission to administer your own Web site within the larger site, but most give you limited permissions: author permissions or, perhaps, only browser permissions unless you notify the administrator of a pending update.

NOTE NOTE NOTE NOTE NOTE NOTE NOTE NOTE NOTE NOTE NOTE NOTE NOTE NOTE

Administering and securing a public or corporate Web site are beyond the scope of this book. However, you should have a basic understanding of user permissions, how they are assigned, and how to secure your web. For more information on Web site administration, see *Mastering Microsoft FrontPage 2000* from Sybex.

Assigning Permissions

To change permission settings for the active FrontPage web that you opened from a FrontPage-enabled server, choose Tools ➤ Security ➤ Permissions, which displays the Permissions dialog box. For a typical Web server, there are three tabs in this dialog box for defining the access rights to this web:

Settings Choose to let the active web inherit all permission settings from its parent web (for example, from the root web for the first web you create within the root), or set unique permissions for the active web.

Users When you are setting unique permissions for a web, you can specify the users who have access to this web.

Groups   When you are setting unique permissions for a web, you can specify a group of users who all have the same access to this web. You cannot create new groups in FrontPage—you must do so in your Web server's administration tool. See your system administrator for more information on creating groups or adding users.

You can assign one of three levels of access rights to an individual, a computer, or a group for each FrontPage web on a server:

Browser   In this context, a browser is a user who has read-only rights in a web and cannot make any changes to it (cannot open a web in FrontPage, for example). In most cases, a person with browsing rights is accessing that web in a Web browser.

Author   An author has all the rights of a browser, *and* can view or make changes to the files in a web, but cannot create or delete entire webs or change permission settings. Therefore, if you have logged in with only author permissions, you can't invoke the Tools ➤ Security ➤ Permissions command in FrontPage.

Administrator   An administrator has all the rights of an author, *and* can do just about anything in the way of editing or viewing webs and their files and can also grant or revoke access rights to a web.

NOTE NOTE NOTE NOTE NOTE NOTE NOTE NOTE NOTE NOTE NOTE NOTE NOTE NOTE

If you are running your FrontPage webs under Microsoft Personal Web Server (PWS) version 4, you will not be able to set permissions because this version of the PWS does not have built-in security. If you are using an earlier version of the PWS, however, you will be able to set permissions as described in this section.

Assigning Unique Permissions for a Web

Each new FrontPage web inherits the permission settings of its parent web by default, so anyone who has access rights in its parent web has those same rights in a new web within that web, unless you specify otherwise. To assign unique permissions for a web, open that web in FrontPage and choose Tools ➤ Security ➤ Permissions, then choose the Settings tab in that web's Permissions dialog box (shown in Figure 14.8). Remember that this tab is not available for the FrontPage root web, which has no parent.

SKILL
14

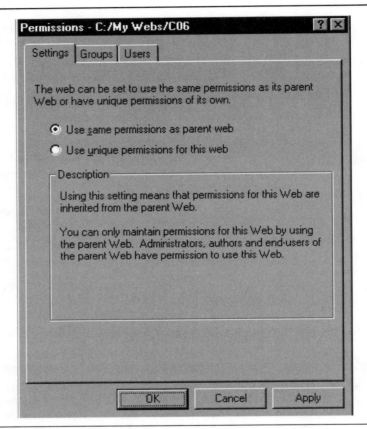

FIGURE 14.8: Assign unique access rights for the active web in the Settings tab of the Permissions dialog box.

The two options in the Settings tab let you specify how the permissions are set for this web. By default, the Use Same Permissions as Parent Web option is selected so whatever permissions have been set for the parent web also apply to this web. To apply different permission settings to this web, you must first select the Use Unique Permissions for This Web option and click Apply, which allows you to make changes in the other two tabs in the dialog box. If there are no unique permissions assigned for this web, you can't make changes in the other two tabs.

At this point, if you make no other changes in the Permissions dialog box, the access rights in this web are still the same as those in its parent web. You use the other two tabs in the dialog box to restrict access to the site further or specify permission settings for other users.

Assigning Permissions to Users

When you have chosen Use Unique Permissions for This Web, you can assign access rights for the active web in the Users tab (shown in Figure 14.9).

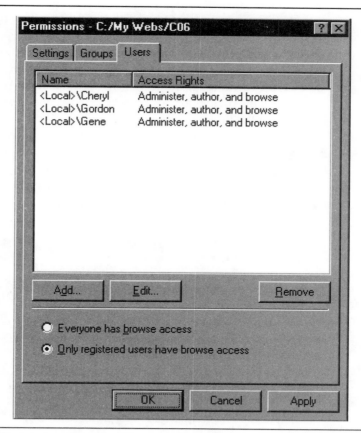

FIGURE 14.9: Specify the type of access that users have to the active web in the Users tab of the Permissions dialog box.

If you do not want to restrict browsing rights in this web, leave the default setting: Everyone Has Browse Access. That way, anyone can view pages and other files in this web (this is the default setting). If you want to limit browsing only to those you specify, select the Only Registered Users Have Browse Access option. Now when anyone tries to open a file on this site, their browser displays a dialog box prompting them for their name and password. Only those users whose names appear in the list in the Permissions dialog box can browse this web (assuming they remember their passwords).

To add a new user to the list of registered users for the active web, click the Add button. You can only add users and groups that are already registered with the server, so if users you wish to add aren't on the list, contact your server administrator.

Select the type of access for this user, either as a browser, an author, or an administrator. Remember, an author's access rights include the rights to browse the web, and an administrator's rights include all the rights of an author. Click OK to close the dialog box, and you'll see the new username in the list in the Users tab of the Permissions dialog box.

To change the access level of a user, an administrator can select a name in the list in the Users tab and click the Edit button. Then choose one of the three permission settings for this user (see Figure 14.10) and click OK. To remove a user from the list, thereby excluding that user from working on this web, an administrator can select a name in the list and click the Remove button.

FIGURE 14.10: To change a user's access level, use the Edit Users dialog box.

Working with the Personal Web Server

Earlier versions of FrontPage came with a small, "personal size" Web server that would host your sites as you built and tested them. FrontPage 2000, however, does not come with a Web server, nor do you need one to build your webs and test most of their functionality on your local computer.

NOTE NOTE NOTE NOTE NOTE NOTE NOTE NOTE NOTE NOTE NOTE NOTE NOTE NOTE NOTE

If you had an earlier version of FrontPage on your computer when you installed FrontPage 2000, you probably already have a Web server installed from that earlier version. FrontPage automatically updates the server extensions for that server. In this case, all of the webs you then create in FrontPage will be server-based (with an http URL).

SKILL
14

If you want others to access your FrontPage webs in a real-world environment, you can run FrontPage under a Web server that supports the FrontPage Server Extensions. There are a variety of servers on the market that support FrontPage, and one is available for free from Microsoft, the Microsoft Personal Web Server (PWS), which is a subset of Microsoft's popular Internet Information Server (IIS). You'll find this server on the Windows 98 CD, or you can download it from Microsoft's Web site. We'll be discussing this version here.

Running the Microsoft Personal Web Server

The Microsoft PWS starts each time you start Windows 95 or 98 by default; therefore, it's available to FrontPage at all times. When it's running, you'll see an icon for it in the system tray on the right side of the Windows taskbar.

You really don't see any interaction with the Microsoft PWS while you're working in FrontPage; the server is pretty transparent. You can stop or start the Microsoft PWS at any time via the Personal Web Manager, where you can also adjust a few settings and access its administration utility. You can start the Manager in two ways:

- Right-click its icon in the system tray and choose Properties.

- From the Windows Start menu, choose the Personal Web Manager command, which you should find on the Internet Explorer menu.

The main screen of the Personal Web Manager is shown in Figure 14.11. It displays the URL of the PWS root web and home page on your computer (`http://gordon` in Figure 14.11) and the physical address on disk (`C:\Inetpub\wwwroot`).

The Personal Web Manager also displays activity statistics, including the number of visitors, file requests, and bytes served. There's a small chart that displays a graph of the statistics you chose from the pull-down list (Requests per Day in the figure).

You can stop the server by clicking the Stop button. When stopped, a Start button is enabled.

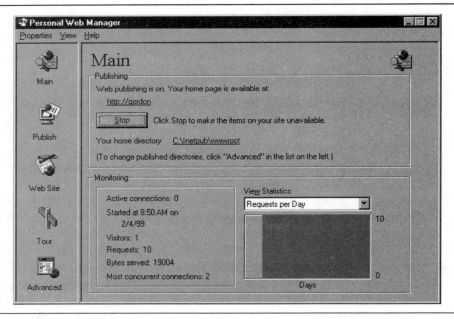

FIGURE 14.11: The dialog box where you can adjust the settings for the Microsoft Personal Web Server

NOTE NOTE NOTE NOTE NOTE NOTE NOTE NOTE NOTE NOTE NOTE NOTE NOTE NOTE NOTE

Taking care of administration duties in the Microsoft PWS is outside the scope of this book. If you're in charge of administering all aspects of the server, you might want to read Sybex's *Mastering Microsoft FrontPage 2000*.

This concludes the discussion of Web site management in FrontPage, and this is also the last Skill in this book. Your head is undoubtedly brimming over with ideas for creating sites, pages, hyperlinks, tables, images, frame sets, image maps, and all the other Web and HTML features you can produce in FrontPage. Don't forget to visit the Microsoft FrontPage site for themes, tips, and information:

```
http://www.microsoft.com/frontpage/
```

Good luck with all your projects on the Web!

Are You Experienced?

Now you can...

☑ **Test your Web site**

☑ **Publish your web on a server that has the FrontPage Server Extensions**

☑ **Publish your web on other servers using FrontPage's built-in FTP or the Web Publishing Wizard**

☑ **Set user permissions when your webs are hosted by a FrontPage-enabled Web server**

APPENDIX A

Installing and Starting FrontPage

- ➔ **Learning about RAM and disk space requirements**
- ➔ **Installing FrontPage**
- ➔ **Choosing which components to install**
- ➔ **Starting FrontPage**
- ➔ **Getting help and running the FrontPage tutorial**

Installing FrontPage and its additional software does not take long, but it does involve several choices and considerations. If you have already installed Front-Page and have it up and running, you may not need to read this appendix. For further help with FrontPage, be sure to check out Microsoft's Web site:

```
http://www.microsoft.com/frontpage/
```

NOTE NOTE NOTE NOTE NOTE NOTE NOTE NOTE NOTE NOTE NOTE NOTE NOTE NOTE NOTE

Unlike earlier versions of FrontPage, you do not need a FrontPage-aware Web server in order to create webs in FrontPage 2000. Therefore, during installation there is no option for installing the Personal Web Server.

Running the Setup Program

To run FrontPage either alone or as part of the Microsoft Office suite, you'll need a computer that supports Windows 95, 98, or NT. Although you might get by with a 486 processor in your computer, it is recommended that your computer have at least a 90 MHz Pentium processor with 32 MB of RAM. A faster processor and more RAM will improve your FrontPage experience.

If you have an earlier version of FrontPage installed on your computer, you can either overwrite the earlier version by installing FrontPage 2000 in the same folder, or you can install the new version in its own folder and leave the earlier version untouched and still available. You don't need to keep earlier versions; your existing FrontPage webs work fine in FrontPage 2000.

Installing FrontPage 2000

The setup routine uses the standard Windows Installer, and the process is essentially the same whether you're installing the stand-alone version of FrontPage or installing it as part of the Microsoft Office suite. We'll be referring to FrontPage in this discussion, but you can simply substitute "Office" for "FrontPage" if you're installing the Office suite.

Here are the steps to install FrontPage:

1. When you insert the FrontPage or Office CD into your computer's CD-ROM drive, the setup program should start automatically. If you do not have AutoStart enabled in Windows, go to Windows Explorer and double-click the program SETUP.EXE on your CD drive.

2. The setup program will first prompt you for your name and the CD key that identifies your copy of the program. You'll find that string of letters and numbers on the CD's storage case. Click Next to go to the next step.

3. In this step you can either accept or reject the Microsoft license agreement. (Hint: If you choose not to accept the license, you won't be able to install FrontPage.) If you accept the terms of the license, click Next.

4. The next screen offers two buttons, and is shown in Figure A.1. One button will be labeled Install Now if you do not have a previous version of Front-Page on your computer, otherwise the button will be labeled Upgrade Now. Choosing this option will create a standard installation of the most commonly used components, and FrontPage 2000 will replace and overwrite a previous version of the program. The second button is labeled Customize. Select it if you want to choose which components to install or if you want to install the new program without replacing the existing one. When in doubt, choose Customize and take that extra minute to establish without a doubt just what is getting installed and where it's being installed. For this discussion, we'll continue with the Customize option.

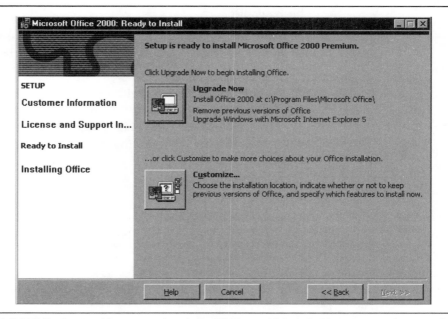

FIGURE A.1: You can select Install Now or Upgrade Now to create a standard installation or select Customize to fine-tune the choices.

5. After clicking the Customize button, the next step lets you pick the location where FrontPage will be installed. Unless you have a reason to specify otherwise, the default location should be fine. Then click Next.

6. If you have earlier versions of FrontPage or Office applications, the setup routine will offer to delete them for you. If you do not want them deleted, be sure to select the Keep These Programs option. Then click Next.

7. Now you'll be asked if you want Internet Explorer 5 installed along with FrontPage. You can choose the standard or minimal installation, or choose not to install it. If you don't install it, you won't be able to take advantage of all the new features in FrontPage or Office 2000. Click Next to continue.

8. Finally, you'll get to the step where you choose which components to install. Figure A.2 shows this screen when FrontPage is being installed as part of Microsoft Office 2000. A component with a plus sign to its left includes other components from which you can choose. As in Windows Explorer, just click the plus sign to expand the list. The Windows Installer offers several ways to handle each component:

   • Install a component on your computer or network so it will always be available.

   • Run the component from the CD. This saves space on your hard disk, but will require that you have the CD available whenever you want to access that component.

   • Install only the command that starts the component, but not the component itself. This option is called Installed on First Use. When you later try to access this component, you will be prompted to insert the CD so that this piece of the program can be installed. Once installed, it will always be available. If you're not sure you want a program installed, this is a convenient way to get the program later without running the entire setup program again.

   • Choose Not Available if you do not want the component installed. Remember that you can run the setup program again in the future and select new components.

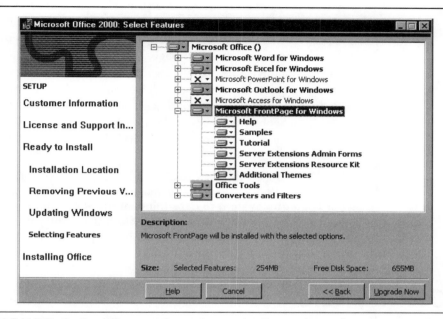

FIGURE A.2: When you have chosen the Customize option, you can select which components to install.

9. As you make your selections, watch the Size indicator beneath the list of programs. When you're finished making selections, click the Install Now (or Upgrade Now) button to complete the job.

The setup routine will begin copying files; the time required depends on the number of components you selected and the speed of your computer, hard disk, and CD drive.

Starting FrontPage

The most important thing to remember about running FrontPage is that you should always use it when you want to make any changes to the files or folders within a FrontPage web. In other words, don't use Windows Explorer to delete, rename, or copy files into a FrontPage web. Doing so will just make it difficult, if not impossible, for FrontPage to keep track of all the files and folders in that web.

You normally open FrontPage from the Windows Start menu. Remember that FrontPage 2000 is now fully integrated, so once you've started the program you have access to all its features: creating a new FrontPage web, opening an existing one, or creating or revising web pages.

If you do not have a FrontPage-aware Web server running on your computer, the webs you create in FrontPage will be disk-based. If you already had a server installed when you installed FrontPage, such as the Microsoft Personal Web Server, by default the webs you create will server-based. Either way, when you're creating a new web you can choose to make it disk-based or server-based.

NOTE NOTE NOTE NOTE NOTE NOTE NOTE NOTE NOTE NOTE NOTE NOTE NOTE NOTE NOTE

If you have a Web server running, the first time you start FrontPage, it examines your computer system to determine information about the computer's host name and TCP/IP connection information (on a network). It then displays a message to let you know what it found.

Getting Help

You'll find plenty of help available in FrontPage, which you can access in several ways:

- To open the standard Windows help screens, choose a topic from the Help menu, press F1, or click the Microsoft FrontPage Help button on the Standard toolbar.

- To learn about a command or button, press Shift+F1 and then choose the command or click the button.

- To get up-to-the-minute information from the Internet, choose Help ➤ Office On the Web. This will open your Web browser and connect you with Microsoft's Web site, where you can choose from a variety of FrontPage topics, browse the answers to FAQs, and download files.

You should definitely set aside some time to browse the Microsoft Web site. The tutorial, product information, web-design tips, and sample Web sites you can visit are invaluable tools for learning not just about FrontPage, but about designing Web pages and sites.

Index

Note to the Reader: First level entries are in **bold**. Page numbers in **bold** indicate the principal discussion of a topic or the definition of a term. Page numbers in *italic* indicate illustrations.

Numbers and Symbols

D

G

H

I

T

W

GET THE SKILLS FOR SUCCESS!

NO EXPERIENCE REQUIRED

Focus on skills and succeed with today's most important software!
Learn skills through a tutorial-style approach, with practical, real-world information

ISBN 0-7821-2128-4
544 pp. 7½" x 9" $24.99
May 1998

ISBN: 0-7821-2293-0
704 pp. 7½" x 9" $24.99
February 1999

ISBN: 0-7821-2385-6
496 pp. 7½" x 9" $19.99
November 1998

ISBN: 0-7821-2374-0
432 pp. 7½" x 9" $19.99
February 1999

ISBN: 0-7821-2184-5
560 pp. 7½" x 9" $24.99
February 1999

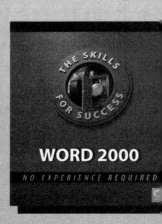

ISBN: 0-7821-2400-3
496 pp. 7½" x 9" $19.99
February 1999